InRage

InRage

Linda Y. Callaghan

CONTENTS

I dedicate this book to all of the survivors of child sexual abuse, those who have healed and those who are still among the walking wounded. Every day they waken holds a promise of a better life, and every breath is an affirmation of their inner strength that has triumphed over their abuse.

*The names of all patients and family members,
and some locations have been changed to protect patient privacy.*

ACKNOWLEDGEMENTS

I'm grateful for the opportunity here to acknowledge publicly and thank those who helped me through the physically and often emotionally difficult process of writing this book.

- To Audrey DeLaMartre, my dear friend and editor, I offer gratitude for her faithfulness through a long and difficult process, even to cheering me up when the remembering got too heavy. She has ability to read and understand what I write and then knows what questions to ask to get at the deeper meaning. She was the one who read the first edition of *Inrage* and recognized the value of expanding it, and then she guided and nurtured the process to produce the present volume. I'm so grateful that she is part of my life.
- To Paul, my spouse, I offer thanks and love for being strong and constant, for picking me up when I felt down, for being gentle and loving when I was so ill, and for always having faith in me.
- To my sisters Mila and Del, thanks for their emotional and financial support.
- To my patients, thanks for permitting me to tell their stories sharing the good news that the wounds will heal and that joy is possible.
- To God, who strengthens daily me to rise above the pain of telling my patients' stories, and reminds me that suffering like theirs must cease.

FOREWORD

As a film director and producer I have had many opportunities to meet people from distant countries and all walks of life. Several years ago when I was shooting a film in Poland, I spent three days at the Auschwitz concentration camp. I walked among the barren wooden barracks, the tall guard towers and barbed wire fences, but its tragic history came alive for me when I was joined by two of its survivors. Ted Wojtkowski and Adam Jurkiewicz had spent five horrific years in the camp before they were liberated in 1945 and their nightmarish daily life there became vivid again as they recounted the merciless abuse, hatred and death. And they cried.

When I read Linda Callaghan's book, I realized how similar to Adam Jurkiewicz and Ted Wojtkowski raw emotions of rage, grief and loss are those of the children who have been sexually abused. Both experiences show the strange and extreme power of the human heart to manifest destruction. Not only in Auschwitz do we find unbearable abuse, hatred and death. Some homes, like those described in this book, are like concentration camps with family members and assumed friends as cruel enemies. And the children cry.

In the pages that follow you will read about deep despair in human hearts caused by conditional love, contaminated love and absent love. But also you will read about healing and redemption.

Many young people today live isolated in barren and hostile environs. Their hunger to feel included, accepted and loved by those around them drives them to extreme means to maintain what little self-worth they can find. Envy and hatred build as they think that love will surface through possessiveness and authority. And, of course, it never does.

The ideal support structure for every child is a healthy, loving family but unfortunately this isn't always so. Mother Teresa of Calcutta offered powerful insight into this crucial need. When I interviewed her a few years ago in New York City, I asked why there is so much suffering in the world. I'll never forget her answer: "Want of prayer." Throughout her life she repeated that "a family that prays together, stays together." Children are a product of the family and reflect the faith it has in God. That is why she stressed praying as a family is so vital, allowing as it does for each member to connect with the divine as well as each other in a continuous and protective atmosphere of healing. It is this atmosphere that provides the unconditional love that is our birthright and our destiny. The unconditional love that we need heals, lifts, supports, consoles, guides and gives.

God has called all of us, professional therapists and filmmakers alike, to restore to humanity the components of love, mercy, compassion, respect, dignity and honesty. This book will help those who want to advance the healing process and end the hidden rage and horrible legacy of the victims of child sexual abuse. Dr. Callaghan shows that survivors can be helped and the cycle broken with focused and sustained effort.

John B. Clote
The Mercy Foundation

INTRODUCTION

Some of the stories on these pages are stark, cruel, vicious and horrifying. Even for professional therapists the material can be traumatizing. Nonetheless, I have not softened them because in my opinion as a woman, a mother, a physician and a psychiatrist, the reality of child sexual abuse is too excruciating to be softened or minimized and must be faced honestly if we are to help its victims and eliminate the problem. And I believe firmly that we can go a long way in our lifetime to eliminate the problem of child sexual abuse, but it will take presence, understanding and work. Therefore, I present the cases in their stark reality to offer tools to therapists and, through them, hope to survivors and those who love them.

Please keep in mind that those whom I describe as victims are in reality *survivors* who are in the process of healing. I have not used the real names of either patients or other persons involved in their cases, to protect their privacy and guard their healing process.

INTRODUCTION

The title of this book rises from my patients' letters and poetry about their sexual abuse. Their emotions show on their faces, spill into their diaries and drawings, haunt their nightmares and pierce the souls of those who hear them. Rage, pervasive and organic, is the primary emotion of survivors of childhood sexual abuse.

One of my patients wrote of that rage:

> "My body is flailing violently. I'm scared. I'm alone. I'm isolated. I'm fighting memory. My legs are shaking. My

arms are shaking as I try to write. In a dream I took a big knife and diced through sheets of the paper I'd been writing on. Then a violent voice said, "You little son of a bitch." My body keeps flailing and falling. I can't write. Why can't I write? I can't write. God help me write.

Tonight I fantasized about disemboweling my father and stomping on his guts. I pull out his intestines with my hands, reach right up to his stomach that I've sliced vertically with my big knife. I feel like I'm fighting with a force. He is my father. Earlier, when he called me a little son of a bitch—I'm starting to shake again—I know he was threatening me not to reveal the secret."

Rage like that destroys; it murders the soul. Sexual abuse in childhood can cause sexual excitement of traumatic intensity, as well as rage of helpless frustration. Together the feelings generate murderous impulses. Those impulses, in turn, promote massive defenses against such overpowering emotions. Then, when other stresses threaten to liberate those repressed feelings and bring them back into consciousness, survivors repress them again with denial, intellectualization and rationalization. And so the deadly spiral goes through a lifetime.

For example, a woman who had been abused as a child by her father might continue to deny the facts by telling herself that she is remembering a movie, or a nightmare. Another person might rationalize away the past by saying that children naturally fantasize about physical relationships with their opposite sex parent. Such defensive reactions can't hold back the damaging effects of repressed emotions forever. One day they will rupture and emerge as severe anxiety, or a panic attack, unexplained pain, overwhelming depression, or even an engulfing need to become a sexual victimizer.

To manage the continuing effects of suppressed rage, it is absolutely vital that the rage is released, but that rage usually is separated from the rational mind, a split demonstrated in a patient's diary entry:

"I am terrified. I hurt. I'm scared. No one is home who I can call to help me. I hurt so bad. I want to own this pain so I can let it go forever. Oh, God, help me own this pain. I don't want to hurt this way any more.

"It is real! It is mine! Oh, God, it is my pain. He hurt me. I wish I could have killed him for the things he did to me. This pain is real. It is not imagination. Let me feel it and let it go. Help me. I am ready. I am ready. Please open this wound enough to let the shit out that is killing me. I hurt! Oh, God, help me!"

As she wrote that, her emotion was flowing openly and powerfully. But when she resumed writing later that day, she denied and reduced them to trivialities and then explained them away, shutting off her feelings and engaging her rational/logical process.

"That was silly. I don't really feel all that pain. I was just scared when no one was here to answer my call. I've settled down now. I must go and get a meal ready, and then I have to get Mom's apartment ready for her to move into. I feel like crying. I wonder if recovery work causes headaches?"

A victim's rage denied and concealed lies compressed in a small compartment of the subconscious, building pressure until it erupts in a sudden activity or fury. Eruptions aren't necessarily healing because they may not be a direct and conscious confrontation of the feelings. Eruptions may take the form of highly emotional writing, screaming, tearing paper, self-abuse, spontaneous role playing or compulsive exercise. Fantasizing murder and mutilation of the victimizer releases pressure, too, and can be beneficial, but only when the victim recognizes that it is a fantasy and what its motivation is. The benefit comes from making the rage conscious and ventilating it, as does the following writer.

CARNAL KNOWLEDGE

Around each bend, just inside darkness
A tiger lurks, wearing my father's stripes.
I long to stroke the silken fur of orange and black,
But instead I lie down beneath his merciless jaws.
Grisly teeth rip open my chest.
He devours my heart and races off on blood stained paws.
I feel nothing
nothing
except sadness at a death that is not complete.
For years I wait.
Then, again, I tackle the mountain
This time armed with gun and knife,
determined
to kill the son of a bitch who ate my heart.
I will blow off his head
and slit his dead guts till my heart pops free.
But my bullets are only blanks, words
begging
that he love me.
I turn and run, his hot breath inches from me.
Again he does not kill me and he does not love me.
I am a failure. An empty shell of a woman
with no heart.
People tell me that the tiger is dead now
and cannot hurt me.
But he took my heart to his grave.
I see him in my sleep.
I see him in the eyes of house cats
Guarding the door to paradise.

Painful as the poem is, it is a healthy form of acknowledgment and an unusually creative verbal step along the hard path of survival and recovery. However, recovery seldom is complete; there are always scars. Sadly, survivors who lack treatment or don't finish it, don't reach such full awareness, but continue to suffer the consequences of the trauma, often without even knowing why.

In my practice of general adult psychiatry I became increasingly aware of the prevalence of sexual and incestual child abuse among adults being treated for a wide variety of psychiatric disorders. Although child abuse is a small and integral part of the literature of mental health questions, the primary focus of the literature lies elsewhere. There is an urgent need for literature that deals exclusively with the long-term effects of sexual and incestual child abuse and the therapeutic treatment of the survivors. To that end, then, this book is directed.

The general public as much as the therapeutic community needs to know that sexual and incestual child abuse occurs more frequently than we realize. It is the cause of mental illness[1] in its victims, and it can be treated successfully.

PART I

CONTEXT

CHAPTER ONE

DIAGNOSING CHILDHOOD SEXUAL ABUSE

It has been my professional experience that sexual and incestual child abuse can cause any one of the illnesses, or several in combination, that are classified in *The Diagnostic and Statistical Manual, III, Revised* (DSM IV-R). One patient at a time, it became obvious to me that a child who has been abused sexually or any other way, has been scarred emotionally. It is perhaps less obvious how specifically and tightly that abuse is linked to forms of mental illness, especially since those forms are normally considered in terms of a clinical label, or as a syndrome of patient problems, without a common link to other mental illness. That link, that underlying cause, is sexual abuse during childhood, and it is particularly true of incest, the most prevalent form of sexual abuse.

Incest has a broader definition in this book than used generally. In clinical discussions incest refers to any sexual activity between a child and a related adult, no matter the specific kinship, and may even be used when there is only a symbolic relationship. Thus, parent-child sex is incest, as is uncle-niece, or grandmother-grandson. However, in terms of the damage done to the child, step- or foster-parent sex with a dependent child, or teacher-child sex and even clergy-child sex is also incest, *because the child is compelled to be sexual with an authority figure.*

Incest has been judged differently from one culture to another, one family to another, and one historical time to another.

Assessment has ranged from condemnation as criminal behavior, to acceptable social behavior. Some literature shows that incest isn't necessarily violent, nor does adult-child incest necessarily constitute child abuse, although today's cultural standards automatically regard it as such. No matter how it is regarded, incest has the power to damage a child severely and cause mental illness, most especially if violence is used in any form.

Sometimes incest claims victims who were *not* part of the sexual activity. One of my adult patients had been involved in child-adult incest with her biological father, and in adulthood still found adult-adult incest pleasurable with him. At age 48, through 22 years of marriage, she continued to have sex with her father, claiming to enjoy it more with her father than with her husband. Her husband learned about their secret sex life accidentally, and then discovered that his father-in-law had been molesting his 15-year-old daughter as well. Shortly after that, he had a psychotic breakdown marked by a collapse at work. It took four years in therapy for the underlying cause to surface and be dealt with. The history of this case is detailed in the chapter on Psychogenic Amnesia.

Identifying incest is important because of its devastating impact, usually on both the victim and the family unit. During therapy, inevitably family relationships will change. Currently there are laws mandating reporting all types of child abuse through the Department of Protective Services, or similar programs. This reporting causes an adversarial relationship between families and state authorities and often between individual family members. Within a family it provokes a mixture of anger, shame and guilt.

CHILD ABUSE IS COMMON

People deny and try to suppress evidence that child sexual abuse is no less rampant now than ever before in history. Today in Africa, the world's hotspot of AIDS, children are getting AIDS from rape in increasing numbers:

"An alarming growth in rapes of children, often by relatives who believe that sex with a young virgin brings mystical powers or can even cure AIDS, is devastating families across much of Africa by spreading HIV to otherwise sexually inactive girls…as young as 10.

Unscrupulous practitioners of traditional herbal and spiritual medicine, which are hugely popular across Africa, are fueling the problem by prescribing pedophilia as a remedy for everything from money woes to AIDS. In some instances, poor relatives quietly tolerate the crime, allowing a daughter to go with an older man for much-needed cash or as a compensation for a debt or ancestral transgression. Others demand payment from the rapist and then remain silent."[2]

The article observes that AIDS is simply a new complication to an old attitude that a "girl child has no value in African society; she is a thing to be used to make men's lives better."

The very next day there was a news article about how female children are being used today within polygamous clans in Utah. The whistle-blower in this case was a 16-year-old who had run away from an arranged marriage as the 15th wife of her uncle. What she told launched many studies, which in turn revealed that pregnant women in such marriages often receive no prenatal care, live hidden lives in poverty as single mothers on food stamps and welfare who must never question male authority. Adolescent boys as well as adult males have sex with female children commonly, teaching little girls that their "bodies are not their own."[3] So commonly that the children referred to it as "an evil spirit visiting them at night," which they thought was a bad dream.[4]

While it's easy to be outraged at such a news story, child abuse and child sexual abuse goes on everywhere, even in our own quiet hometowns. In Traverse City, Michigan, where I lived and practiced in 1989, there were 350 referrals of child abuse and/or neglect. Of that number, one third were substantiated. Of the substantiated cases, 23% were physical, 29% were sexual and 46% were neglect.[5]

One family asked for my help. Their 12-year-old daughter had reported abuse by her adoptive father and stepbrother. The family was uncomfortable with the court appointed therapist and asked me to be their support. During our first session I could see that there was nothing wrong with the other therapist and that my role was simply to provide moral support to the family and validation of their feelings. As a result, the therapy sessions provided a safe place to vent their anger.

A word about false reporting of abuse: it happens and can be weeded out by a competent therapist. Even if the incident or incidents reported are false, the act of reporting is a clear call for help that must be heeded. The need for help may lie in the family system or in the reporting individual, but either way it points to a serious glitch in the family's relationships that needs to be addressed with the mediation of a therapist.

Unfortunately, as sometimes happens, in a different case the daughter reported sexual abuse by her father and she was lying. She was angry and getting even with her father and stepbrother. Tragically, the therapist and the court ignored her retraction. An intensive family therapy process that would have been difficult at best was too great an obstacle for this family and they have never recovered fully.

Most often families enter therapy only because the law requires it. Sometimes the victims cause such disruption in the family that the family seeks therapy to deal with the victim's rage and depression instead of pursuing resolution of their own emotions. Too often no family therapy is done because the incest remains a secret until the perpetrator dies or is physically separated from the victim. That lack of therapy allows the concept of sexual abuse that is woven through the family system to move unchallenged from one generation after another.

Domeena Renshaw, M.D., lists the various relationships encountered in incest covering a broad range of categories, types and relationships.[6]

- Consanguineous (related by blood)
- Consensual, coercive, or forceful
- Coital or non-coital
- Heterosexual or homosexual
- Adult-child, child-child, adult-adult, or group
- Rape
- Pedophilic
- Exhibitionistic
- Multiple deviance (e.g., prostitution, transvestitism, child pornography, sadomasochism)
- Fantasy or dream
- Incest craving or envy
- Incest-accepting family, culture or religion

I haven't added to Renshaw's list. In fact, in most of the following cases only a few of the terms apply because most cases in my practice involved adult-child coercive incest. Usually, but not always, they were consanguineous.

To demonstrate the impact incest has on the victim, especially when the victim is an abused child, I will recount case histories with specific diagnoses found in the DSM IV-R. The relationship between incest and mental illness becomes sharper as it repeats in case after case, even when the illness emerges later in the survivor's life.

Sexual child abuse is a crime. It is a forceful act against a child that is classified as a criminal act, not as a mental illness or mental disease, except pedophilia.[7] Many perpetrators fall under other descriptors, but not categorized as mentally ill. As researchers uncover more about perpetrators of all forms of sexual child abuse, their victims, their physical history, and their mental health, I believe that all forms of sexual child abuse will, and should be, considered a sign of or a type of mental illness.

CHAPTER TWO

THE ENVIRONMENT

What causes child sexual abuse? Where does it come from? I hear this anguished cry from every sector of society and every corner of the world and I must admit that the answer is still a chicken-or-egg impasse. The roots of sexual abuse of children are buried so deep in history that we can no longer isolate where it began, and despite increased reports of abuse, I don't believe that it is any worse now than previously. It's only that reporting is up. Increasingly, survivors recognize that being a victim of abuse doesn't equate with responsibility for the guilt, and they are rising up in great numbers to say No More!

There is evidence of child abuse all through the literature that influenced Western civilization. Sodomizing boys in early Greece was common and approved of as part of the culture. The Bible tells about the man who would have sent his "virgin" daughters out "to have intercourse" with a crowd of men in order to protect his two visitors (Genesis 19). Charles Dickens wrote about children in Victorian England who were used, abused and neglected and allowed generally to be vulnerable. The message: children are expendable and exploitable.

Ivan Turgenev, playwright from 1840s Russia during the Age of Realism, wrote of incest in his first play, "First Love." Reclusive poet Emily Dickinson's works have prompted speculation about the reasons for her bleak and morbid tone and her withdrawal, which are behaviors consistently demonstrated by those who have been abused.[8] Research into the writings of writer and essayist

Virginia Woolf revealed that she and her sisters were victims of incest at the hands of a live-in uncle. That element of her childhood affected her attitude and writing profoundly, and predisposed a brilliant woman to depression.

It goes on and on. The seeds of current child abuse, including sexual abuse, go back in history as far as we can trace. There are those who would use such evidence to justify the practice. There are those who would like to rewrite the past to change it. What we need to do is change the *present*, and an excellent way to begin is to identify the risk factors.

In the more than 300 cases of child sexual abuse where I've worked with adult survivors, the perpetrators, mothers of the victims and the families of the victims have shared common traits. These characteristics have high statistical representation and are a distillation of my cases. I offer them here so they can serve as warning signals to alert professionals who can apply appropriate deterrents *before* abuse can occur. You will note necessary redundancy between risk factors and warning signals.

RISK FACTORS

There are risk factors that signal a predisposition to abusing children sexually. The common factors among abusers that I've discovered in my practice include:

1. **Substance abuse**: Alcohol and drug abuse disinhibits, increasing significantly the risk of sexual abuse.
2. **Mental disorders**: The presence of emotional disorders such as bipolar disorder, depression of any etiology, personality disorders, schizophrenia, and so on, can create an environment receptive to the development of child sexual abuse. One of my patients who had undiagnosed bipolar disorder sexually abused his seven-year-old daughter for about two years during the manic phase of his illness. Then the child told her mother, who reported her husband, who later was referred to me. He

couldn't remember abusing his daughter and, when his wife and daughter confronted him, he went into a catatonic state. He was treated with lithium carbonate, came out of the catatonia, learned about his behavior and was horrified. In his opinion, no more detestable behavior was possible. When his wife divorced him, he surrendered custody of the two children readily, and requested visitation rights *only* if the daughter agreed. She refused to respond to his apologies, which made him very sad. He was sent to jail where he continued to take his medications faithfully and underwent intensive psychotherapy. When he got out of jail he devoted his life to religion and doing volunteer work in nursing homes on weekends. Eventually he married a woman who shares his interests. He continues to pay child support and doesn't try to force his children to visit with him. He perseveres in his treatment and hopes that someday his daughter will forgive him. He has not re-offended in ten years.

3. **Isolation:** Sometimes incest happens because the people don't know that it's against the law, and a socially unacceptable practice for hereditary reasons. In these cases violence may or may not be a factor.

   One of my patients was forced by her brother to have sex with him. When she informed her mother, she was told that it was a family practice. Her paternal uncle, her mother said, had sex with her regularly until she was married. She told her daughter not to make too much of it. My patient, however, told her school counselor, who notified Child Protective Services, who investigated the allegations. The family was more upset by interference by strangers than by the information, and they blamed the daughter.

   When the 17-year-old brother was separated from the family and told to get treatment, he threatened to kill his sister, so he was admitted to a closed facility for children. Later I heard he joined the army. The girl was found to be four months pregnant, decided to keep the baby and live on her own. She got ADC (Aid to Dependent Children), finished high school and lived away from her family. I have lost track of the patient since she finished treatment, but she was doing well when I saw her last.

Also, in isolated circumstances some people practice zoophilia, the act or fantasy of engaging in sexual activity with animals as a preferred or exclusive method of achieving sexual excitement.

4. **Parental discord:** In some cases the victim is parentified, treated as a parent, by his or her opposite-sex parent and later may become a sexual partner to this parent. These patients report initial feelings of entitlement due to their relationship with the offending parent, and anger and contempt for the same sex parent. Later, when they get interested in peer relationships and the offending parent interferes, they transfer these feelings to the offending parent. They feel trapped and hence act out by reporting the offending parent, or escaping through drug or alcohol abuse, running away, dropping out of school or other adolescent delinquent behaviors.

5. **Poverty and unemployment** have been linked to enhancing the risk of child sexual abuse. In my experience these factors alone were not associated with the abuse unless complicated by some of the other factors cited above.

WARNING SIGNALS

Characteristics of perpetrators, both male and female:

*   History of drug and alcohol abuse.
*   History of incestuous victimization, usually in combination with emotional and physical abuse.
*   Marital problems, usually involving poor sexual relationship with spouse.
*   Severe personality disorder, including inadequate personality, narcissistic, antisocial, psychotic and sadomasochistic behaviors.

- History of cultural acceptance of incest, such as in families and communities where incest is a matter of privilege. Usually these communities and families are geographically isolated and extremely poor.
- Sexual deviance, including pedophilia.

CHARACTERISTICS OF
ABUSED CHILDREN'S MOTHERS

- Chronic physical or emotional illness so she can't protect her children. May be abused herself.
- Drug or alcohol abuse.
- Frequent absence from home, possibly to work full time, so the adult male tends to the children.
- Highly codependent, causing mother to blame child of causing the abuse and justifying father, stepfather, brother or boyfriend's abuse.
- History of being abused.
- Cultural acceptance, as above.
- Symbiotic relationship with daughter including role reversal. May consciously or unconsciously contrive to make daughter recipient of abuse.
- Sexual problems. Usually dislikes sex.
- Character disorders: passive-dependent, avoidant, and immature behavior.

CHARACTERISTICS OF FAMILIES
WHERE INCEST OCCURS

- Dysfunctional; poor communication and interaction between family members; distant or rigid manner, lacking healthy demonstration of affection; home environment usually chaotic; sex not discussed with children.
- Alcohol or drugs abused by one or both parents.
- Overt sexual behavior between parents in front of children, including intercourse.
- Isolation of family, lack of socialization.
- Incest considered normative and acceptable. In some cases of

extreme wealth, intermarriage with blood relatives is considered acceptable to keep wealth in the family.

THE VICTIMS

Of the sexually abused people I see in my practice, 95% are female. All of the males of the remaining 5% were perpetrators themselves. Of those who commit sexual abuse on both genders, 95% are male. Of all of the perpetrators in this group, fewer than 10% had ever received counseling of any kind, and then only through court mandate, family pressure, or intervention by others, such as clergy. All of the survivors in this study have reported similar characteristics of their abusers by direct observation or by history culled from relatives who knew the history of the perpetrator.

Studies have shown that male sexual victimizations are underreported by both the victims and their families. The most likely reason for this is their shame at their inability to stand up to the perpetrator and the consequent damaged self-image as males, especially if they were in their early teens at the time of abuse. Thus, their trauma is unresolved and later they retaliate by victimizing other children, usually their own. Their own gender identity usually is a subject of distress and confusion because of their sexual experience with another male. Even though essentially they were powerless at the time, they fear that the experience makes them, or means they are, homosexual. That isn't true, of course.

My experience is that 97% of perpetrators had drug and/or alcohol problems, and claimed to be impaired at the time of the incident(s), so they don't remember. I believe that their claim is a protective falsehood and that they use chemicals to dull the pain of their own victimhood, which puts them at greater risk to become offenders.

A significant number of perpetrators have reported having sexual problems with their spouses. These problems are be wide-ranging and can include frigidity, impotence, premature ejaculation, retarded ejaculation, dyspareunia (pain on intercourse) and unorgasmia (inability to attain orgasm). I believe that for some of these individuals sex is a weapon, a way of getting back at their perpetrators. In their marriages, sex as an act of love gets lost, and the act becomes a reminder of their abuse.

From unconscious prompting they may turn to pedophilia. That provides an encounter in which they feel more powerful than their victims, while at the same time expressing their rage and feeling victorious instead of victimized. Some of them have told me that, when they have sex with children, they actually feel like children themselves. In a way, they are trying to recreate the unresolved trauma. It's as if their instincts tell them that they can't get rid of that old trauma until they go back to it psychiatrically and heal the wound. And that's exactly the case. Intellectually, they realize that they are adults, but during the sex act they are unable to integrate intellect and emotion. Afterwards they feel a great sense of inadequacy because of their inability to deal with adult sexuality.

PERSONALITY DISORDER

All of the male perpetrators I have treated carry a diagnosis of Personality Disorder, particularly Antisocial Personality Disorder. They have difficulty with interpersonal relationships, show absence of compassion or remorse, tend to blame others for their problems, and justify their wrongdoing. They show marked difficulty keeping jobs, have a high degree of repeating unacceptable behavior and appear to be unable to learn from their mistakes. Many of them are habitual liars, by self-admission and demonstrated by family history.

A great number of perpetrators have dissociated their memories of abuse and so are not conscious of what motivates their behavior. Nonetheless, they over-compensate through pathological identification with their abuser and show signs of hyper-sexuality, aggressiveness and antisocial behavior. The key to helping these offenders is with competent therapy to uncover, work through and lay to rest the memories of abuse. Only then will they be free from their unconscious motivation to criminal behavior, in both a legal and ethical sense. Without such therapy, perpetrators are condemned to re-offend.

PART II

THE DISORDERS

CHAPTER THREE

DISSOCIATIVE IDENTITY DISORDER,

(FORMERLY MULTIPLE PERSONALITY DISORDER)
[DSM IV-R 300.14]

Media portrayal of multiple personalities is dramatic. The heroine, it's rarely a male, slips from one personality to another, impelled by forces beyond her control. Not only can't she control the changing personalities, often she isn't even aware of them, or if she is, only in retrospect. Soon it is apparent to the viewer or reader that she isn't playing games; she's a prey of her disorder and she's not a happy, fulfilled person. Usually it is a reasonably accurate portrayal of Dissociative Identity Disorder, DID (formerly Multiple Personality Disorder or MPD), which is one of the psychological conditions that can result from sexual child abuse.

PERSONALITY COMPONENTS

A healthy, integrated personality is made up of three generally recognized components that Freud called the Ego, the Superego and the Id.

- The *ego* is intellectual and interpretive, identifies problems, seeks solutions, and specializes in "head talk."
- The *superego* has learned all the shoulds and oughts, reminds us of our duties and what to feel guilty about, compels us to get chores done, and specializes in censorship and control.

- The *id* loves pleasure, is impulsive, inventive and creative; doesn't care if chores ever get done; often is called unrealistic and doesn't care.

FORMATION OF ALTERS

DID patients host multiple personality components that are less analogous to a nuclear family, and more like an entire extended family, in-laws and outlaws included. However, a DID person doesn't *know* she hosts a crowd of alternate personalities, or alters, but she may suspect something from the voices she hears in her head, criticizing, giving opinions and orders. Even so, that is her reality so she may dismiss the idea that hearing voices is abnormal, and continue to cope as best she can.

Formation of alters is a response to abusive events too traumatic for the host or core personality to endure, but the host doesn't know the formation is occurring. There may be few, three or four, or there may be multitudes numbering in the hundreds, usually depending on the duration and severity of the abuse. They form families or alliances based on their age, which in turn is based on the host personality's age when the particular abuse occurred. Alters in different families may or may not know other alters outside their particular alliance, and they may not recognize or know immediate family members of the host personality.

Alters can and do choose to be male or female, regardless of the gender of the host personality. For example, an alter may choose to be the gender of the perpetrator, hoping that when the abuser recognizes that they are the same gender, he or she will cease. Sadly, it doesn't work. Alters have autonomy from each other, can be in strong conflict with each other, and can sabotage therapy effectively enough to end it. Thus, conflict resolution becomes an important part of therapy.

ALTER POTENTIAL

All healthy personalities contain the raw material of alters, the seed of other personalities, but lack the psychological provocation to make the split. Without that provocation their personalities continue to exist as elements along a continuum, a smooth flow of potential, possibility, variety, variations on a theme that are never splintered. Because these variations are normal, it is possible to incorporate them into a unified personality.

APPEARANCE OF AN ALTER

When an alter takes control from the host personality, or one of the other alters emerges as the dominant persona, the host may experience a period of amnesia. Or she may realize that an alter is pushing her back and taking over but she is powerless to stop the takeover and to regain control. Understandably, these episodes provoke enormous dread. Not only does the host personality fear losing control, but she's equally afraid that other people will find out about the alters, suspect that she's different from other people, and she'll lose her credibility.

She reacts by increasing her hypervigilance, controlling her external environment more tightly, obsessing about order, time, diet, exercise, weight, cleaning, personal appearance, what she says and how she says it, everything. This effort to keep all her internal chaos from spilling out causes escalating stress and anxiety, which precipitates depression. The pressure builds and she fears a complete breakdown, so she is forced to seek help, but even that may not last.

THE SHOCK OF MEETING ALTERS

"Jane," a 35-year-old woman, was referred to me for a sodium amytal interview. She was waking in the morning with aches and bruises and no idea of how she got them. Her husband, a police-

man on night shift, accused her of adultery, pointing to her foot-
prints in the snow that led out and back into the house while he
was at work. Tearfully she denied having an affair or even leaving
the house. When the bruises appeared more frequently she got
frightened and she and her husband asked their physician for a
referral. He sent them to a colleague, who sent her to me for the
interview.

Jane was not aware that she had been sexually abused as a
child, but she remembered that her childhood had been unduly
sad. Her father, a minister, was dour and strict, and her mother
was immature, emotionally unavailable, and seemed to dislike her.
Jane's memory of childhood was vague, almost dreamlike. She
couldn't place in context or memory what few photographs she
had of herself as a child. Hearing that made me suspicious, but I
said nothing.

During the sodium amytal interview an alter emerged who
asked me to call her Kay. She was vivacious and had a facial tic. She
disliked the name Jane because her father had chosen it and he
had abused her sexually from age 10 to 16. It might have gone on
longer but her mother discovered them together in bed and kicked
Jane out of the house. Nothing was ever said between the three of
them about the sexual abuse, and her father behaved as though
nothing had happened.

At that point, another personality emerged, calling herself
Sylvia. She was seductive and belligerent, with speech seasoned
liberally with foul language. It was she who had taken over and
went out to bars while the host personality slept. She was the
reason for the bruises. She picked men up in the bars and had sex
with them. When the men got rough, she left, went back inside,
and left the host personality to cope with what she found. Jane
told that when she woke up in the act of intercourse with a stranger
and surrounded by other men she didn't know, her state of undress was more important to her than her safety.

After the interview, Jane and I together reviewed the videotapes of the session. She was staggered by what she saw and heard,

and refused to continue that session with me, with her other therapist, or any other therapist, saying she couldn't afford therapy. She was in total denial. Whether the refusal was the work of Jane, Kay or Sylvia, or some other alter I hadn't met yet, I don't know. Both my colleague and I offered to work with her on a sliding fee scale, or any other basis she found comfortable, but we haven't heard from her in four years.

DIAGNOSING DID

DID is diagnosed when a patient exhibits more than one distinct personality, each with her own particular pattern of perceiving herself and comprehending and relating to her environment. Each separate personality takes full control of her behavior recurrently. The continuing skepticism that DID generates is far more customary than with other, more commonly recognized psychiatric disorders, such as character disorders, bipolar disorders and anxiety disorders. Possibly that's due to sensationalizing such books and films as *The Three Faces of Eve* in 1957, *Sybil* in 1973, and *Loose Cannons* in 1989.

Even today DID is considered to be so rare that, even when the evidence can't be denied, therapists prefer to go for a different, more acceptable diagnosis for fear of being called on to defend their conclusion. That caution can lead to some pretty funny rationalizations. One therapist ventured that his patient's claim that "she feels like she has a split personality" is caused by the patient's "inner child work." This inner child, he said, has been repressed for years and is fighting for acknowledgement and nurturing denied by emotional deprivation in childhood. Eventually, this same therapist requested that I do a sodium amytal interview, during which we uncovered several other personalities. I'm pleased to say that, in light of what we uncovered during the interview, he accepted the evidence and today his patient is making very good progress.

LEAVING THE PAIN

Carl Gustav Jung, Swiss psychiatrist and break-away student of Sigmund Freud, observed that a neurotic person evades awareness because her consciousness is reduced by self-fragmentation and that this process does gross injustice to her potential. "Only a unified personality can experience life, not that personality which is split up into partial aspects, that bundle of odds and ends which calls itself man."[9]

Individuals suffering from DID have dealt with severe, repeated trauma by going into a trance, leaving the pain, taking away its power by denying it. Over time, the trances come more easily, and eventually memories of the events detach and coalesce into separate identities. The identities or alters assume the feelings experienced at the time of the trauma—terror, passivity, hate, combativeness, anger. These feelings may be so unacceptable to the host personality that she can't assimilate them into her consciousness, so they are denied and flash-frozen in her unconscious at that age. Thus, the eight-year-old alter who hides in terror in a dark closet, remains there until she is thawed from her frozen state by the process of psychotherapy.

DISSOCIATION

In DID the primary defense mechanism is dissociation, a split of consciousness. But then, most people employ dissociation on an every-day basis. Normal dissociation involves losing awareness of one's immediate environment through total absorption in some activity like reading, watching television, or listening to music. Dissociation places a barrier between the person and her environment. As a result, her thoughts, feelings, actions, memory, and sense of identity may be altered so that they are inconsistent with what is happening around her. This can happen in small and large ways. For example, dissociation alters one's sense of time, so that while driving one may suddenly become aware that she has arrived at her destination and has no memory of the drive there. Her cognitive abilities—discrimination, memory, temporal continuity, sensory perception, judgment and reasoning—were constricted to "auto pilot."

A DID uses an extraordinary form of this loss of awareness to escape, and once established as a tool of escape, it becomes more and more easily employed. Thus, she falls into it for even relatively minor stressors, such as a job promotion or layoff, preparation for a significant social occasion, holidays, events others take in stride consciously. This extraordinary capacity to go into a self-induced trance-like state gives DIDs a predisposition to hypnosis.

An indicator of dissociated memories that I watch for is when a patient describes traumatic events without showing emotion. Showing emotion about an upsetting situation, however contained, is normal. Showing no emotion is a sign that something is interfering with a normal response. Another indicator of dissociation is extreme sensitivity to external stimuli, a reaction that is inappropriate to the current circumstance that indicates possible severe trauma in the past. Even though the memory of the trauma may not be accessible, the external stimuli triggers a reaction incongruent with the present.

Generally, DIDs are multi-talented, exceptionally intelligent, creative and imaginative people. Sadly, most often they are misunderstood and these traits are used as weapons against them by people who don't or won't understand and who label them theatrical, hysterical, neurotic, psychotic, *or any label other than DID*. The histories and evidence they offer causes them to be accused of manufacturing stories. Too often they accept that charge because so much of their past is buried in the fog of dissociation, and the longer memories are repressed, the more unreal they feel. Also, perception is affected by age at the time of the trauma. Together, these two factors make exact recall of times, places and dates problematic.

Even when a memory does rise out of the fog, it seems to be out of any logical context and the person assumes that it must have come from another source. Two of my DID patients, both of whom happened to be counselors, ascribed their memories to their clients' experience, assuming that they must have internalized their clients' problems. It took a long time for them to accept the memories as real events from their pasts, even after validation from family members, hypnosis and sodium amytal interviews.

One patient encountered her own error-through-repression. Initially she remembered that her father's brother, a fraternal twin, had raped her. Then one day while she was looking at family pictures, she saw a picture of the brothers standing side by side. She stared at the picture and then burst into tears because she recognized that it was her father, not his brother, who had raped her. At the time of the rape her mind couldn't accept that her father was the perpetrator because she was close to him and adored him, while his twin brother was despised as an alcoholic wastrel.

It is striking that 95 to 98% of patients with DID are survivors of severe child abuse. Characteristically, the abuse has been administered by parents or close family members over a long time, periodically but inconsistently interspersed with expressions of love. The patients' degree of fragmentation is related directly to the severity of their abuse.

All of my DID patients have a history of severe physical, sexual and emotional abuse. Further, and typically, they have been brainwashed not to tell. If a survivor does screw her courage up enough to report the abuse, almost predictably the family will call her a liar. She is fabricating, they insist, and treat her like a pariah. She is crazy, they tell her, just trying to get attention. No one in the family has ever acted like this before. They respond to the therapist with hostility, even suggesting that she or he suggested the abuse and diagnosis to the patient.

Most often, however, the patient doesn't remember the abuse. She has pushed recollection of the traumatic events from her memory as too vile to be borne and cannot access the memories consciously. Usually, what brings her to me is another condition like severe depression, or pain that another physician can't find a reason for, Somatization Disorder.

Together the survivor and I work gently and patiently to recover all the fragments of self buried with their respective memories and reunite all the selves into one whole, complex and complete woman. It's an exhausting process for both the survivor and the therapist and it's well worth all our effort.

CO-CONSCIOUSNESS

Co-consciousness is natural in a healthy mind. For example, when children are in a classroom, they are aware that the playground is there and what its play potential is, but they focus, presumably, on their lessons. Then later on the playground they are still aware of the classroom, but they focus on play. Thus they hold consciousness of both places and the events appropriate to each and elect on which they will focus. Someone who has dissociated bitter memories no longer has that power to elect. Part of my psychiatric responsibility is to return that choice to my patients.

Co-consciousness, then, is the goal of reversing dissociation. Those memories and experiences that a patient has dissociated still exist along with unrepressed data. Treatment removes the barriers hiding the repressed trauma and brings to consciousness knowledge of the abuse. Once we access the information held by separate alters and reintegrate it into ordinary working consciousness, alters lose their function. It's a difficult process in which, while accessing repressed material into the co-consciousness, a patient feels again the original episode's pain.

BODY MEMORIES

As a patient reintegrates thoughts, feelings and events during treatment, body memories begin. Body memories are the physical sensations and the pain felt at the time of the original attack that are felt afresh, as though the sexual assault were just occurring.

Other events can trigger body memories: a vaginal examination by a gynecologist; an adjustment by a chiropractor; a massage

by a masseuse to loosen tight muscles; making love with her husband. Touching specific body areas, certain sounds, a particular
tone of voice or facial expression, and smells and tastes can trigger
body memories and strong, even violent reactions. Many massage
therapists, chiropractors and others who do body work have been
startled by a survivor's sudden and extreme reaction during an
otherwise calm and peaceful session.

BLOCKING

Dissociation, sometimes called *blocking,* is predictable because it
is used so commonly as a coping mechanism in cases of physical
and emotional abuse. Survivors become expert blockers when abuse
is ongoing, even if a particular abuse has ended and a new and
different stress triggers old feelings. Suppressing traumatic memories further enhances dissociation mechanisms, blocking habits,
because probably survivors have been brainwashed. Indeed, most
abused children are brainwashed, literally indoctrinated by their
abusers to believe what is untrue and against their best interests
and, just to cover all the bases, often they are threatened with even
greater violence against their persons and families should they remember and tell anyone, anyone at all. The threat usually is compounded by the fact that the abuser is an authority figure, a person from whom the child should be able to expect nurturing, or at
the very least, protection.

Adult patients who were sexually abused as children often have
little or no memory of their childhood because of a strong denial
system. Often they maintain certitude that they had loving parents despite overwhelming evidence to the contrary. Not unexpectedly they tend to ascribe their memories to dreams, books,
films, or even their therapist's invention, anything but the truth
that is too painful and too threatening.

Despite a survivor's heroic efforts to block the truth to preserve her sanity, her subconscious will strive to resolve the conflict
between truth and falsehood, and deliver the truth to her con-

sciousness, usually through dreams and body memories. The following letter from a patient illustrates my point. Following the letter I will offer some insights into her comments.

> After I talked to you on the telephone I had an abdominal spasm that made it hard for me even to stand up. I had to rub it to make it go away. That has never happened before. I'm afraid to go to sleep tonight.
>
> I'm trying desperately to remember something. I was considered the favorite [child in our family]. I seldom clashed with my father. My brother and sister both had violent arguments with him. I seldom [made] waves. I was an ass-kisser. I was a great tiptoer not to get anyone upset. I feel so lucky inside.
>
> I feel so dirty after the dream. [She alludes to an earlier letter describing a dream in which she was raped by a faceless man whom she suspected was her father.] I feel bitter and scared, and even excited. The kind of excitement I [felt] while watching him fighting with my sister, brother or mother. The feeling I had while [I was] pinned down during the rape, is the feeling I have experienced when my husband has been goofing around with me [and] the same terror. I still feel like nothing physical happened to me.
>
> My sister has never had any problems about her outright hate and rage [toward] my father. She says she would like to dig up his dead body and put it through a meat grinder. I never felt that I could identify with any of this until recently. I was Daddy's little girl.

1. The abdominal spasms are both symbolic and body memories of pain and pleasure intermixed. The vicious sexual attacks caused pain, yet she had orgasms also. The experience confused her. She can't reconcile how she can feel so disgusted, hurt and frightened and still have orgasms. The memory of her rape brought a flashback of the pain, her anger at her father's betrayal and her

desire to expel him. She was barely into her teens when the attacks began. Without sex education she couldn't identify the orgasms as such, only that there was pleasure with the pain. In therapy she was able to understand that the orgasms were a physical response beyond her control.

2. The spasm was a body memory repressed from recall and then summoned to mind by some form of stimulation of body part involved in the original incident. In this case, the pain was regenerated when she reclaimed her memory of the event. Incidentally, blocking can't be overcome with willpower because it isn't voluntary. Voluntary forgetting is called *suppression*. Suppressed memories can be recalled with effort. Involuntary blocking is called *repression*. Repressed memories require intensive work with professional help to break through the barriers.

3. She called herself an "ass kisser" because she tried to please everyone and keep everyone happy. Her "tiptoeing" was her efforts to keep her family from explosive issues, her vigilance at deflecting triggers of arguments by changing the subject or creating a distraction. For example, when her father was drunk, she made sure there was a hot meal and the house was clean. If he complained about anything, she fixed it fast so he wouldn't blow up. Her apparently contradictory comment that she feels "lucky" means that her efforts worked well to avert family arguments and deflect attention from herself and so stay safe. Obviously, not safe enough, since ultimately she was her father's rape target.

4. For all her vigilance, there were violent physical and emotional fights between family members, adults and children alike. The mixed feelings she alludes to in the dream includes excitement, which draws on the still repressed pain/pleasure memories of rape. Her "goofing around with her husband" refers to mock fighting, but the physical contact accesses the same mixed feelings.

5. She says she feels both excitement and terror. Her dreams blend with her reality because she is beginning to remember, but she can't always discriminate between the two, and she doesn't know what provided the memory recall.

6. Her comment that she still feels like nothing physical happened to her is continuing denial that is both involuntary and unconscious. During therapy, when she voiced her denial again, it was followed immediately by nervous laughter, then uncontrolled crying and even twitching. It was almost as though her body was trying to expel the abuse it received.

Despite her denial, physical signs that are offshoots of the mental process demonstrated that her denial system was breaking down. Her body was reflecting the emerging memories' effect on her conscious.

7. Calling herself "Daddy's little girl" had a double meaning. First, she literally was the favored child. Second, and this is the ironic part, she was also daddy's little woman at night. Also, she's expressing some guilt feelings here, from her sense that her father raped her because she failed to be or achieve something that would have appeased him. Also, her orgasmic reaction still caused feelings of guilt.

DISSOCIATING INTO MULTIPLE PERSONALITIES

When a patient must deny herself and the reality of her experience so intensely that she subdivides into multiple personalities just to cope with the horror of her experience, it is the ultimate in creative dissociating. Actually, all dissociating is creative survival, even when it is destructive to a survivor's integrity. Thus, while the human psyche is both as fragile and as tough as a kitten, survival is its goal, and creativity is its benchmark.

When a person dissociates into separate personalities, each personality is called an *alter*, and is defined as another self. (I repeat this explanation here for readers who jump and search through the text instead of reading straight through.) In reality, alters are designated holders of specific traumatic memories, which split off or separate from the host personality at the age and time of the trauma. Thus, one trauma that causes one split can result in one alternate personality, whereas a life filled with terror, humiliation, pain, and desertion from its earliest years can generate dozens to hundreds of repository personalities. Each personality has its own name and will stay the age at which it was generated.

NAMING THE ALTERS

Most patients have names for their alters; some don't. Sometimes they know how the alter came by her specific name; often they don't. Usually the host personality feels confusion and anguish, which the poem "Samsara" (See Appendix I) shows clearly, because of the presence of the alters and the rage they carry that hasn't been resolved, and which is in large measure responsible for their emergence.

Sometimes a DID patient, to her great consternation, will dissociate into an alternate while she is working, traveling, shopping or doing any normal activity. Any kind of stressor, as I said earlier, can trigger a dissociative episode.

Alice, one of my patients, was afraid to drive because of her illness, so she took a bus. During the trip she dissociated to her four-year-old personality named Sandy. Her trip ended when she was led by the hand to her own door by the bus driver who said to her husband, "This little girl, Sandy, is lost. Does she live here?"

Her husband, who didn't know that she was a DID and had never seen her alter, reacted with shock and consternation. Yes, she lived there, he said, but she was his wife, Alice, not Sandy. The bus driver turned and walked back to his bus, shaking his head. Alice felt understandably distressed and decided to seek treatment.

TWO CASE HISTORIES

Below are case histories of two patients whom I diagnosed with DID. Both cases involve satanic cult activity, which further complicates their treatment. Some readers will find the facts that I present implausible. To that skepticism I can say only that I have treated too many survivors of this kind of ritualistic abuse to dismiss or even discount what they report. Many of the facts were confirmed by sodium amytal tests and through testimony of survivors' family and friends.

A word about satanic cult abuse. Skeptics are inclined to say that there is no such thing as satanic cults and that such outrageous events as described below are figments of overwrought imaginations. Further, they assert that claims of satanic cult abuse are figments of therapists' imaginations. As insulting as their allegations are, I would rather they be true than the alternative, which is that there really are people who are such cultists and that they really do such vile things to their victims.

It isn't necessary that you and I believe what cultists believe. All that is needful is that we comprehend fully their belief system and frame of reference, and thereby equip ourselves to help our patients. If we have a patient who is convinced that he is Napoleon, then a good place to start might be Elba. Our comprehension doesn't *compromise* our professionalism, it *informs* it.

The history of belief in Satan is prebiblical. More contemporarily, Anton LaVey shaved his head in 1966 and announced that he had just "founded" the Church of Satanism in San Francisco, CA.[10] Consequently, it is now a recognized religion in which Satan is worshipped in a hedonistic parody or reversal of Christian beliefs and worship practices. Soon after his formal creation of the Church, in 1972 he published *The Satanic Bible*.[11] This attempt to legitimize what had existed for thousands of years served to make satanic rituals practiced under cover of darkness and in secrecy only marginally more public. An organization devoted to hedonism, focused on hostility and willfulness, that supports ritualized acts practiced in secret, is a ready-made nesting place for sick, twisted personalities, and a breeding place for perpetrators of many kinds of abuse, among them, child sexual abuse.

However, in terms of therapy, whether a therapist finds believable the existence of Satanism or cult abuse is not the issue. A patient's healing comes first. If a therapist is so put off by the emotional context that constitutes the patient's reality that the context must be denied in order to continue, then it's imperative for the patient's sake to help him or her find another therapist who can work with the patient's reality. Therefore, believe or disbelieve as you must, but don't punish your patients with your beliefs; recuse yourself instead.

DELIA

Delia was 37 years old, twice divorced and remarried when I first saw her as a patient. She had sought help from a therapist who specializes in DID survivors of cult abuse and then soon after her father died she became deeply depressed and suicidal. Since she would need to be hospitalized and would probably need medication, he referred her to me.

THE SOCIAL DELIA

I had worked with her in two places: a local nursing home while I was still in Family Practice, and when I worked as a staff member and Director of the Psychiatric Residency program at the State Hospital in the area. I remember her as quiet, hard working and compassionate with the patients, but not friendly with the staff. But she was changeable. At times she could be quite jolly and talkative, and other times almost morose. In fact, one of her outstanding features was that chameleon quality.

She enjoyed acting and was considered one of the best actresses in the area. She had directed a very successful play for a local theater group, an accomplishment that gave her pleasure. However, she had memory lapses, she heard voices in her head, discovered purchases she didn't remember making, met people who knew her but whom she didn't know.

Beginning at about age eight or nine she realized that she had other selves but she had no way of knowing that it wasn't normal.

As a result of this fragmentation, her core symptom was her lack of continuity of self, of identity.

DELIA'S FAMILY

Delia's mother was sexually abused by her own father as a child and was forced to quit school at the end of the eighth grade. There was a lot of drug addiction on her mother's side of the family, including her mother. Delia's father was ritually abused in a satanic cult for years and his parents began practicing incest on him as a child, a practice that lasted through his lifetime and which was probably supported and exacerbated by cult alliance.

There were "neurotic characteristics" in her mother's family, Delia told me, mainly involving hypochondriacal symptoms that justified use of prescription drugs. Alcoholism was prevalent in her father's family. Her father was career Air Force, discharged honorably after 25 years as a technical sergeant. Then he was employed by the Federal Aviation Agency as a meteorologist. Delia's family looked like ordinary, law-abiding citizens.

PHYSICAL PROBLEMS

Delia had an abundance of physical problems:
- Hyperacidic stomach with esophageal widening.
- Diverticulosis.
- Hysterectomy, presumably from endometriosis.
- Cholecystectomy, gallbladder removal.
- Many intestinal problems.
- Scoliosis, abnormal curvature of the spine that she believes was from frequent beatings, falling and violent mistreatment during childhood.
- Spondylolisthesis and retroscoliosis of lower vertebrae, L5 and S1.

My experience with cult survivors is that drugs are used on them liberally, so when they need medically prescribed drugs or medication, their tolerance is extremely high. That was true for Delia, whose tolerance was so high that a normal dose didn't reach her need. Later I learned that some of her alters were alcoholic. While it wasn't a big problem, it was a factor.

SOCIAL HISTORY

She was the oldest of four children and a bright student, but quiet and fearful. She avoided interacting with classmates and went directly home after school because they called her weird and shunned her. For the most part she remained passive to their taunting, graduated from high school, went on to college and earned a degree. She worked well in her profession, although she remained isolated from her peers.

Delia's first husband was abusive, self-serving, led her into prostitution and was her pimp and source of illegal drugs. She became pregnant and her husband divorced her shortly after the birth of her first son. Two years later she remarried and had another son with that husband. When for no apparent reason she tried to stab him, the marriage ended and she married her third husband. Since the drugs and prostitution were secret, to the rest of the world her life seemed normal.

My initial interview with Delia was no different from any other psychiatric interview. It included the history of the present illness, the presenting symptoms, mental status and family history of mental illness. Delia said she felt no pleasure in activities that she used to enjoy. She couldn't concentrate at work, she had mood swings, difficulty falling asleep, fluctuating appetite and energy, feelings of hopelessness, helplessness, a lot of anger, frustration and frequent suicidal thoughts. She was already well into her individual psychotherapy with her therapist. I proposed using antidepressants to alleviate her depression. I kept track of the dosage, explaining the benefits and side effects and asked her husband to help monitor her medication intake due to the danger of overdose. Every depressed patient is a possible suicide. Even if there is no intention at the time the medication is prescribed, stress can provide a temptation to end one's life.

It took most of a year for Delia to learn to trust me. She perceived me as an auxiliary therapist, especially when hospitalization and medications were needed. To her I was the ideal surrogate mother, a counterpart to the surrogate father she found in her primary therapist. She trusted us because we accepted the history of her past and were supportive and empathetic. She relied on us when in crisis and we were always dependable. She felt that her wellbeing was our main concern. Her primary therapist and I made sure that we kept each other apprised of new information so that her therapy could proceed as smoothly as possible.

During the course of her therapy Delia began to remember the gruesome details of her early childhood, especially being used sexually by her father. It is not unusual for DID patients to have little or no memory of their childhood when they first come into therapy, as I mentioned earlier, because the memories have been blocked. Also, it isn't unusual for patients to seek help shortly after the death of the perpetrator because either there is some safety for the first time allowing disturbing memories to return, or one of the alters is so devastated by the death that the alter is suicidal.

As her memories unfolded, Delia's mother and siblings had mixed reactions to her disclosures. Their initial guarded support turned to anger as they discounted her memories.[12] She described her mother's reaction as total devastation. Her only brother, his father's favorite, refused to respond because he felt any comment would be a betrayal. No other family member sought counseling. To this point, only the memories of incest had surfaced.

Delia's mother had worked at night while she was still in school. Her father, a practicing alcoholic, worked days. While he was in the armed forces his family followed him from base to base as he was transferred. One of Delia's memories involved sexual abuse by a maid and her boyfriend while the family was stationed in Spain. An alter formed as a result of that abuse, and it was the alter who told me about an episode when she was about seven years old. The maid and her boyfriend put a pickle in her vagina and then forced her to allow a dog to lick her vulva while they laughed as she shook in fear. The maid threatened to hurt her if she told her parents. Being a child, and already conditioned not to tell by her father who was molesting her already, she obeyed. Besides, she felt, as is common in these circumstances, that she wouldn't be believed anyway, and if they did, they wouldn't care.

After the incident she tried to overdose on aspirin, became very sick and had her stomach pumped. During the overdosing incident she dissociated into another alter who carries the memory of the severe abdominal pain. Every alter took on the memories of different abuses which unfolded painfully in therapy. The memories that came back during this stage of her treatment were so disturbing that she became suicidal again and had to be hospitalized. I worked with her primary therapist and other professionals in the psychiatric unit taking turns providing her with support while she worked through the memories of abuse. She switched often from one alter to another when the alter who was out could no longer stand the pain of the memories. One particular alter, a child who always came out when I was present, appealed to my maternal instincts. She called me Doctor Mom, and gave me information on other alters who refused to come out to talk.

Some of Delia's abuses involved her paternal grandmother who continued to have sexual involvement with her father, possibly until the grandmother committed suicide. She was forced to witness the intercourse between her father and grandmother and then forced to join. The pet dog was included also.

It took about two years in therapy before she remembered the episode involving her mother's culpability. She had thought that her mother had never been a part of the abuse. Then one night during one of her stays in the hospital she became very restless and asked if I could hypnotize her to help her free the memory.

Once she was under I asked her, "Delia, how do you feel?"

"I don't know," she paused. "I feel very strange." She paused again. "I see my Dad. Oh, no! Not my mother, too. Oh, Mother, how can you?"

She leaped out of bed, ran over and began to slam her head against the wall. Then she ran to the window and tried to break it to jump out. I went to her and put my arms around her to comfort and calm her, and to control her violence. I spoke to her in whispers, holding her, quieting her, and gradually led her back to the bed where eventually she fell asleep. When she woke the next morning she was helplessly suicidal.

The following day Delia, her primary therapist and I met with her together. We validated her feelings and allowed her to ventilate her despair without judgment. Due to her deep depression, I gave her an option to have a trial of an antidepressant medication and told her that I had ordered general suicide precautions for her. She agreed to the wisdom of that. Also, I used an existential therapy method called "the courage of despair," in which the patient's recognition and acceptance of despair is seen as an act of faith that ultimately will allow her to pursue self-definition and self-affirmation.[13]

As treatment continued, other episodes of abuse in her past came out. For example, one day when Delia was in her early teens, her father and his brother, her uncle, had been out drinking together. They came home so her uncle could have sex with her at her father's insistence. "Make sure you please him," he growled at her. As time went on, her uncle came to have forced sex with her as his right, with and without her father. One time, when she refused to submit to him, he forced her into the trunk of his car and locked the lid.

She didn't know how long he kept her closed in there to punish her because she dissociated while in the trunk. The alter formed from the trunk experience was claustrophobic. She remembered that he used her as amusement with his friends, bringing men to have sex with her while he watched and photographed. The men used her like a sex machine, even to forcing her to submit to having sex with dogs. The alter who split off from the dog experiences had a dog phobia that wasn't shared by the other alters.

Somehow she got copies of the pictures and confronted her

uncle with them a few years later, to his great alarm, and in the presence of his wife. He denied her charges, but she was pleased with her own ability to overcome her terror of him and confront him. While her uncle fidgeted and squirmed, she looked at him steadily, she told me, and said, "You know what you did. I do, and I can prove it." Walking away from him with the pictures in her hand, she felt confident that she wouldn't have to deal with his abuse again.

She didn't, but the anguish she carried in the personalities of her many alters would take many years to uncover, heal and integrate. It wasn't until after three years of intense therapy had passed that Delia began to remember her satanic cult involvement.

SATANISM

Geraldo Rivera, sensationalist talk show host, did a show on Satanism in 1989, to which several of my patients reacted alarmingly. While Rivera loves the sensationalism, I don't know that he ever expected to impact so acutely the lives of many of his viewers, if indeed, he ever knew. They decompensated. They simply fell apart. The Rivera show pushed their dissociation button to off and the unblocked memories came flooding back into fragile and unprotected minds nearly drowning the survivors in terror.

Delia had begun to have memories about her cult involvement even before the TV show, but then, in response to the show, the memories became an avalanche that buried her. She remembered being a "breeder" for the cult, one who had babies for the cult's use. There were several young women and men used exclusively for breeding, she remembered. The resulting infants were used as sacrifices and eaten by members of the cult. The revulsion she felt at the recovery of this memory seemed to be too great for her to express fully.

Satanism, her memories told her, seemed to go back five generations before her. Her paternal grandmother, her father and mother were all involved. She could remember her mother being very drugged at the meetings. Some of the people who she remembered being involved in the cult's activities included a prominent physician and some police officers. Several of the cultists had warned her that she would be killed if she disclosed anything at all about the cult. One of her alters was a witch, a member of the cult, and heavily involved in its activities. The alter held most of the cult memories, and it was most resistant to therapy. She, the alter, continued to practice Satanism until she was caught during one of Delia's hospitalizations.

When incest survivors dissociate and develop multiple personalities, one of the known causes is vicious traumatization. Delia remembered incidents of people being sacrificed and murdered. As her witch alter, she remembered having to sacrifice her infant daughter and cannibalize her little body, and that both her paternal grandmother and her father were present and strong advocates of that ritual.

Now that she has left the coven, she fears for her life. A decapitated cat was thrown at her front door as a warning to reveal nothing. When she went to the police for help and protection, she was told only not to go out at night.

FAMILY TREATMENT

Conflict between alters isn't unusual. Delia had to resolve the conflict between her witch alter and her core personality. In fact, she had to resolve conflicts between several of her alters, which is called family treatment. The parallel with family treatment in chemical dependency recovery is obvious and accurate: the goal is to resolve conflicts between personalities by sharing, learning, empathic understanding, and removing the barriers between them by disclosing their secrets.

A recovering family in chemical dependency treatment becomes closer and has a healthier relationship. Ideally, a DID patient integrates all her alters into one whole and harmonious personality, and in the process of doing so, gains insight into her condition and confidence in her ability to deal with stress. A less ideal but acceptable relationship develops as the alters re-experience their trauma. Even if all the personalities never are able to move beyond co-consciousness, at least it's better than mutual exclusivity. And there is always the possibility that integration will occur when the alters are ready to trust the host personality's readiness to assimilate their memories and cope.

Delia's primary therapist tried family treatment first, but her alters' resistance was impenetrable, possibly because that therapist was a man. Since her father was the more dominant and traumatizing parent, and because she feared him, and because so many of her abusers were men, she could have transferred that fear to her therapist. It was obvious to both the other therapist and me that she feared his possible disapproval, and that by working more closely with me, we could help Delia more. Together, then, and using hypnotherapy carefully when it seems indicated to pull out stubborn memories, we three together continued making progress in Delia's healing.

Her children were unaware of her problem. They didn't realize that when their mother acted more like a playmate than an adult, that it was her younger alters who had come out to play. In spite of her different alters' choice of playmates, Delia's children are well cared for and show no signs of physical or emotional neglect or abuse. All they saw, and wondered about, were her mood changes. Delia's husband, however, was aware when he began to get acquainted with her different alters, each who saw him differently, but positively for the most part.

He was having his own problems with *situational depression*, that is, depression caused by external events, as opposed to *endogenous depression* which is genetically transmitted and can occur without recognizable external stressors. He was depressed about losing his job, the chronic nature and duration of Delia's illness, and their mounting medical bills. Then their medical insurance provided through her job was discontinued. Although things must have looked bleak for them, he was always there for her, considerate and constant. At the most, he appeared a little detached at times and he didn't seek therapy for himself.

While he was trying to deal with a marriage seemingly on hold and the absence of sex, the alters were getting used to him. Most of the alters didn't see him as their husband. Some saw him as a friend, some as a foe. Some of them seemed to need to test him because he is a male and probably interested only in sex. After all, that had been their experience. One alter decided to seduce him to prove their worst fears. He declined. At first she was angry, but then her anger turned to admiration, respect and relief, and then trust. The reason he didn't press for sex is because he felt he wasn't dealing with the personality he married, and he preferred to wait. His admirable resolution was helping his wife win her private war.

GROUP THERAPY

One of the therapeutic methods that helped Delia was group therapy, both in-patient and outpatient. In addition, she attended support groups for DID and survivors of incest at a Women's Resource Center. Another helpful therapy was the cognitive therapy that her primary therapist combined with his own alertness to emergence of manipulative alters who were trying to sabotage therapy. Delia's "center" felt that she knew her primary therapist from "another time" and so she was a cooperative force in the integration process. Another alter, a male, represented her negative force and he misled the therapists, had a violent streak and promoted suicide.

CORE, CENTER, HOST, ETC.

By psychiatric convention, the terms core personality, center, host, etc. are used to describe certain phenomena.

- **Host:** The *host* personality has executive control of the body the greatest amount of time during any given period.

- **Presenting:** Host is also a term used for the *presenting* personality because of psychiatric symptoms: depression, anxiety, time loss, etc. The presenting personality is the one that presents itself for therapy.
- **Original:** The *original* personality is the theoretical construct that denotes the identity from which the first other personality split off and usually has no knowledge or awareness of the alters.
- **Self-helpers:** There are often personalities called *inner self-helpers* that assume a serene, logical, benevolent bearing.
- **Centers:** Self-helpers also are called *centers, protectors, advisors, keepers, scanners,* and so on. The terms assigned depend on the sophistication and education of the patient. The centers are often positive figures in their lives, or culturally sanctioned protective figures, such as the Virgin Mary, archangels, guardian angels, saints, protective older relatives or friends.
- **Core:** The *core* personality usually refers to the birth personality or the *original* personality. Also, it is referred to as the *nuclear* personality.

LAYERS OF ALTERS

In Delia's case, where there were more than 300 alters and whose abuse spanned over 30 years, there were five layers of consciousness with the lesser trauma, as Delia called it, emerging first. As the abuse became more horrific, there was more fragmentation to ensure the individual's survival. When Delia referred to the core personality in each layer, it was not her birth personality, but the particular alter that seemed to be the leader or strength of that layer. These core personalities also knew of the existence of all the alters at that level, as well as their memories.

Among Delia's alters child-like personalities are quite common. Some are polarized into love/approval seekers (Sunny), distrustful/angry /suicidal/homicidal (Lillith), and yet there are alters who try to deny the trauma and preserve the healthy expression of feelings and thoughts. There are personalities who take on the perpetrator's characteristics and sometimes defend or apologize for the abusers. There are personalities who serve specialized functions (keeper of secrets, obstructers to alters who want to tell, alters immune to pain or drug effects, etc.). Since their structures are fragile, these alters will fuse with the core personality once their functions are worked through.

Personalities who are not in control overhear and see one another as hallucinations and may have totally different descriptions of each other (hair color, gender, voice timbre) than what they see when they watch themselves on videotape. Alters who are not in control also try to threaten, intrude upon and even take over the presenting alter. When they contend for control or power, the result is confusion, chaotic thoughts, severe headaches and physical symptoms that arise without overt or laboratory evidence to corroborate the complaint. For example, palpitations may be believed to be a heart attack.

Alters' handwriting differs, and in the case of satanic ritual abuse survivors, some alters write backward. Often stronger alters feel distinctly separate from the others and that killing the others would give them full control of the body. This high degree of autonomy makes them resistant to integration because they equate integration with death.

(That belief has given rise to a bit of foolishness that psychiatrists are prone to. It is one I can share with patients only at the end of their therapy, and with other therapists: Old alters never die; they just fuse away.)

The existence of male alters in female patients is a form of defense against male abusers. It's an effort to be as strong as their male abusers so they can fight them off. Once these alters are empowered in therapy, and no longer have need for their maleness, they integrate.

As treatment of Delia as a collection of alters moved toward Delia as a whole and integrated individual, the male alter's behavior changed and a new alter was born to take its place. That event represented her hopes for the future, her forgiveness of her father, letting go of the past and focusing on the present.

At this time Delia has attained almost complete co-consciousness and partial integration. The changes in her life have been positive and I believe that one day she will attain full integration.

THE COMPLEX OF DELIA'S ALTERS

I'm going to address this subject out of the flow of Delia's story because it's so convoluted and is a story in itself.

Delia's alters involved *five levels of consciousness.* The first level consisted of alters who had suffered physical, sexual and emotional abuse by many perpetrators, including parents and extended family members. This very organized level had separated into families. There was an androgynous alter named Scanner, who was the core alter at the first level and seemed to be responsible for the births of other personalities. Scanner was compassionate, kind, wise and cooperative in therapy.

First level: Alters in the first level ranged in age from six months to 31 years. They displayed different characteristics, one stuttered badly, one was frightened and shy, one was outgoing, one was precocious and wise, and so on. One alter, Sunny, took a liking to me and called me Dr. Mom. Both Scanner and Sunny had co-consciousness with the other levels.

There were violent, vulgar, cigarette-smoking young alters. There was a 12-year-old, proper young lady who spoke with a British accent that probably she picked up when they were in Europe. There was a black alter who is straightforward, had a good sense of humor and was virtually fearless. There was 15-year-old Cecilia who emerged in Spain, was outgoing but had a deep vein of anger, and had a male twin, Tommy. There was suicidal Sad Lisa. There was Cassandra, a witch with a Polish accent who was heavily involved in Satanism. There were unnamed alters, too: a hippie; a flirtatious, flamboyant one; a plain one with low self-esteem; a prostitute/drug addict who was strong willed, aggressive, belligerent and short tempered; and one who always came out complaining of stomach cramps. And there was Jeanne who served as a bridge between levels one and two.

Level two: In level two the alters were as young as three months and as old as 80. The Walkin' Dude was a storyteller, a tall, skinny, black, toothless man who spoke in a soft, slow drawl and smiled easily. He was intuitive and had a warm, easy wit. He told tales about the level one alters, using Scanner as the heroine, yet he was amazed that those at the first level even existed. Delia noted that The Walkin' Dude liberally flavored his stories with principles like honesty, courage, determination, and the idea that it's possible to turn wrong into right.

In the second level there was a persecutor, Ex, who punished the others because he felt they had sinned. Some revealed their function in their name: The Observer, The Interpreter, The Interrogator, The Informer, and the Satanists. Mackenzie was the conscience of this level, carrying a sense of responsibility for the others' involvement and subsequent guilt when they were forced to perform murders, tortures, cannibalism, recruiting of victims into the cult. One was a laborer who assisted in desecration of graves and witnessed necrophilia. One was called The Shark, who carried responsibility for participating in cannibalism and was angry, impulsive, aggressive, fearless and fueled by hatred. There was Tough Girl, Screamer and Recruiter.

Also on this level there was Caitlin, a fun-loving, outgoing, intelligent teenager with an Irish accent, with whom I spent some time because she gave me insight into part of Delia's intellectual process. Caitlin said she detested the memories, yet saw Satanic doctrine as a humanistic invention, an "unreligion," invented by men, not gods or demons, so people didn't have to take responsibility for their actions. She said that, in her opinion, born-again Christians were self-styled people who give Christianity a bad name. But then, in seeming contradiction, she said that if we accomplish something, it is through God's intervention and grace, and if we do wrong, it is Satan's work. Like most adolescents, Caitlin was a charming blend of freethinker and traditionalist.

There was also Bethany, a three-year-old who was mute, deaf, blind and appeared to be catatonic, or paralyzed into immobility. Delia explained that her frozen stance was necessary to prevent her from being stung by bees, or being covered by insects. The reason for that possibility was because she was smeared, "anointed," with honey, a ritual know as "balling." Balling appears to have religious significance, but no one could tell me the reason for or the significance of the ritual. Another alter called Bethany a "retart," with a "t."

There were several more alters in this level who appeared to existence to take over when the existing alters could no longer stand the endless and horrible tortures. Those alters were identified as males, females, Caucasians, non-Caucasians with different and distinct accents, behaviors, styles of dress, bearing and living. I grew to recognize the different alters as they came out. Also, I learned to recognize when there was a danger of suicide. Indeed, certain alters would telephone or come into the office to warn me about suicidal or homicidal threats toward other alters.

Certain level two alters were called fine tuners, a core group whose main purpose was gathering, screening and storing information about the others, serving as intermediaries between embattled alters, and intercessors for non-communicating alters. Their manner was robotic and they seemed not to have specific ages. One called "The Recorder" had transcribed a poem composed by the alter Theodora, AKA Teddy, who spoke with a Southern accent. In the poem which confronts Lillith, another one of the alters, Theodora calls herself "the dead babies."

The alter, Lillith, believed she was Satan's child. She was between six and ten years old, did only infant sacrifices, and drank nothing but blood, urine or semen. Her memories were of burials, tortures, imprisonment, suffocation, and threats to her life. In therapy she was able to brave memories of great emotional and physical pain, was verbal and cooperative. (The poem is Appendix III.)

The level two bridge to level three was Noelle. She had been a level one alter, but then became a traveler between levels, trying to increase co-consciousness. She was soft-spoken, gentle and cooperative, and, although her age was three years, she had adult verbal and social skills.

Level three: This was called the Safe Place. The core personality in this level is The Nurse who attended the "wounded ones." (This alter is probably the one who was in control when I encountered Delia working as a nurse in the same institutions where I worked, before she became my patient.)

The Recorder gave me the following information: Delia's birth personality was on this level, named Ailed, Delia spelled backward. She was fixated at the age of three months, the age when the abuse started. That's when two alters, Jeanne and Noelle, took over. The birth personality is developing communication skills gradually and seems to have no awareness of her life. I believe that Ailed's "growth" is contingent on the process of uncovering and healing from her macabre memories.

I believe that a determining cause for Delia's survival is that her devoted maternal grandmother demonstrated love and concern for her. Grandmother was Polish, which explains the alters with Polish accents, but unfortunately she died when Delia was young. Delia called her Babushka, and kept her alive as an alter in the third level. The alter, Babushka, had characteristics like the grandmother's (pleasant, loving, cheerful) and her role was to be an immortalized symbol of unconditional love in an otherwise nightmarish existence.

Also on this level there was a male transvestite; a devout Catholic named Mary Catherine, quiet and subordinate because of her vow of obedience. Other alters included a seductive, exhibitionistic child (there were other alters across different levels who had similar traits, which explains her lack of self-consciousness as an actress, and her love of an audience); an alter called Nimue who is a memory trace and knows everything about every level; Dog Girl, so named because she enjoyed bestiality, which had been forced on her; Obsidian, a male alter and protector of the birth personality, unapproachable and intimidating. (He had come out to protect Delia during the fight with her previous husband that ended the marriage.)

Other alters included a seductive woman who loved men; a cheerful young girl who loved to play practical jokes; Winter, aloof, unapproachable, judgmental alter; a 30-year-old streetwise and tough alter; a flirtatious woman-hater who loved men and was an alcoholic; one who was a devout Catholic but at odds with herself because she was a lesbian; a 23-year-old shy alcoholic; a 15-year-old, bright, energetic, smart, enthusiastic girl who had a juvenile delinquent twin who was a shoplifter, liar, drug and alcohol abuser, and swore profusely. The last alter in this level is Jessica, a perfect wife and mother whose life revolves around her children, but who has no opinion of her own.

RETRIEVING MEMORIES

As Delia's recovery continued, she confronted her mother with her recently reclaimed memory that she was put in a refrigerator at the age of three months as punishment for crying. Her mother was so shocked that she could remember the incident that she forgot to deny it and admitted it was true. Around the same time her relationship with her husband seemed to be getting worse. Unexplained injuries were materializing: multiple bruises, chest pains, black eyes that didn't seem to be self-inflicted. Also, she was having more flashbacks, amnesia, insomnia, multiple switching of alters and sometimes she talked in what sounded like gibberish. I taped it, and when I listened closely, I discovered that it was Latin, spoken backwards. Her diet alternated between fasting and bingeing, causing wide fluctuations in her weight.

On St. Winnebald's Day, a Christian holiday when Satanists had sexual orgies that ended in bloody rituals in which they dismember systematically a human sacrifice, Delia began to have seizures with loss of bowel and bladder control. At that point she revealed that her husband had accidentally pushed her down the stairs during an argument and she had lost consciousness.

At the time, Delia and her husband were in the process of divorcing, at her instigation. He didn't want the divorce and asked that they remain friends, and he promised to help her any way he could. I recommended that she go to the Columbine Hospital in Denver, Colorado, a dissociative disorder clinic where she could do some intensive recovery work, which would speed her recovery, thus, saving her money.

During her Clinic stay she planned to leave her two young sons with their birth father, who had a stable home to offer them. She intended to wait a couple of weeks but it became apparent that she would have to move them right away. She had been too open about her cult memories and the cult was sending her warnings: her cat was killed and they broke into her tool shed, leaving signs each time.

DISSOCIATIVE DISORDER CLINIC

At the Clinic she was given a thorough physical, psychiatric and psychological examination. Her case was presented in one of their case conferences, which I attended. The Clinic and Delia kept me apprised of her progress, and when she left the Clinic, she came back into my care.

Level four: In her fourth month at the Clinic her fourth level of alters was revealed. She recovered memories of her biological mother being killed by the cult, and memory evidence that her biological father was, in fact, the man she knew as her father. His father's brother, her uncle, was a high priest and the cult Magister or Ancient.

DEFORMING HISTORY

At the Clinic, Delia made rapid progress. After she returned, she discovered that she could chant in the language of ancient Sumeria. That might seem to indicate that the roots of the cult in which she was involved could be traced back to ancient Sumeria and is, there-fore, somehow legitimized. Not true.

The presence of the language demonstrates the historical and very interesting roots of Satanism in Zoroastrianism, which was born with its prophet, Zoroaster, in ancient Persia, now Iran, which was geographically adjacent to Sumeria. Zoroastrian teachings see the world as a battleground between the forces of good and evil and is still today a strictly patriarchal religion. Satanism's roots are in Judaism's and Christianity's belief in Satan, which historically followed Zoroastrianism. From there it became a worship of the power that both Judaism and Christianity regard as the origin of evil.

More contemporarily, nineteenth and twentieth century oc-cultism became the springboard for the present Church of Satan that exists as a justification for materialism and carnality. It didn't take much goading for opportunistic hedonists with twisted minds to determine that Satanism was useful. So, from the Church of Satan, splinter cults were formed by unbalanced people with sa-domasochistic and sadistic penchants to indulge their ugly fan-tasies. That is the kind of cult that had tried to destroy Delia, and discovering the chanting opened another can of worms.

CULT MEMORIES

The cult was called SADST, Sons and Daughters and Satan's Truth. They used a book called the *Necronomicon*, called demons during their masses which were held during Satanic holidays, which, not coincidentally, corresponded with Christian holidays. She remem-bered names and addresses of specific people involved, places used, where artifacts were kept, and so on, and unfortunately, she was open about the information. The cult heard about what she was telling and she was warned more forcefully. The cult held its ritu-als according to Satanic calendar that Delia gave to me, which is reproduced in Appendix II.

A CHAOS OF MEMORIES

The warnings, in turn, alerted her whole alter system and a state of chaos set in. She was called Shiru, Whirlwind, at birth, she remembered. She remembered being forced to kill her birth mother,[14] whom she had loved dearly. Then she was compelled to witness her eight-year-old brother, Newt, a cult child, hung on a meat hook by the neck, which paralyzed him, but didn't kill him. She was six at the time and being trained to be an Ancient, a cult leader. Lillith, a level two alter, was supposed to kill him on the altar of flat stones. When she couldn't do it, she was punished by having her body submerged in freezing water. At that point, Shosa, another level four alter, emerged and skinned her brother. After that, the comatose but still-living boy was brought to the sacrificial altar in the Center Of The Eye and another fourth level alter completed the murder by cutting out the still-beating heart.

Because of the overwhelming horror of these memories, a cascade of alters formed in level four. Since the memories were too harrowing to bear, the alters/bearers were repressed to the depths of unconsciousness. They were Millennium, Magister I, Slasher (who was required to slash the penis, testicles and intestines), and Meghan, the alter who came out to eat the body parts of her mother and brother when Slasher couldn't do it. When Meghan vomited, she was given a drug by injection to sedate her. Later Meghan went into a very painful grieving process.

There appeared to be yet another level and the alter at that level seemed to hold memories about details of the cult and their modus operandi. At the fourth level she had alters called Apazel (or possibly Asasheel) who seemed to be programmed to dig graves. Another, "666," was a maniac, she said.

Prior to her stay at the Clinic, Delia came to an appointment as Meghan on what was a pagan holiday for Firegod, not a Satanic holiday. She was sad, tearful and still grieving. She was having a hard time making the decision about leaving town to go to the Clinic, and leaving Dr. M. and me as counselors. "666" came out and revealed two things: one, he used another alter, Sabbateus, an infernal name, as his eyes, because he couldn't see; and two, he wanted to kill the cult because of the brutal deaths of Delia's mother and brother.

Level five: I met several other level five alters: Raytoff, unpleasant but not violent; Tutu, who wore certain ceremonial garbs with a symbolic seal on it and made offerings on the altar; Magister II, and about fifty free-floaters who were "Sumerians" with intricate and well-defined individual functions, and were known commonly as Elder Gods. There was also Pasuzu and Inana who, along with the Elders, were the ancient ones embodying the demons and who could kill if they had to.

The revelations carried by those alters comprised the reason for all Delia's sufferings.

CORE RAGE

At a recent appointment Delia said that she could feel the inner rage that had been buried in her unconscious for so long, and her fear was receding. While at the Clinic she was given quite a few medications for headaches and to help her sleep, but they were still ineffective even this long after cult drug administration. There has been fusion between levels one through three, and co-consciousness between all five levels. But there was no lack of work required before Delia healed.

Danielle, an emerging dominant alter wrote the following letter, which serves as a kind of internal status report:

> The others do not lie about me. I can be and have been all the terrible things they say. I am not this way because I'm naturally bad. I am this way because I'm naturally cautious. I trust nobody; I have no reason to. Dr. Callaghan, I'm glad we spoke with each other yesterday. I knew that you were upset about Sunny. What you forgot is that I am Sunny. I'm Sunny all grown up, yet I'm Dani all by myself, too. The

things that happened to Anny, Sunny, Little Robin, Cassandra, etc., etc., happened to *me*, too. I own all these memories. When I talk to you, I talk through a closed door that holds in so much rage that I don't believe there's a word for it. If I sound cynical or sarcastic or sullen it's because I have all these memories. I was able to tell you some of them yesterday. They don't make me cry. I've been with these memories for some time. I cried with Dr. M one night because I just wanted him to know how much it hurts to keep this door closed. Please believe this: if I was really as terrible as some think I am, I would just fucking open that door.

Before I leave, it's important that you know this: I have accepted Scanner's challenge. I will be awake again, but Scanner informed me that it will not be for some time. Until that time, I plan to rest. You may be assured that I will do nothing to interfere with the course of therapy the others receive. Scanner can vouch for me when Scanner chooses to do so. Dr. M, thank you. I have never before shed tears for myself. I promise to do everything I can to prevent hurting you or anybody else and I accept whatever precautions you deem necessary to opening that door.

Danielle

HOW LONG WILL INTEGRATION TAKE?

The integration process, as you can guess by now, can be long and complex. Asking how long recovery will take is like asking how long will it take to build the pyramids? It depends on the availability of building materials, and the willingness and ability of workers to cooperate, and what the plans, the internal specifications, for that particular pyramid are. Each project is different.

With each fusion of an alter with the host personality, a vast range of behaviors, feelings, characteristics particular to each alter is incorporated into the host personality. Since every individual is different to begin with, and each has individual experiences, the integration process is different with each individual.

An example of the process is "Sybil," whom I mentioned earlier. After intensive therapy with Dr. Wilbur, about a dozen alters had emerged and the quality of Sybil's life had improved. An individual's ability to function independently can take place within a year after intensive therapy uncovers the disorder and memories are recalled, but one can count on many years of therapy for full integration.

THE ISSUE OF THERAPIST GENDER

Some DID patients have strong feelings about the gender of the therapist, because they fear harm from someone who is the same gender as the perpetrator. The equation is simple: Most DID patients are female who don't want a male therapist, because most abusers are males who abuse females.

Alternatively, I have found also that therapists who are the same gender as the patient's abuser may have certain advantages, as evidenced by Delia's treatment by her primary therapist, a male. He was a non-threatening, soft-spoken man who showed her a lot of warmth and caring, yet gently thwarted the advances of her seductive alters, which made them feel safe as well. At times a lesbian alter might try to seduce a female therapist and then boundaries have to be discussed and set clearly and firmly.

THERAPEUTIC METHODS FOR DID PATIENTS

Whatever the therapist-patient gender relationship, I believe it is essential to adapt therapeutic methods to the patient's unique needs, avoiding rigid molds and approaches. This becomes even more important with DIDs because of the different ages of the alters. My approach is eclectic.

Most of my DID patients have been to a minimum of six therapists and have had multiple diagnoses that defy use of some of the treatment methods recommended, including electroconvulsive therapy, which I feel is contraindicated. Usually they have visited their family physicians with a variety of physical symptoms, such as anxiety attacks, hyperventilation, fear of choking or dying, dizziness, trembling, menstrual irregularities, depressions, suicide attempts, auditory and visual hallucinations, mood swings, feeling dazed or disoriented, gastrointestinal upsets and frequent, severe headaches. They may have become regular visitors to emergency rooms for shots of narcotic pain medication and then diagnosed as drug addicts. They may go from hospital to hospital when the emergency physicians refuse to give them any more injections or pain medication prescriptions. They may be accused of being hospital dependent. They may seek numerous consultations for obscure body aches and pains, body memories from abuse, sundry phobias and poor treatment compliance.

These patients tend to be so chronically in crisis that some therapists develop countertransference due to frequent cries for help. Until the secret of the abuse is unlocked, the symptoms will go on, and some will actually have a physical breakdown. At that point, in spite of good therapy, inexplicably their recovery stalls and their attending physician calls in a psychiatrist. If the psychiatrist is alert to the signs, the abuse is uncovered.

Those alerting signs are:
1. Prior treatment failure.
2. Three or more prior diagnoses.
3. Concurrent psychiatric and somatic symptoms.
4. Fluctuating symptoms and level of function.
5. Severe headaches.
6. Time distortion or lapses, "lost time."
7. Being told of unremembered behaviors.
8. Others noting observable changes.
9. Discovery of inexplicable objects or handwriting.
10. Hearing voices urging good or bad activity (80%).
11. Use of "we" as collective personal pronoun.
12. Elicitability of alters through hypnosis and/or amytal.

Except for the fact that one is treating more than one personality within a DID patient, her therapy is the same as that used to
treat patients with any other psychiatric condition. Thus, one may
have either group or individual therapy with one patient.

Initial sessions of therapy for DID patients are used to accomplish three important steps. *First*, gather vital information to establish a working diagnosis. This consists of the usual mental status exam to ask specific questions about intellectual capacities,
thought patterns, cognitive abilities, behavior, perceptions, and
thought content. Since trust is of primary importance with DID
patients, establishing rapport is critical from the start, so honesty
is essential. Patients should be encouraged to ask questions and
voice concerns to help ease their fear.

Second, work out a treatment plan. Explain to the patient the
anticipated length of each session, and the probable duration of
treatment, sometimes that's only your best guess, and the patient
needs to know that. Discuss patient's and therapist's expectations.
Experience has taught me that my expectations and my patient's
may be entirely different, and failure to explore those differences
at the beginning of therapy can cause problems later.

Third, because DID therapy can be long and very expensive,
financial arrangements have to be discussed. This is a special problem because DID patients' conditions are so unpredictable that
few can sustain jobs. Options need to be considered to avoid add-
ing a financial burden to the patient's other problems.

Usually, options are limited since there are few therapists who
have experience with DID and who will accept payment on a sliding scale basis. Further, some insurers, like Medicaid and Medi-
care, don't pay certain providers. Due to my interest in this field,
I have taken some patients on a payment schedule, accepted their
insurance payments, or remained as a medication provider while
they saw another therapist for individual counseling. Referral to a
Community Mental Health agency (CMH) may be an option,
but some of my patients have had unhappy experiences with them.

I've been told more than once by CMH workers that they don't even believe in the existence of DIDs and as far as they're concerned such patients have "personality disorders." Due to the existence of attitudes like that, patient's treatment options are limited, which makes discussing costs and payment methods in the early sessions necessary.

THE THERAPEUTIC RELATIONSHIP

After that, sessions involve processing information gathered previously, working through issues of transference and countertransference, and frequent assessment of the status of therapy.

Transference is how the patient relates to the therapist. *Countertransference* is how the therapist relates to the patient. Either can be positive or negative. For example, a patient may view the therapist as a parent, which can help or hinder therapy. DID patients tend to test therapists' trustworthiness by acting out, so therapists need to be consistent as well as flexible. A therapist's patience can be tested sorely with recurrent suicidal and self-harm behaviors. Incidents like superficial cuts and abrasions, scratches, misuse of prescribed pills, cigarette burns, or combining alcohol with medications can seem like manipulative behaviors and provoke countertransference feelings. As therapy progresses and the patient becomes more anxious and depressed, the behaviors may increase, and the patient may not even remember hurting herself. Often one is faced with an incredulous host personality who attributes the self-abusive and suicidal behaviors to alters.

When making a verbal or written contract with the patient to forestall self-harm behaviors, all of the alters need to be involved. Limits need to be reinforced and consequences discussed to ensure that the limits are kept. More than once for contract reinforcement I have had to use short-term hospital stays, or increased frequency of the sessions, or invited the involvement of supportive family members and friends, or even used involuntary commitment to a state facility when the self-abuse continued or became threatening.

There have been times when I have had to terminate the therapy in self-defense because the acting out went on and on, the contracts were broken, and I felt too burned out and used up on the case to continue. However, I never terminate therapy until after I have tried hard to work through whatever barriers existed in the therapy. In my opinion, ending therapy mid stream is to be avoided if at all possible, since no matter how well the termination goes, the patient usually feels rejected and abandoned. Usually it confirms their feelings that they are bad and unworthy. It has happened that, patients who were terminated were so fragile and volatile that they took a punitive stance against their therapists, concocted egregiously false charges and sued their therapist, creating all kinds of unnecessary personal and professional havoc. No matter how many years I have practiced, terminating is still the hardest thing for me to do, and something I avoid until there's no alternative. Even then, I make every effort to place the patient with a highly competent colleague before termination.

As therapy continues and new personalities emerge, four things need to be established about each alter. The first is obvious: one needs to know the *name* of each alter to talk to them. Two, establish the *age* of each by determining when they emerged, which offers a sense of the flow and pivotal traumas of the patient's abuse. Three, to guide the course and effectiveness of the therapy, learn the *reason* the alter was created, out of what specific incident. Finally, there is a hierarchy of *power* among the alters that is measured by the length of time they have been present, the knowledge they hold, and the decisions they make. While it's time consuming to become familiar with each alter, it is essential to learn what power they hold in the "family," which is the patient.

There have been cases in which there have been over 200 fragmented alters. The original person fragmented into alters, which subdivided again. I can't tell you exactly *how* such extensive fragmentation happens, but certainly *why* it happens has its foundation in prolonged, intense abuse. In cases of extended fragmentation there is usually a "center" that identifies itself as a "maternal self-helper," "controller," "data bank," or even with a letter of the alphabet. The center doesn't function as an alter; it has no gender, feelings or effect on the alters, and has robotic behavior and tone. Usually it knows about all of the alters, but they don't know of the center.

A VARIETY OF TREATMENT MODELS

The relationship between child sexual abuse and mental illness has never been demonstrated scientifically by any study that I know about. But there's no lack of literature discussing the existence of child sexual abuse in a significant number of people with diagnosed mental illness. In short, the inner rage that can and does develop from child sexual abuse has and does cause a variety of emotional illnesses.

There is no way of measuring or comparing degrees of severity of sexual abuse. Sexual abuse causes pain, and pain is a signal that something is wrong, whether it's mental or physical pain. *All* sexual abuse is damaging, even though the resulting emotional illness may be judged mild, moderate or severe. By the same token, no matter how severe the illness is, it can be treated successfully by drawing from a number of treatment models.

Individual psychotherapy can employ psychoanalytically based psychotherapy using a classical *Freudian* method, or the *neo-Freudian* method. There are many other similar types of psychotherapy, such as Transactional Analysis and Reality-Oriented psychotherapy, and although they have been modified along the way and called by different names, the basic premise remains the same as the Freudian and neo-Freudian models. The generic name for them is "dynamic" psychotherapies.

Freudian: The concept of classical psychoanalysis is that psychological difficulties arise from unsuccessful resolution of (instinctual) childhood conflicts, which were rooted in either real or imagined involvement with significant individuals in the child's life. These conflicts, which were too painful and difficult for the child's ego to handle at the time, were repressed from awareness and didn't go away but remained active and dynamic, waiting to be expressed.

Although repressed, the conflicts exert influence on the individual's feelings, perceptions, reactions and responses to people and situations. These behaviors are involuntary, repetitive and in-flexible, and beyond the individual's voluntary control. Therefore, they impair his or her emotional maturity, judgment and adapta-tion to life. The goal of psychoanalysis is to break down the de-fense mechanisms of the repressions that guard the entrance to the unconscious. Then the freed memories can be worked through, allowing the person's stunted emotional growth to reach full de-velopment. In Freud's opinion, psychoanalytic treatment acts as a second education of the adult, as a corrective to her education as a child.

In the case of DID patients, analytic therapy encourages trans-ference, facilitates regression, not only in thinking but also in feel-ings and behavior, allowing young alters to express themselves in ways that feel comfortable and safe. Patients use the technique of free association, saying what comes to mind without censor. The therapist is trained to recognize that a "therapeutic alliance" is necessary before the individual can trust enough to relinquish these painful memories. Without a therapeutic alliance, therapy may be obstructed by "resistance," which is demonstrated by long silences, forgetting appointments, blocking, and so on.[15]

Countertransference can occur when the analyst responds to the therapeutic situation unconsciously with agenda determined by his or her own needs. Obviously, this will obstruct therapy if it isn't recognized and dealt with. Freud recognized this possibility and recommended that analysts resubmit to analysis periodically, preferably every five years.

Analysts are expected to listen to the patient, observing care-fully both verbal and non-verbal behavior, analyzing and inter-preting elements garnered from dreams, free associations, slips of the tongue, and acting-out behavior, such as suicide attempts, vio-lent verbal and non-verbal behavior. Analysts usually delay sharing interpretation to allow patients their own insight into their issues. That insight then helps patients to psychological and behavioral change.

Neo-Freudian: These are simply modified ways of doing psychoanalysis. The biggest difference is the absence of the analyst's couch. It puts patient and therapist face to face and is more interactive, although other therapeutic elements remain the same.

Existentialism: This is an outgrowth of the neo-Freudian model. Its theory is based on the freedom to define oneself, and the capacity to exercise this personal freedom is essential to being fully human. Anything that interferes with that freedom to make responsible choices is psychologically unhealthy. That is similar to Freud's insistence that reducing our unconscious and enhancing our conscious helps us take more responsibility for our thoughts, feelings and, therefore, our behavior. To be aware, conscious and responsible is the definition of health, he taught.

Gestalt: Another popular therapy. A holistic, here-and-now oriented form of psychotherapy that stresses the value of current experience to organize and structure our concept of ourselves. Based on our awareness of self, either we assimilate or reject experience and use it to define ourselves. A learning experience is one from which we may gain insights and be prompted to reorganize our thinking. All contact with the world outside ourselves influences our thinking, but our awareness comes from our unconscious. These two work together to create a new awareness of self in the world.

To resist this influence and change is called *confluence*, meaning avoidance of contact. Using that word to mean resisting influence seems to fly in the face of reason, I know. After all, the confluence of rivers is where rivers flow together. Unfortunate as the choice of words is, it points to the very paradox of Gestalt, which is that every person becomes an individual, becomes more him or herself, through interaction with his or her environment. It is in the friction of interaction that a personality finds its shape, its unique and indivisible configuration, its gestalt.

Still within Gestalt, the term *retroflection* means providing for ourselves the response we want from others. In short, embodying for others the treatment we want.

Behavior therapy: Another form of individual therapy which sees pathological or unhealthy behaviors as learned, involuntarily acquired, undesirable habits of responding to environmental stimuli. Its techniques are classical conditioning and operant conditioning. The purpose is to replace unhealthy behaviors with healthy ones. The therapeutic purpose is focused and the method used is planned and controlled.

Classical conditioning was made popular by Pavlov's familiar salivating dog experiment, but practitioners and advocates Wolpe and Lazarus actually used it as therapy. The interesting and disturbing aspect of this therapy is behaviorists' belief that a patient's pathological behavior is learned, but a therapist is responsible for the patient's recovery. If a patient fails to recover, according to that thinking, it's because the data wasn't analyzed correctly, or the therapist's technique was lacking. I'm in favor of taking responsibility for what we do and don't do, but try as hard as we might, the ultimate resolve must be in a patient.

A behaviorist initiates his patient to her therapeutic sessions with an information session, telling her about the technique and how it will help her change her learned habits. He assures his patient that her behavior and reactions can all be explained in terms of previous learning and that she is not mentally ill. An example of one technique used is counter conditioning, based on the idea that many troublesome thoughts and behaviors are anxiety-based and the treatment consists of treatment of anxiety. A frequently used treatment is *reciprocal inhibition*. It's based on the premise that, if a response that inhibits anxiety can be triggered by a stimulus that creates anxiety, the association between the stimulus and the anxiety is weakened and, thus, the anxiety will decrease or disappear.

Behaviorists have in their armamentarium such questionnaires as "Life History Questionnaire," "Fear Survey Schedule," and "Willoughby's Neuroticism Schedule." These are used to gather information about family history, and how rewards and disciplines are determined. The patient's educational, interpersonal and sexual history is taken. Then, after all the information has been gathered, the patient usually is told immediately what can be hoped for in therapy and how it will be pursued. After my years as a psychiatrist, and knowing how a patient's case can grow, change and develop, I find such dispatch astonishing and certainly unrealistic.

One of the more popular counter-conditioning techniques is *assertiveness training*. Others include *systematic desensitization*, which is self-explanatory; *modeling*, in which the therapist assumes the role of the patient to demonstrate a desired behavior; *flooding*, the opposite of desensitization, in which the patient is exposed to an overwhelming flood of the stimulus that evokes maximum anxiety. The idea there is that one can feel only so much anxiety, so after surviving a flooding, the anxiety will lessen or disappear. If not, treatment continues until the anxiety and phobias are mastered.

Support groups: Certainly there are other strategies for treating the ravages of child sexual abuse. One of the more successful has been support groups. These may deal with peripheral issues, outgrowths of the abuse, but not the abuse itself. These can include any one of a number of Twelve Step groups based on Alcoholics Anonymous, such as A.A. itself, Narcotics Anonymous, Overeaters Anonymous, Sexual Addiction Anonymous, Agoraphobics Anonymous, Adult Children of Alcoholics, and a host of others. There is also Women for Sobriety, Secular Sobriety. Finding the right group, one that addresses the issues important to the individual, can be a search. Specifically, survivors need a group that addresses dysfunctional behavior.

Incest support groups do exist that deal directly with sex abuse issues, but these groups tend to suffer from a low-energy problem. Due to the stress levels survivors have sustained, their physical and emotional stamina tends to be depleted and, more than any other recovery group, they succumb to depression, panic attacks, anorexia and bulimia, alone or in combination. Often they require long-term antidepressant and antianxiety medications.

Spiritual counseling: Some survivors benefit from spiritual counseling, if the church has been a source of strength and support for them. However, therapists need to be careful about recommending counseling from clergy. Some churches deal heavily in guilt, and guilt, inappropriately felt, can cause more decompensation or deterioration of the patient's condition. Also, full knowledge of the patient's history is necessary for any counseling to be effective, and depending on the clergy and the church, that may or may not be appropriate.

Other supports: Exercise, maintaining a nutritionally balanced diet and balanced sleep pattern are important to recovering people. Relaxation tapes and visual imagery are useful, as well as a form of self-hypnosis to drive out negative thoughts, all of which provide respite from psychotherapy. Family therapy is useful, as well, when it is appropriate, and obviously that depends on whether or not there was any family involvement in the victimization.

All of these modalities of treatment may be used in conjunction with one another. Since we deal with individuals, it is necessary to recognize each patient's uniqueness so the therapy provides maximum benefit.

MY PREFERRED TREATMENT MODE

I prefer to use a combination of techniques, determined by an individual patient's needs. Among the factors I consider are educational background, age, personality traits, and experience both in terms of abuse and life experience. Obviously, as therapy continues and new information enters the picture, I may need to shift between or into new modalities. Therapists have to be light on their professional feet. Recovering people have to be resilient and patient.

GOALS OF THERAPY

Integration is the ideal goal of DID therapy, consolidating all of the personality fragments into one entity, one whole, healthy, happy, contributing and functioning person. Unfortunately, the alters may resist integration as analogous to their death. The stronger alters may even create a crisis to prove their superiority over the host personality, and attempt to unseat the host, to take control from what they see as an unstable, untrustworthy wimp who can't even own her own memories. This possibility demonstrates the need to know the name, age, reason for and power of each alter, because it helps the therapist form the alters into family units. Family units are the beginning of cohesion.

The alters may have formed alliances and enmity among themselves already. I have seen these big sister/big brother arrangements encouraged between younger and older alters in most cases of great numbers of alters. Forming them further into family units promotes a closer, more supportive relationship and allows the center a choice of alters with whom to identify, and allows the alters and center to become conscious of each other. Sometimes non-dominant but co-conscious alters simply are absorbed into the persona of the dominant ones. The remaining alters explain the disappearance as "going into the black hole," "growing up," "gone to sleep," or simply "gone."

The alters' dramatic behavior often puzzles, frustrates and angers therapists, since the conduct can appear contrived and manipulative. Small wonder they are often misdiagnosed as having Borderline Personality, although the two diagnoses don't necessarily have to be mutually exclusive.

One therapeutic technique that I have used with great success when alters don't relate well to each other is Internal Group Therapy. I use video taping to allow patients to see their different alters and their respective agenda, feelings, behavior, appearance and knowledge. One of my DID patients, 38 years old, described her alters to me as an 11-year-old male, a 16-year-old female tomboy, and several adult women distinguishable by their manner of dress. While her description was useful, personally I prefer video tapes used specifically in later stages of therapy when most of the alters have emerged and participated in therapy. If video is used too early, however, I find that patients have great trouble accepting what they see and are inclined to terminate therapy abruptly, to their great disadvantage.

Incest survivors who have been involved in cults, like Delia, are extremely hard to treat because of the preventive programming planted in the survivor's mind. Programming for self-abuse is a common tactic in satanic cults, and is used to effect a periodic check of the strength of the programming's control over the survivor. The control is based in one alter, who wields power of control over other alters and the center not to tell, or to instigate punishment if even a small slip in secrecy is considered, which explains exhausting acting-out behavior.

Programming for suicide is implanted for several more reasons:

- To test the force of the cult's control over the survivor.
- To demonstrate the power of Satan and the cult.
- To bind the survivor more tightly to the cult in case she's "rescued."
- To punish her should she talk after the rescue.
- To show how powerfully she has been trained, which terrifies her more deeply than keeping silent.

As if that isn't irresponsible, self-serving and destructive enough, survivors have been programmed to attempt suicide, not only if they reveal cult secrets, but also at *specific ages or on command*. The following abbreviated case history will illustrate my point.

SHARON

Sharon, 22-year-old DID patient, recalls incidents of cult involvement at a very early age, possibly from infancy. As far as cult-caused DID, sadly her case is textbook. She believes that her paternal grandparents and parents were cult members, and recalls severe multiple sexual abuses by those grandparents, her father, and other cult members. She remembers her mother beating her with a wooden spatula. When it broke, her mother took her to the store to choose the next beating instrument.

She has more than 175 alters, but fewer than 50 are primary alters. Her younger alters remember being sexually abused over and over. She suffered vaginal penetrations with assorted objects, including a snake. She remembers being forced to submit to oral sex and to witness and at times participate in sex between adults, between children, and between adults and children. Her sexual abuses were described as sadistic and always accompanied by pain or threats of pain.

She has vivid memories of people being sacrificed, asserting that several of these people, including children, were street people from Chicago. She recalls infants being sacrificed at an altar, including her own infant when she was 16 years old. She has nightmares of seeing blood all over. She recalls being forced to eat the flesh of the murdered people and to drink their blood, a corruption of the Catholic Church's rite of Holy Communion. She recalls being put in a coffin and thrown among the dead bodies.

She recalls people being skinned alive in front of members of the cult. She recalls robed worshippers chanting and what seemed to be Satan coming out of a fire. There is a strong probability that she was drugged at the time. She recalls seeing an inverted cross and people defiling the cross with excrement. She recalls her father being publicly beaten and tied to a cross. She thought at the time that he might be killed. She was spared, she believes, because she was being groomed to be a high priestess, to follow her mother, but apparently that never happened.

Sharon became an extremely self-controlled child to escape death. She said she learned not to cry in spite of the pain. At no time during the four years that I treated this patient did I ever see her cry.

At age 22, she appears much older. She is tall and beautiful, with a gentle voice. She lives a very secluded life with her maternal grandmother, who was not involved with the abuses and may not have known of them. Sharon likes order, and when she is under stress, her need for organization intensifies. Her DID was discovered when she attempted suicide at 18, around the time her parents divorced.[16] Despite that, she still was able to graduate from high school. While she was in the hospital, a staff nurse found her regressed into a child with a different name. Her psychiatrist at the time was skeptical of DID, so a sodium amytal interview was conducted. Some of the horrors I related above were revealed during that interview. Not long after that her psychiatrist moved to another part of the States, and I took over her care.

Initially my reaction to Sharon's bizarre history was skepticism, so I decided to go forward with Reality Oriented Therapy. I discouraged her from dwelling on the past, urged her to release therapist failures in the past and move forward with her healing.

Shortly after we began therapy she became very frightened because one of her more violent alters started to cut cult symbols on her arms. The cuts extended to other hidden areas of the body so that her grandmother wouldn't see them. Sharon swore that they were just there when she woke in the morning. She found herself driving to places without knowing why, including wooded areas, which frightened her since cult rituals usually were held in such places. She began to suffer from insomnia and headaches, partly because she was so afraid of dissociating and losing control. At about the same time, 15 additional alters came out. They brought no new memories and had no apparent purpose except to exercise tight control. For example, they kept her from eating by telling her she was too fat.

I put her back in the hospital for about a week to get her stabilized on her medications for headaches, anxiety and panic attacks, nausea, and auditory hallucinations. As it turned out the hallucinations were the voices of several of her alters that kept her mind so busy that she couldn't concentrate or sleep. I cut her medications down, since they didn't seem to be effective in spite of high dosage. The side effect of tiredness she had complained of in the hospital left. I encouraged her firmly to recognize her own strengths and learn to use them in her healing. She had expressed a lot of anger at the people who had hurt her, including a former therapist. That anger was righteous and healthy, I told her, and urged her to use it as a source of strength to aid her healing. Be more assertive, I encouraged her.

I should have been more specific about what to be assertive about because when she took my advice, she turned her anger on me! She said I didn't trust her and that I was taking her problems lightly. I assured her that I took her problems seriously, which was why she was in the hospital, but I was skeptical about some things she said, and I was concerned about her dependency on the hospital. At that, she got angry and demanded to be discharged. I complied . . . in a week. Her self-mutilation had improved, but subsequently she was readmitted for dehydration and starvation.

I have met both of her parents. Her father offered to help, but declined my suggestion that he help Sharon with her bills. His resources were limited, he said, although Sharon noticed that he had just bought a new house, a new car and a boat, and that he lived with his girlfriend. He didn't bother to ask what Sharon's problem was. "He knows," Sharon observed wryly. Her mother I met twice. Neither time did she ask what Sharon's problem was. Her stepfather scolded her for hurting her mother by returning to the hospital for dehydration and starvation. Her mother visited a couple of times and said she was tired of visiting and Sharon should come home and help her clean the kitchen. Only her grandmother, with whom she lived, seemed to be willing to care or help.

During summer solstice she was admitted again briefly for suicidal thoughts. The Feast of All Souls, Halloween, and many other Christian holy days are high-risk times for Sharon and others who have been abused by satanic cults because those are days on which Satanists are most active and vicious.

(Those who practice the venerable Craft of the Wise, Wicca or Witchcraft, also have rituals that mark solstice dates and other seasonal events, but they do not present the vicious destructiveness of Satanism. Wicca is an ancient nature-based religious cult

that predates Christianity in Europe. The most remarkable difference between Witchcraft and Satanism is that the former is life-
based, and takes its momentum from the flow of the seasons. Its
hallmark is unity, respect and cooperation. Satanism, on the other
hand, is based in selfishness, violence, control and revenge. The
fruit of one is life; the other is death.)

Since Sharon had a significant amount of therapy and multiple sodium amytal interviews prior to seeing me, I decided to
begin video taping her alters so she could see them for herself.
That was a sound decision. Her response was quick and positive,
and her prognosis was better, including self-affirming work on
channeling her inner rage. Her hospital dependency diminished
and she began doing volunteer work.

Recently she confronted her father about his sexual abuse. Very
few survivors get the chance to face their abusers. Even though he
denied it, which is predictable for sexual abuse survivors no matter
who the victimizer is, Sharon says the confrontation felt cleansing
for her. Now we're working on how she can learn not to be
revictimized, always a very real danger, and how to accept feelings
of self-worth that are beginning to emerge, and that she finds disturbing.

Sharon is eager to resume her education, even though it will
mean sacrifice. She is happier than I've ever seen her, and she has
direction, hope, a sense of purpose and a sense of self-worth and
vindication.

CONCLUSIONS

Both Delia and Sharon were diagnosed with and are recovering
from DID, and both are survivors of cult abuse. I have many other
clients who are multiples who have had no contact with cult abuse,
but all of my clients with DID are survivors of child sexual abuse.

Any kind of abuse is traumatic. Child sexual abuse is probably
the most traumatic, especially if incest or cult activities are involved. These children are not protected, as any child has the right

to expect to be, nor can they defend themselves, so they do what they have to do to survive: they retreat inside themselves, but even there they haven't the emotional or intellectual resources they need. So, emotionally and mentally they are ripped and shredded into multiple personalities. It's not surprising that, as a consequence, they have a burning rage buried inside. Nor is it surprising to realize that the rage must be uncovered, brought up and out into the open, and dealt with before they can reintegrate.

It is a constant source of joy for me to see again and again that these survivors can and do survive, reintegrate, and are healthy, happy, contributing members of the global village. Their recovery is a tribute to the vitality of the human spirit.

I can't leave this chapter without admitting to a sense of dread caused by two events. The first was that Margaret Mead's now classic book, *Coming of Age in Samoa*, published in 1949 about teenage sex practices in Samoa, was challenged and mocked in 1983 by Derek Freeman.[17] The second is a film clip I saw of one of the oldest informants of Dr. Mead's research, in which the subject, a woman now in her 80s, claims that every person interviewed for the study lied in a cultural practice called *recreational lying*. The woman claimed that she and all the other girls interviewed were just having fun at Dr. Mead's expense, but Dr. Mead took them seriously.

After watching that I sat back and wondered in dismay what defense Dr. Mead had under those circumstances? As I shook my head, a thought shot through my mind: What defense do therapists have if their clients diagnosed as DID decide to do a little recreational lying? Then what can a therapist do when these same clients, when their lie is unmasked, tell some additional lies while suing their therapist? What defense does a therapist have, especially given how lively the False Memory Syndrome pot boils? How can reality be sorted from fantasy and maliciousness? Will we, because of a few liars, be forced to throw survivors back into the cold prison of child abuse memories?

CHAPTER FOUR

PSYCHOGENIC AMNESIA

300.2 [DSM IV-R]

Psychogenic Amnesia is a persistent or recurring feeling of detachment from one's body or mental processes, as though living one's life as an automaton, or watching a dream. It is also a sudden inability to recall important personal information that is not caused by an organic mental disorder. The extent of the disturbance is too great to be explained by ordinary forgetfulness.

There are four types of recall disturbance:

Localized, or circumscribed, amnesia, is the most common type. It is characterized by the failure to recall all events occurring during a circumscribed period of time, usually the first few hours following a profoundly disturbing event.

Selective amnesia is less common and is the failure to recall some but not all of the events occurring during a given period.

Generalized amnesia is one of the two least common types, in which failure of recall encompasses the person's entire life.

Continuous amnesia is the second least common type in which the person can't recall events subsequent to a specific time up to and including the present.

During an ongoing amnesia episode, perplexity, disorientation and purposeless wandering may occur. When the episode is past, usually the person recalls the disturbance. The amnesia begins suddenly following a severe psychological stress, usually involving a threat of physical injury or death. During the period of amnesia there may be indifference toward the memory disturbance. The impairment varies from mild to severe, and termination of the amnesia is typically abrupt with complete recovery as a rule. Hypnosis or a sodium amytal interview usually brings about a rapid recovery of memories and recurrences are rare.

RAY

Ray is a 47-year-old incest survivor who grew up on a remote and isolated farm with nine sisters and brothers. The children walked a mile east to their one-room school on an unpaved country road. Their nearest neighbor was several miles west on the same road. That remoteness, I would learn, played a part in Ray's early psychiatric history.

RAY'S HISTORY

His tendency to compulsive behavior was expressed as workaholism. He put his company's needs ahead of his own and his family's, often working long hours without compensation. As a result, he was promoted to a supervisory position.

Fifteen years earlier Ray had seen another psychiatrist as a result of depression following a lumbo-sacral, lower back, injury and surgery, and the way the company treated him. He had always put the company even before his family, and when he returned to work he discovered that he had been demoted from foreman to assistant and suffered a substantial pay cut. At the same time there was intense, prolonged union conflict causing firings and stripping of employee privileges.

His family situation compounded his stress. He had four children. The oldest, a son, quit school due to school phobia. The second, a 15-year-old daughter, had sexual interactions with a neighbor boy that provoked severe stomachaches. The 12-year-old son was having severe headaches, and the eight-year-old was school phobic.

A history of problems in his birth family intensified his psychiatric vulnerability. His mother had spent time in a psychiatric hospital for a major bout with depression. A sister had tried to choke her baby while in the throes of depression. Another sister had epilepsy and was developmentally disabled.

Everything crashed in on Ray and he became severely depressed, psychotic, suicidal and unable to function. That's when he sought psychiatric help originally. During treatment Ray became impotent, which caused marital problems. He blamed his impotence on his prescribed antidepressants and antipsychotic medications and wanted to stop taking them. About that time his psychiatrist referred Ray to me prior to leaving the area.

AS MY PATIENT

When Ray and I discussed his medications, I told him that to stop his medications abruptly would be ill advised psychiatrically and dangerous physically. Instead, we agreed that I would help him to reduce the dosage. I titrated his medications, reduced the dosage gradually while observing Ray's reaction carefully, to the point that he wouldn't suffer withdrawal complications when he quit.

After that, Ray's appointments were on a monthly basis due to the long distance he had to drive and the unreliability of his car. Also, another important piece of data that I noted in his file and waited to see what it would reveal was that he was unwilling to spend more time talking. I had no choice but to wait; since we can never go faster than a patient can tolerate, patience is essential in therapy.

Ray was always detached, even appearing to be disoriented. He volunteered no information and answered only direct questions. I attributed his reticence to the change of psychiatrists, and even though I wanted to be forbearing, I was sure our process could move faster. I asked him if his emotional distance was due to his efforts to adjust to me and his grief over loss of his original therapist?

"No," he said quietly. "I'm always this way."

Abruptly, he burst into tears. When he could talk again he said he felt so guilty and ashamed. Since our last appointment, he told me, he had molested his 15-year-old daughter while he braided her hair.

THE INCIDENT

He had been standing behind her braiding her hair and the repetitious movement of his hands and the warm closeness of their bodies had caused him to slip into a trance-like state. He reached out and fondled her breast, unaware of what he was doing until his daughter began to cry and pulled away. Ray regained awareness and jerked his hand back, mortified, shocked, and ashamed that he could do such a thing to his own child.

As he told me about the incident tears stood in his eyes and he was so embarrassed that he looked at the wall, making eye contact with only brief glances. Stumbling over his words, he told me how ashamed he felt and wanted to know how he could help his daughter to prevent long-term emotional damage. He had offered to pay for counseling sessions for her, he said, but she refused. What could have caused such a thing, he asked me in anguish?

By that time Ray had been with me for three years, and I had worked with him to get him off the medication, as he requested, even though I wasn't convinced that it was the best psychiatric decision, which I told him. The incident with his daughter and his self-destructive thoughts confirmed my reservations. During his next appointment a few days later he told me that he was feeling extremely suicidal again. He fantasized about blowing his head off and staging an accident with his car or motorcycle, he told me. Yes, he agreed that it was a good idea for him to check into the hospital.

A phone call from his wife confirmed what he told me. They

had been sitting in their living room, she told me. She had been doing some handwork, and he appeared to be lost in thought, staring into space. Then, almost as if he were in a trance, slowly he raised his hand, pointed his index finger at his temple like a gun, and pulled the trigger.

"What are you doing?" she asked, puzzled.

He turned to her, eyes absolutely blank, and shook his head. He had been unaware of his actions. The following morning, Ray had telephoned to make an appointment with me, and then agreed to be hospitalized. During that hospitalization we learned what prompted his reaction.

PULLING THE PLUG

During this hospitalization we recovered more repressed memories by using sodium amytal, but it took three weeks before I could convince him to do so. Ray is a very quiet and reserved man and would never offer any information spontaneously; I had to pull it out of him, and even then he tendered only the bare essentials. I theorized that his repressed conflictual and unacceptable memories kept him inarticulate and unwilling to delve beyond the spare material we'd extracted in three years. To speed his process and save him money in the long run, I suggested that we try some short-cut methods. He agreed eagerly.

We began with hypnosis, but he couldn't concentrate. His other therapists had tried other uncovering techniques, such as relaxation and a concomitant use of medications, but the results had been fair at best.

I don't use sodium amytal lightly, nor do I avoid using it. In the few thousand cases in which I've used amytal over the past 17 years,[18] the worst side effect to my patients has been an allergic response. The patient developed hives, which I treated with a Benadryl injection, and the hives went away. There was no permanent harm. Probably the most serious side effect is a spasm of the larynx, which is another allergic response, but I have never seen this happen. If it should, it would be treated promptly with Benadryl and oxygen.

The sodium amytal interview is a good adjunctive procedure to get to deeply buried memories that may be hard to access because of the extreme trauma associated with the memory. (See chapter 16 for a clinical discussion of sodium amytal use.) It serves to get past a stalemate in the discovery process and can cut short a long process of normal memory recall.

Often the memories are repressed and won't come out naturally. When they do come out under sodium amytal, the memories can re-traumatize the patient. Nonetheless, the poison that causes the infection must be found before healing can begin. The possibility of re-traumatization is diminished by the presence of a safe individual—the therapist who walks with the survivor through the minefield of memories. I remind my patients often during the procedure that these are memories and they aren't happening now.

The drug is injected into a vein as the patient lies on a bed. When she or he slips into a hypnotic state, I begin asking questions to encourage the patient to release repressed memories. The procedure disinhibits patients to the point that they are unable to screen out memories held in their subconscious. During the interview they may rage, scream and cry, and even get up and move around in their anguish. That's why I have a psychiatric nurse present, to keep them from injuring themselves.

Overall, in my experience, it's a positive technique. Releasing repressed memories is beneficial, facilitates therapy and has never, that I have seen or heard of, re-traumatized a patient longer than temporarily. On the contrary, patients have asked me to repeat the procedure when they feel that the three or four hours spent wasn't ample. Further, shortening the duration of therapy by uncovering repressed memories faster saves patients' money and helps them get through and beyond their trauma faster.

RAY'S AMYTAL INTERVIEW

During Ray's sodium amytal interview, he remembered that, when he and a neighbor boy were around six and seven years old, and their sisters were in their early teens, the sisters had used them sexually. At the time the boys thought of it as "playing mom and dad." Later, while he was in his early teens, his sister, older by three years, had forced him to have sex with her. Her tool of persuasion was her threat to share her knowledge that Ray and a neighbor boy had done some sexual experimenting with a neighbor girl five years older than they. There were even times, Ray recalled, when he and his neighbor had sex with their docile cow. (If that stretches your credulity, you may be surprised to learn that bestiality is fairly common for farm boys who are learning about sex in isolation.)

Since our subject is sexual abuse, reading that Ray's sister forced him to have sex obliges us to conceive of a penis as something beyond a tool of aggression and/or abuse. So, setting aside the issue of abuse for just a moment, let me point out that the penis is a vulnerable organ, hanging outside the body, in front of the testes, with only skin to protect it from injury. Not only can it be injured easily, but it can be teased into service, as Ray's sister apparently had learned. A man who has been so victimized may find that later in life his organ will not respond normally and he is impotent. That was part of Ray's problem.

The atmosphere of Ray's youth was radically sexual among the children and incestual in his family. Obviously, Ray's sister had previous sexual experience, but Ray didn't know if it was abusive or consensual. Even though Ray was a child and the sex was forced, he knew that sex with a sibling was wrong and he felt deeply guilty. His sister had threatened to tell their parents about seeing Ray and his friend with the cow and masturbating together. Masturbating, although viewed as normal now, was considered a sin in Ray's family, and even something that could cause blindness and insanity. As a result, he had buried the memory.

PROCESSING THE INFORMATION

As a boy, at some level, Ray felt that what he was doing was repulsive, wrong, and he felt guilty, but he felt unable to control his compulsion to be sexual. His normal reticence as an adult, and the guilt and shame he harbored about these incidents, caused him to bury the information until the sodium amytal disinhibited him.

After the interview, Ray and I listened to the tapes together. He cried while he listened to himself tell me that his daughter had revealed that her maternal grandfather had sexually molested both her and her girlfriend by fondling and attempting to have sex with them. Grandfather had told the girls, who were both about age ten at the time, that he was instructing them in the correct ways to please a man sexually, a highly inappropriate activity between grandfather and granddaughter at any age. Her telling of that incident(s) had excited Ray sexually, which led to him fondling her. But then, afterwards, shame and guilt overwhelmed him and he had repressed the memory so deeply that it was available only under sodium amytal. It was the only time he ever molested her.

Whether she was aware of it or not, and I believe that she was more aware than not, Ray's daughter behaved seductively toward him often, requesting behavior that would be intimate between adults. For example, she asked him to comb and brush her hair and liked to sit with him, her back nestled between his legs. Before the fondling incident he had admonished her about her behavior and about how she walked around the house scantily dressed and asked her to be more modest.[19] She complied for a while and then reverted to immodesty.

Before Ray and I uncovered his father-in-law's malfeasance, I asked Ray if it wasn't possible that her behavior wasn't more childlike and trusting than seductive. He considered the possibility for a moment and then shook his head. She wasn't like that with her mother or anyone else, he said.

In her defense, I believe that her behavior was a reaction to her grandfather's improprieties several years earlier, which she had never

processed intellectually or emotionally. I offered to do some sessions with her, to help her understand how her grandfather's behavior was abusive and how it affected her still, but she refused. At
the time of this writing she still refuses any help.

Later Ray confronted her again about her seductive behavior
and apologized again, taking responsibility for his behavior and
refusing to use his dissociation as an excuse. In fact, he was so
acutely embarrassed by all the information that he had uncovered
that he had a hard time talking with *me* about it. He blushed and
refused to look at me. He tried to dismiss it as a dream. He even
cancelled appointments in an effort to avoid the subject. Ultimately, though, he faced the truth squarely. Not only did the
recovery of the memories allow him to work through the feelings
he had repressed, but it freed him of the impotence that he had
attributed to his prescription drugs.

Then, after that, during an argument, Ray's wife of 22 years
blurted out that she had been having sex with her father all during
their marriage. She said that it had gone on since before their
marriage and, furthermore, she enjoyed sex with her father far more
than with him! He told me that he had been aware that her father
had been around a lot and he had his hands on her more than
necessary and in an unfatherly way. She, too, made excuses to spend
a lot more time with her father than with Ray.

By then Ray was aware that there was a lot of incestuous behavior in both his and his wife's families and he was determined
that it had to stop. At first he didn't feel comfortable talking to his
wife about her relationship with her father, and her other infideli-
ties. I encouraged him to use the tapes of his amytal interview to
help him talk to her.

She came in for a joint session with him, but retracted her claim
about sex with her father and other men. She had spoken only to hurt
him, she claimed, but I'm uncertain what to believe since she's an
evasive, inarticulate woman. When she and Ray came to sessions together, she seemed anxious about what Ray might say, and Ray glanced
at her frequently to assess her reaction to his words.

She came in alone for one session with me. I was direct with her. I told her that it was not customary to admit to a sexual relationship with one's father, and that such an admission could be dangerous. For one thing, incest is a criminal offense in this country, and for another, not all husbands might remain as passive as Ray had. Some, in fact, have been known to get homicidal. She got defensive and insisted that she was telling the truth and, at the same time, Ray was making too much of it.

She never came in to see me again.

As a basically passive man, Ray was no good at confrontation, so he chose to accept what his wife said. He felt he had only two choices, to accept her denial, or accept the end of their marriage.

He talked with his daughter and tried to make amends. At first she was angry, and rightfully so, but she forgave him and worked with him at improving their relationship.

At this writing, Ray is still working at his job, but he's not as ambitious and hard working as he used to be. He chose to stay on a low dosage of a combination of antipsychotic and antidepressant medication for a period and appeared stable and content.

Yet, I'm not convinced that his contentment is authentic nor that it has any power to endure because he accepted his wife's denial too easily and he didn't work through the issues that came out under the sodium amytal. All of that ticks away like a time bomb in the storeroom of his mind.

He has lapsed back into a detached state, and while the gains made under amytal remain unexplored, they aren't lost either. He's just put them on the shelf until he's ready to pursue them. That, I believe, is exactly why he has chosen to stay on the medication, to keep open the door to further therapy.

As his doctor, I'm not comfortable with the way he set aside his problems without resolution. While it is self-destructive to some extent, it *is* his decision. All I can do at this point is to respect his wishes and let him know that I will be available for therapy when he is ready to resume.

CONCLUSIONS

Now, several months later, Ray's life is unresolved and he goes about in a fugue-like state. While he has insight into his marital strife and, though he may be denying reality by choosing to ignore his wife's obviously conflicting messages about her indiscretions and incestuous relationship with her father, he may be wise to keep his peace until she is ready to deal with her problems.

Since Ray's disclosure of inappropriate family sexual behavior by both the grandfather and himself, such conduct has stopped. Ray's self-esteem has improved and he is no longer impotent.

He has been off the antidepressant for over 18 months and he continues to do well at work. At this time, although we have not terminated our therapeutic relationship, Ray feels no need to continue seeing me on a regular basis.

NANCY———————————————————————

Nancy is a 44-old transcriptionist who consulted me for chronic low-grade depression over 20 years. It began when she discovered her father's body hanging from a rafter in the barn. She remembered that, as she stood looking at his feet, her heartbeat had thundered in her ears. Then she felt nauseated. Then she went blank. The blank lasted until he was buried. Her sister told her that Nancy appeared calm and poised while everyone else was weeping and hysterical with grief.

Nancy told me that she had no other memories of her life between 10 and 18. There was no abuse, not much contact or communication between members of her immediate or extended family. Her family was just like everyone else's, she insisted.

Shortly after her father died, she married a distant and cold man. They had one son, but she wasn't close to their son either. After 12 years her husband divorced her unexpectedly, refusing all efforts to identify or repair whatever he felt might be wrong.

That was when she had her first major depressive episode. She was admitted to a psychiatric facility where she was treated with medication and intensive counseling, but she never recovered fully from her depression. Five years later she remarried, but her husband died within two years from liver cancer. Although her depression exacerbated, she continued to function with the help of therapy.

A year later she married a man who had been divorced recently, and who was still feeling deeply guilty by how the divorce had affected his children, all of whom were adults. The daughter, 22, lived with them and accepted no responsibility. When Nancy tried to talk with her husband about his daughter assuming some duties, it brought nothing but arguments followed by strained silence. He spent more time with his daughter than with her, but Nancy felt nothing. She seemed to be outside her body, just watching.

NANCY'S FAMILY HISTORY

A series of hypnosis sessions helped Nancy recall her past. She was conceived unexpectedly ten years after her sister was born. Her mother told her that, if she weren't such a good Christian, Nancy would have been aborted. Nancy's mother was an unhappy, pessimistic, frequently ill woman. When I first met Nancy, her mother was still alive, living in a nursing home, afflicted with Alzheimer's disease. Her father appeared to feel nothing at all. As the years went by her parents became more distant. When she was six or seven, Nancy noticed that they slept in different bedrooms.

When Nancy was ten, she began to menstruate. Since there had been no discussion of such things, she was terrified. Rather than upset her mother, she stuffed a wad of toilet tissue in her pants and ran to her father. She thought the bleeding meant that she had leukemia, like the girl at school, and would need blood transfusions. Her father said, no, these were called monthly periods and they prepared women for motherhood. Then he sent her to her mother. Mother found the whole matter an annoyance. She handed Nancy some pads, told her how to use them and dismissed her. Nancy went back to her father for more information.

Then she went into the only bathroom in the house to take a shower and change into clean clothes. While she was in the shower, her father came in to use the toilet, as was the family practice.

For the first time, Nancy felt self-conscious of her nakedness. Her father showed a new awareness, too. His eyes traveled from her budding breasts to the darkening patch of pubic hair. She hurriedly drew the shower curtain and turned on the water, but her father lingered in the bathroom. When she stepped out of the shower, he father was masturbating frantically and he stared at her pubic area while the semen shot out.

She froze. She had never seen a penis before, let alone an erect one. Then she grabbed her clothes and ran to her room, feeling dirty and strangely guilty. Mom was never told a thing. Father, on the other hand, became quite interested in her period's cycle and instructing her about hygiene.

When she was 16 she had fumbling, painful sex with another uninitiated adolescent who was rough and vulgar as he forced himself into her. The experience frightened her. She told me she felt like she left her body and watched from outside, yet some time later she had no memory of the event. One day her father asked if she'd ever had sex. Caught off guard, she said yes. Enraged, her father took her to her room where he told her to undress. He examined her vagina and then had intercourse with her. That was her punishment, she thought. Again, memory of the incident became lost to her until later, in therapy.

After that she tried to stay close to her mother when her father was around, even if mother asked her to do chores or watch soap operas with her, which she hated. In spite of her precautions, father continued to force himself on her. She locked her door. He took the lock off. She stayed away from home. She was needed at home.

Fortunately, she didn't get pregnant. When she graduated from high school, she left home immediately, just as her sister had. She went to school and made excuses not to come home, just as her sister had. Her mother asked her to come home once and talk to her father because he had been drinking a lot. Her sister wasn't even asked because her mother felt Nancy was the only one who could talk to him. Her sister had returned home possibly five times since she left, and one of the times was to introduce her new husband to her parents, after the wedding.

It was when she responded to her mother's summons that she found her father hanging.

THERAPY

Once in therapy Nancy regained her lost memories quickly and began to work through her anger and grief. She was angry with her mother for her rejection and abandonment, and with her father for his abuse.

She tried to talk with her sister to see if she, too, had been sexually abused, but her sister was remote. When she told her about the abuse, the sister said coolly, "Oh, really? That's too bad." The subject was never brought up again.

Nancy was able to work through her other losses: her divorce; the death of her second husband; her lack of closeness with her only child, which she is working on presently; and her relationship with her third husband and his daughter. When her mother developed Alzheimer's disease, she became her guardian and the conservator of the estate. Consequently, it was a propitious time to work through her anger at her mother for her rejection and ensuing lack of nurturing.

CONCLUSIONS

Nancy had localized psychogenic amnesia. Ultimately, she has recovered her memories and has no further blank spots or amnesia. Her sexual abuse caused long-term problems with normal sexual relations and interpersonal relationships. Her latent distrust of people can still be triggered by the right circumstances, such as the closeness she sees between her husband and his daughter bring to mind her father's coercive relationship with her. I believe that she will work through all remaining issues successfully.

CHAPTER FIVE

DISSOCIATIVE DISORDER
NOT OTHERWISE SPECIFIED

300.15 [DSM IV-R]

Dissociative Disorder Not Otherwise Specified means simply that there is a dissociation that doesn't fall into established categories of dissociation.

JOE————————————————————

Joe was referred to me by his dermatologist, with a diagnosis of scrotal pruritus, severe itching of the scrotum, for which no dermatological reason could be found. My examination revealed nothing either. During my interview he denied feeling depressed, anxious or agitated. He was, he told me, married, a recovering alcoholic, had a good job and enjoyed his family life. While he took Naldecon, an antihistamine for sinus trouble, he'd never had skin problems before, nor was he aware of any food allergies.

He hated crunchy sounds, he said. As a result, his wife and son couldn't eat crunchy foods like potato chips or raw vegetables when he was around. In fact, Joe's annoyance to sound was so extreme that his wife bought and prepared only foods that could be eaten silently. Should someone at the table inadvertently make a noise while eating, Joe would leave the table in silent anger and stay silent and angry for days.

LOOKING FOR A DIAGNOSIS

Symptoms can suggest a diagnosis. In the case of Conversion Disorder (Hysterical Neurosis, Conversion type), symptoms that suggest a neurologic disease actually can reveal the inner conflict. For example,

- Vomiting can represent revulsion and disgust.
- Pseudopregnancy (Pseudocyesis) can represent either fear of or wish for pregnancy.
- Blindness can represent conflict about acknowledging a traumatic event.
- Muteness (Aphonia) can represent conflict over acknowledging inner rage.
- Paralysis of an arm can represent curbed desire to strike out with responsive rage.

An individual gains twice from such a conversion. First, the *primary gain*, is the successful suppression from consciousness of an internal conflict. In other words, when something prompts memory of a disturbing or conflictive event, the physical symptom represents a partial, if temporary, solution. Second, the *secondary gain*, is getting support that might otherwise not be forthcoming. In Joe's case, he got away from what bothered him and his wife was supportive and attentive.

Recently Joe had turned down a promotion at work, feeling that the job would be more stressful for him, which ultimately would be more of a disadvantage than a benefit for him and his family. His decision caused management to turn cool toward him, excluding him from meetings, and subtly making him feel like an outsider.

Although some of his idiosyncrasies caught my attention, nothing in his presenting symptoms and history gave me a clear sense of a significant pathology, that is, mental illness. At that particular time my caseload was full to capacity, so, with Joe's agreement, I referred him to a psychologist for testing and a second opinion. His diagnosis was that Joe was a schizophrenic. I was startled to read the diagnosis in his report because it flew in the face of my observations and instincts.

I considered his case again, going over the details. Joe was a warm person, interacted easily with those around him, and had no thought disorder. For example, he didn't think that thoughts were being put into his mind, nor that his thoughts were being broadcast.

Joe and I discussed the troublesome diagnosis and he agreed to submit to another evaluation by another psychologist. The third opinion was again schizophrenia. I wondered how could these two psychologists come up so easily with a diagnosis that was so clearly wrong to me? Obviously, someone was wrong here. Was it I? My gut instincts told me that we were missing something vital, possibly something hidden deeply.

During his next appointment, Joe and I talked again. He confided to me that he had been taking a mild antianxiety medication.

"Oh?" I responded. "Why do you take that? You told me you're not anxious."

"It helps me sleep some nights when I can't get to sleep," he answered, looking down at his hands.

I noted his disclosure in his chart without further comment, and sent him back to the psychologist for follow up, since my case load was still too full to accommodate him. I would serve only medication purposes on his case, or so I thought.

DEPRESSION

A year later, his second marriage was in crisis and so was Joe. He was suicidal, and when he was hospitalized, I was called in on his case again. His first marriage had lasted only a year when his wife, who had pursued him avidly before they were married, divorced him. To this day he doesn't know why. His second wife also was the pursuer, telling his mother that she was going to "get him at any cost." Now their marriage was unhappy, she said. She couldn't talk to him, he was jealous of her social life and didn't want her to wear things like low cut dresses and bathing suits. His attitude intensified, she said, when she lost a lot of weight and became a counselor for Weight Watchers. Their relationship was more like mother and son than wife and husband, she said, and while divorce was inevitable, she was afraid to leave him for fear that he would kill himself.

She left him anyway and divorced him, and Joe plunged into despair. He requested further counseling with me instead of with the psychologist, which seemed to make sense since he needed medication for his depression, which the psychologist couldn't provide. When our sessions resumed, he was open with me, but he was unable to provide much more information than that his relationship with his mother was poor, and he "couldn't stand being around her." He didn't know why.

We decided to try hypnosis to break through his memory block. Under hypnosis he remembered being an outcast in grade school, but he didn't remember why. His memory refused to yield anything more. We moved on to sodium amytal, but his mind had sealed away his memories too tightly even for its powers to reveal. Whatever it was that had been too much for Joe to handle, apparently during childhood, had been locked firmly away from recall.

Trying to find a clue, Joe talked with his sister—he had two siblings, an older brother and a younger sister. She revealed one of the things that his conscious memory denied, that he had been a bed wetter until he was 12 years old. When he was younger he didn't realize that he stank until his sister told him, and told him he had to take showers. Because he stank, other children shunned and tormented him.

Joe was shaken. Then fragments of memory began to filter back into his conscious mind. He remembered being hanged by his arms in a tree during recess and heckled by the other children. He remembered the nightly torment of not being able to find a dry spot in a wet bed that wasn't changed from day to day. He remembered sitting up in bed and picking maggots off his scrotum from the flies that laid their eggs in his bed.

As Joe remembered, he sat there in my office twisting, jerking, shuddering, his teeth clacking together in horror, eyes wide in terror, mouth opening and shutting without sound. Also, he remembered discovering his father in bed with his parent's friend, a married woman, attracted by the noise of sexual activity.

Joe remembered, and I felt certain that we had the answer to both Joe's itchy scrotum, his obsessive cleanliness and his aversion to noise. But I said nothing to interrupt the flow of his memories. It was important to let light into the dark closets of his memory.

He remembered seeing a dead body. He remembered seeing a horrible face at his window, a "boogie man," not unlike his mother's face, he commented, appearing faintly surprised, or perhaps amused. With that, the flow of memories stopped, and an exhausted Joe sat silently absorbing what he had learned.

We held a joint session with his mother and sister, which proved to be fruitful. His sister told that their father, who had been a practicing alcoholic and was now dead, had molested her sexually when she was a child. She told how the parents and children had sat together in the living room, the parents openly indulging in sexual petting, while the children pretended they didn't see anything.

When I turned to look at the mother to see her reaction to this information, she appeared unperturbed. She took my attention to mean that it was her turn to talk, and smiled at me, saying that, yes, Joe had wet his bed. She used to waken him to go to the bathroom. According to her, it was nothing significant. She told that her husband had been a jealous and possessive man. To hear her, their family was only one step removed from the Cleavers.

In a family like this, where there is little or no loving support or nurturing from the parents, it's not unusual for the children to turn to food and/or alcohol as a substitute, as well as insulation from being hurt. There was evidence that this was the case here. While Joe's mother was gaunt, both his sister and brother were extremely obese, and Joe was a recovering alcoholic. I could understand better his obsessive fear of gaining weight and it helped me understand his compulsive dieting, exercising to the point of injury, and even his occasional eating binges. Also, he said, at infrequent family gatherings, there's little interaction; everyone just sits around and drinks.

STUCK IN DENIAL

Joe spent the next four years in denial, neither willing nor ready for intensive psychotherapy. Although he had uncovered horrible memories, he hadn't internalized them. He hadn't hit bottom yet, as recovering addicts say, meaning that things weren't so bad yet that he felt he couldn't handle them. He saw a psychologist who diagnosed him as a schizophrenic and who used supportive psychotherapy dealing with the present, not the past. I saw him periodically to monitor his progress, review his physical status and review his need for medication.

BACK TO CRISIS

After four years of coping like this, two things combined to make Joe more vulnerable: there was a major shakeup at work and his wife filed for divorce. The combined stress caused Joe problems with concentration and memory. Then he began to abuse his anti-anxiety medication because it helped him forget his distress, as alcohol had, but it backfired and added to his troubles. His coworkers caught on quickly, so management knew what to do one day when his pill abuse caught up with him.

I learned about his self-medicating that day when the personnel manager brought him to my office. He was confused and trembling uncontrollably, he stuttered, stared into space and was unable to comprehend the situation. I hospitalized him immediately and long enough to detoxify him. Then I put him on a new medication that was neither abusable nor addictive. It worked well and he returned to work and did very well for a while, until he encountered at work what for him caused more stress than he could handle.

The company had a large layoff and reassigned the remaining employees. As a result, Joe had to learn the computer. While readers may smile in empathy, remembering their own frustration at trying to learn to use an artificial intelligence that seems more arbitrary than intelligent, ultimately most readers managed to learn. For Joe, it was intolerable. His anxiety attacks destroyed his ability to function at work. His inability to work made him afraid that he would lose his job, then his house, and then he'd be unable to pay his child support obligations. His thinking went round and round obsessively. He couldn't sleep.

Then strange things began to happen that convinced him that there was another person inside him, an alter. But alter or no, someone was leaving the garage door open, which was something he absolutely never did. Someone was mixing crazy concoctions at night, such as cola and cereal, which he found in the morning. He was afraid to go to bed at night, so he slept in his street clothes in the living room. But when he woke in the morning, the television that had been off when he went to sleep was on. We tried hypnosis to coax out the alter, the "other one," but no one came out. We decided to change his sleep medication, which helped him to sleep just fine, but his life became even more bizarre.

Joe and his friend planned to go on a trip together. On the day of the trip, Joe sat and waited and waited for his friend to pick him up. Finally, worried, Joe called his friend to find out what was wrong and when he was coming. "But, Joe," the friend protested, "we've already been on that trip. Don't you remember? I came over to pick you up, and you had wet your pants. I had to help you take a shower before we could go."

On another occasion, Joe called my office to tell me that he found his garage door open and his brand new car was gone. However, his two other vehicles were still there. He had reported his missing car to the police, but told them also that he had a problem with "forgetfulness." He drove around to places where he might have gone, hoping to find his car, but without luck. Finally he walked over to a friend's house, just to talk, and there was his car, parked in the middle of the front lawn.

His friend told him that about six the previous evening Joe had driven the car onto the lawn and come to the door. It was apparent to the friend that Joe shouldn't be driving, so he took him home in his own car, leaving Joe's car where it was. When he saw Joe walk straight for his truck, the friend also took those keys away and took Joe into the house and put him to bed, then took the truck keys home with him.

It was apparent from these stories that Joe was dissociating. During that time the medication, Halcion, a hypnotic, which was what I had prescribed for Joe, was in the news. It caused amnesia, the reports said, for people who took larger doses than a quarter of a milligram. Something, the drug or something else, was causing problems for Joe. He had taken the drug twice, and on both occasions he had acted strangely. The last incident seemed to point to the drug as the cause of his behavior, since he had taken it two hours before the incident, intending to go to bed early. The cause of the other incidents remains a mystery, and he hasn't had a recurrence.

He had become wary of women. Even while he was still married his feelings were ambivalent: he told me that he was eager to have sex with his wife and felt rejected if she refused him. Yet, when they had sex, he felt compelled to leave their bed and sleep on the couch because his feelings had changed to revulsion.

He still had frequent suicidal thoughts, fantasizing about killing himself with a gun. During one of our sessions, he took a bullet from his pocket and put it on the table without saying a word. His action appeared to be a request for my permission not to kill himself. I asked him if that was the case and he said that, yes, he had carried the bullet in case he decided to kill himself, but now, because of his relationship with his son and me, he didn't want to any more.

Almost in the same breath, he asked if I was going to give up on him since he had failed as a patient. Of course not, I assured him. Why did he ask? We had decreased our sessions to twice monthly due to his concerns about his finances, and he had interpreted my agreement to mean that I had lost faith in his ability to recover. I reminded him that he instigated the change in our appointment schedule, that I hadn't thought of giving up on him, and that any time he felt he needed more frequent appointments, I would make time for him. He appeared relieved, and after that he had fewer suicidal thoughts.

Joe took some positive and healthy steps on his own. He was doing some journaling, which he calls "keeping a diary." It seemed to help him stay grounded in the present, and to identify and gain insight on his feelings, which we discussed in our sessions. He hasn't had any more dissociative episodes recently, and is more "present" in our sessions. He is becoming less reclusive and is doing some volunteer work, and has begun to attend support groups for recovering substance abusers and also for people dealing with loss.

Touching or showing affection has always made Joe feel uncomfortable, but lately he asks me for a hug after each session. I see this as a positive step toward overcoming his alienation from women. He has began to date again, tentatively, and with no desire to remarry in the foreseeable future.

Determined to conquer the computer, Joe returned to school to study computer technology. He surprised and pleased himself by earning a 4.0 average and a meritorious award for excellence. Nonetheless, his low self-esteem kept him from attending the ceremony and receiving the award publicly. Little by little, though, almost in spite of himself, he began to believe in himself and his worth.

CONCLUSIONS

It remained unclear if Joe has an alter or not. Some things are certain:

- He dissociated with and without medication.
- He was abused physically, emotionally and, my professional instinct says, sexually. I base my judgement on his difficulty with relating to women, his marked discomfort and revulsion after sexual intercourse, his avoidance to the point of panic of discussing sex, his fear of having a child, some body memories centered around his scrotum that include pain.
- And that this abuse contributed significantly to his dysfunctionality.

It is important to note that his childhood memories weren't accessible to recall until his sister and mother began to unlock the past for him, and then, only fractionally. He is still in therapy at this writing, and progress is very slow. His inability to establish the validity of his feelings often prevents him from accepting the veracity of his memories, and delays him from accessing deeper and more painful memories.

This disjunction is a typical feature in patients who have histories of sexual abuse as children. As issues of neglect, emotional abuse and lack of nurturing from his parents were confronted, Joe accepted the fact of the occurrence, but he couldn't connect emotionally. He feels guilty about betraying family secrets and unconsciously punishes himself with obsessive exercising and depriving himself of food.

When he denies and tries to push back traumatic memories that try to emerge, I coax him slowly and gently to tune into his feelings, taking great care not to push too hard. Over the years of trying to unlock the mystery of his past I am alert to the signs that Joe is close to being overwhelmed, and I back off before he gets to the point of re-engaging old defense mechanisms.

Joe's insight is increasing, as well as his self-esteem, and his self-destructive urges are diminishing apace. In the past six months he hasn't thought of suicide once. That's the longest period ever.

CHAPTER SIX

SOMATIZATION DISORDER

300.81 [DSM IV-R]

A patient with this disorder has multiple ailments, pains and other symptoms (a minimum of 13 must be present for this diagnosis) that cannot be explained by normal medical diagnostic methods or by a specific event such as a fall or an accident. The pain, however, is very real.

In both case histories in this chapter you will notice that I mention that the patients are overweight. This is true in the vast majority of both women and men whom I have treated for sexual abuse. At least a dozen of them have undergone by-pass surgery for weight that had reached the stage of morbid obesity.

A minority have Anorexia Nervosa, or Bulimia, or a combination of both called Bulimarexia. Recent studies have substantiated my observations that these individuals develop eating disorders because they feel they have no control over their lives, so they control their bodies.

- Efforts at control may come through extreme denial of food, over-exercising, self-induced vomiting, and abuse of laxatives or diet pills. They're trying to get small again, return to infancy, a time when, theoretically, they were too small to abuse. Unfortunately, evidence demonstrates that no age is safe from abuse.
- Or they may go the other way and overeat because it fills an

unmet need for the nurturing they never had. Or the weight serves as a protective layer to discourage intimacy; or unattractiveness will provide insurance against re-abuse. Or that fat will make them too big and intimidating to victimize again.

- Eating fulfills the desire to return to an infantile stage in which, normally, a baby's discomfort is relieved by feeding or changing or cuddling. Even if a survivor didn't have this experience, she is understandably inclined to accept the cultural norm. This thought process promotes a tendency to other forms of oral gratification, which is why many survivors abuse oral drugs, tobacco products and other substances.
- Rarely do survivors fit neatly into only one of the categories above, but combine them freely into their own survival formula.

Once in therapy and actively clearing out the bad-memory attic, patients begin to move to what is an appropriate weight for them.

CARLA————————————————

I walked into the hospital room and looked at the young woman sitting on the bed. She looked back at me. I smiled. Her expression didn't change. Her enormous fawn-like eyes were empty of presence, as though no personality lived behind the face.

"Good morning," I said. "I'm Doctor Callaghan." I paused. When she didn't respond, I continued to speak, quietly but insistently, trying to draw her out of her silence. When she spoke finally, he voice was low, slow, flat, robotic, as though programmed into a grudging and alien body.

Her chart told me that she had come to the emergency room because she felt that she was choking and couldn't breathe. The ER doctor, her attending physician, as well as an ear, nose and throat specialist had all examined her and couldn't find a physical cause for her problem. They thought perhaps I could find the reason for her problem and I was here in response to their request.

I pulled up a chair and continued to talk with her, noting that she was, possibly, a hundred pounds overweight. When she answered my questions honestly, intelligently and without affectation, I heard in her soft voice a slight idiosyncrasy that might have been a regional accent or a slight speech impediment, but no emotion. None.

No, she had no marital problems, she said. Her husband was a loving, kind man who was devoted to her and their children, a boy and a girl, both ideal children. The only problem that she could think of was her difficulty in accepting her father's recent death from a sudden heart attack. She hadn't been with him when he died, nor did she go to the funeral, because they didn't have the money for the plane fare. She felt so guilty, she said, showing just a fleeting shade of emotion.

After a pause she continued her passionless report. She'd had middle ear problems that had been diagnosed as Pseudo Meniere's Syndrome. Carla's condition had no physical basis, but possibly a psychological basis, which is what I was there to determine. There were times when she had double vision, headaches, and such difficulty swallowing that she feared that if she were left alone, she would choke to death.

Although she loved her husband deeply, she said, she was indifferent to sex. She submitted only to please him, but there were times when intercourse was painful. No physical reason could be found for the pain. (This indifference and pain, I would learn, was a clue to the incest in her past. It's a clue that a lot of physicians miss or misread altogether. At times she experienced dizziness, back and neck pain, fainting and loss of consciousness which had caused a head and an ankle injury. At times she felt that her muscles were weak or even paralyzed.

She had trouble remembering her childhood, she continued. Her appetite was usually good. In fact, she overate at times. Sometimes she felt nauseated, bloated and had abdominal pains. She didn't like going to doctors, but she thought she should have her symptoms checked, especially since they began after she had turned

30. Carla paused, looking down at her fingers picking at the blanket.

We talked further for a while, and then I concluded the interview, making plans for our next visit.

As I walked down the hospital corridor from Carla's room, I knew that the puzzle she presented to me would test my powers of detection. The first person I wanted to talk to was her husband, to see if he could share any further information that would help me to help my patient.

LOOKING FOR CLUES

A quiet, pleasant, diffident man sat in the other chair in Carla's room, trying to remember anything he could to help me. Yes, what she had told me was true. She did have problems with balance, her vision, choking, pain, fainting, and pain during sex, Will concluded, looking faintly uncomfortable with the last piece of information. Other than that, he couldn't think of anything that would help me.

I saw Carla three times a week and then two times a week in my office with little progress. As the time approached for her husband and their daughter to go to her mother's to help her move, Carla became increasingly tense and her swallowing problems worsened. I recommended that we do a sodium amytal interview to get to the root of the problem. Although she was terribly anxious about it, she agreed and checked into the hospital and got settled in bed for the necessary overnight stay.

During the amytal interview, which lasted about three hours, her memory revealed how her grandfather had sexually abused her from age seven or eight to about age 14. In addition to sexual abuse, he tormented her sadistically, just for his entertainment. On one occasion, he chained her to a log in the lumber mill and threatened to run her through the saw that whirled and screamed a few feet away. Another time, he forced her to dig for worms and eat one. When she tried to refuse, he said either she could choose one, or he would make her swallow the fattest one. Another time, he tormented her with the chainsaw he was using, pushing it at her closer and closer, until he nicked her hand.

One day when the family was at her uncle's funeral, a day when a normal father would have been grieving his son's death, the same grandfather threw her to the ground and raped her. She bled profusely and had several visible scrapes on her body. Her grandfather warned her that he would kill her and all of her family if she told the truth, and explained away the damage by saying she had fallen out of a tree. She knew the extent of his strength and his evil, and kept the secret. She kept it so well, in fact, that she buried it away from even her own conscious mind.

Memory of many other rapes returned during the interview: in a cave with another man watching and then participating, in the basement, the bathroom, the garage, and always accompanied by threats. She called the intercourse "breeding," apparently applying a term used when talking about farm animals, and her beloved horses, and possibly because it was the only term available in her child's vocabulary. Devoting all of her energies to raising horses helped her survive years of sexual abuse, and her horses probably gave her part of the limited sense of safety she knew. In support of this assumption, she cried only twice during her interview, once when she talked about her father's death, and again when she told that her horses had died.

As the wall of secrets and lies was torn down, Carla's problem with choking and falling improved dramatically, returning only when new memories broke through. Even so, she felt no sense of connection to the events nor the child she had been, and she couldn't understand why her family wept when they were told. The violence against her child-self had driven a wedge of numbness between her child and adult selves. Only after months of therapy and medication could she accept the past, grieve for her child-self, forgive and let go.

Carla worked well under hypnosis and proved to be adept at self-hypnosis. Since finances were a problem for them and full psychiatric fees were a burden, she asked if her husband and mother (who visited Carla and Will's home for extended visits after her husband's death) could help her with self-hypnosis at home. We met together, the four of us, and talked about it. They respected one another's boundaries and they were eager to help. I explained that they would be functioning as information gatherers and not as therapists, and that the practice could be stopped any time they felt uncomfortable or unsafe, which Carla did later. I recommended that they record the sessions with a cassette recorder as I did in the office.

We terminated therapy by mutual decision, agreeing that we would resume if the need arose, and together we would work through the pain that followed. She continued to write to me about her progress, including her pleasure about her steady weight loss. Previous to treatment her weight was 349 pounds, and it went down to 106.

A TEST OF COURAGE

In 1990 she had an experience that proved to her how strong she had become and how much in charge of her own life she became. While her husband was at work and her children were in school, she was down at the stable tending to her horses, paying special attention to the one that recently had foaled. Suddenly a man with his face covered grabbed her from behind, put tape over her eyes and mouth, and raped her. Because of her rapid weight loss and recent surgery on her elbows, she couldn't fight off her attacker. But she was no longer the easy victim, and her senses were alert to something familiar about him. His smell. His mannerisms. She couldn't quite put her finger on it, but she formed a plan.

She decided not to report the incident to the police, but she knew she would be prepared if he returned. And sure enough, a few weeks later he came back. A faint noise behind her warned her that he was back. She moved to grip the small and extremely sharp knife in her pocket. As he tried to subdue her, she struggled mightily and got a glimpse of him. It was who she thought! She slashed out and cut his wrist.

"I know who you are," she gasped, "and now I've marked you. You can't rape me without me cutting you real bad. If you go away without hurting me, I won't report you. If you hurt me, I'll run your balls up the flag pole with or without you attached, *then* I'll see you to prison."

He stopped. She had surprised him. He let go of her, jumped up and bolted out of the barn. She sat up, brushed herself off, and felt most pleased with herself.

Will wanted revenge. Naturally he was furious, but he didn't know who the perpetrator was, and Carla steadfastly refused to tell him, and the incident was never reported or repeated. Apparently the man left the area, because she never saw him again.

I had urged her to report the incident and I was disappointed when she refused, but I could see how her self-confidence and self-esteem had risen so I let the matter drop. She would need her newfound strength when a new round of memories rose to challenge her a few months later.

MORE MEMORIES

Early in 1991 Carla began to have memories of physical and emotional abuse at the hands of her mother. Until then, she thought that her mother was one person she could trust, one place where she was safe emotionally, so the return of the memories left her feeling vulnerable and abandoned.

Shortly thereafter, while under self-hypnosis monitored by her husband, she said that the woman she knew as her mother wasn't her mother at all. The hypnosis had helped her access the memory of her paternal grandmother giving her this information on her deathbed.

Carla's birth mother was a little, black-haired, blue-eyed native American of the Oregon Mandan people, who was pregnant by Carla's father, even as her adoptive mother was carrying his child in another state. In a complex series of events, Carla was taken from her birth mother and given to her adoptive mother as a substitute for a baby who had died. We have no information about the manner in which she was taken or how it affected her birth mother, but if Carla's father's behavior was consistent with what she grew up with, we can't assume any sensitivity toward her birth mother. In addition, Carla's birth date was "adjusted" to make her two and a half years younger, and thus younger than her younger sister. Consequently, she has always been unnaturally large for her age, and very sensitive about the fact.

The family fiction was that her adoptive mother was in bad mental and emotional shape when Carla was brought to her, and therefore she never knew that Carla was not her own baby. Once Carla remembered her adoptive mother's abuse, however, she had reason to believe that she knew more than she admitted, and that her mother's abuse was prompted by her "half-breed" status.

There was a woman whom Carla called Aunt Hazel, who Carla now believes was her true maternal grandmother. She had an old horse, a trailer and was the spiritual leader of the local Mandan people. It probably was from her that Carla learned her love of horses. Although her adoptive mother forbade her to see Aunt Hazel, Carla sneaked over to see her consistently. They would have little ceremonies in the middle of the living room floor and played with bones. Actually, what she was remembering was shamanic ceremonies of her grandmother's Plains Indians. Probably the grandmother was a tribal Shaman, a position of great respect. Aunt Hazel was full Mandan, as probably was Carla's birth mother. Carla's father, too, had Indian blood in him, but he denied it because Indians were an underclass in their town. That prejudice hadn't escaped Carla at home. Her hair was kept too short to braid, and she wasn't allowed to get suntanned, because she would look like a "filthy Indian." Later, when she was a little older and grew her hair long enough to braid, her adoptive mother said she looked like a "disgusting slut and a whore."

When the family went to visit the (abusive) paternal grand-parents, they rented a motel room with two double beds. Mom would sleep with sister Bea, and Carla had to share her father's bed. Predictably, as Carla's memories returned, she recalled that her father forced her to have sex with him on those occasions, with his hand over her mouth, a fact she had blocked from memory because he was her savior, her hero.

Telling her mother about her grandfather's abuse wasn't safe either. Mom said she was making up stories. Later, when she was 16, she tried again and Mom called her a filthy, disgusting whore. Carla doesn't remember specifically if that was the time when her mother smacked her and locked her up in the rolltop desk to "teach her a lesson," or if that happened on another occasion. On other occasions Carla's sister locked her in the desk as a prank.

Later, when her mother cried and claimed not to have known about the abuse, Carla stopped listening, and hung up the phone to put an end to the fraudulence and betrayal. "She knows and so does my sister," Carla said, nodding grimly. "That's why they haven't visited me for almost three years. They used to visit once a year, but no more. Also," she added with a chuckle, "Bea has gained weight as fast as I have lost it."

PROGRESS IN THERAPY

Carla became more present in therapy sessions as well as in her own life, more present than she had ever been. She was off all medication and had none of her original symptoms. Then against my advice she decided to take a year's vacation from therapy. I recommended strongly that she meet with me once a month so I could monitor her if she recovered additional memories and her presenting symptoms returned, something that experience dem-onstrated was a good possibility, but she was immovable. She did promise that she would contact me or her family doctor if there was any manifestation of physical problems.

Carla's memories had been peeling off in layers, like an onion, and like anyone who has been ill for a long time, she was eager for life without the complications from dissociated memories. In her eagerness, she rushed her process and paid a big price. Late one summer afternoon about a year later, her husband called. Carla was having more memories return, he said, and her headaches, lack of appetite and insomnia had returned with a vengeance. She felt worn down and felt trapped in her own body; all she wanted to do was run away. His words tolled a warning in my mind. We made an appointment for her to come into the office to see me. When she walked into my office for her appointment, I was startled by the gaunt, haggard, yellow-bronze face that topped her usual jeans and shirt, which now hung on her 100 pound, 5'7" frame.

She resumed therapy with me, and she and Will began marriage counseling to repair their faltering marriage which neither wanted to lose. Her adoptive mother was concerned about her and insisted on coming to town for a visit with them. Carla didn't want her there because her overblown concern felt false and was hard to bear, but she wouldn't hurt her mother's feelings by telling her not to come.

ANOTHER LAYER OF MEMORIES

Late in the summer of 1993 a movie was released about a dead rock icon. When Carla saw it she became very upset about what she called "all the lies" about his life, actions and motives. "I was married to him!" she declared to me, and beginning then and over many months, she proved it. Then another movie that became a big hit and made a star of the male lead prompted more memories. Specifically, the way he rode his horse made her remember how, as young men, he and her first husband had ridden her horses, in her presence, in the same manner, with head back, arms out, eyes closed. Carla attempted to close off all memories. "It serves no purpose. It hurts too much. He's dead!"

But the memories wouldn't be denied and her physical symptoms worsened. Alarmed, her husband begged her to purge the memories. When she finally relented, she pursued the details of every memory, verifying public and private occurrences, dates and corroborating incidents with family members and public record. Her family combed their home for documents, photos and mementos. They found hidden away a surprisingly large and possibly complete cache of the rock singer's works, including notes from him and some of the poetry that he'd set to music. The cache included a rare videotape of the singer in performance, and a young woman who looked like younger pictures of Carla, face averted, partially shielded behind a huge bank of speakers. She had turned her head, Carla said, because they were careful to keep their private life away from the prying eyes of the press and his fans. When her mother saw the video, she exclaimed, "Why, my goodness, that's the young man who used to come to our back door and you went riding together!"

As the year went on and Carla filled notebooks with recovered memories, her physical health began to improve and psychologically she became stronger. She had decided to write a book about her first husband to correct the misinformation, but first she wanted verification. She sought validation of her memories from the by now scattered band members, to no avail. She sought the validation of her memories from the by now famous men who had ridden horses with her and her husband so many years ago, and they stiffed her, protecting their celebrity.

The more she dug into the past, the more severely the memories affected her. When the memories returned, she lost enormous amounts of weight, down to a size six. When the memories became too painful and she refused to give them release, she gained weight back, up to a size 18. Meanwhile, as family life and its requirements became more demanding with her daughter's pending wedding, her physical symptoms returned. Once again she had severe anxiety, insomnia, dizziness, headaches, became depressed and reclusive, able to function only at home and left the house only to come to me for medications. Again her weight plunged. Looking for a comfort level with her memories, she abandoned the book idea and pulled back into herself more and more. At one session we discussed cutting back on her medications because of the potential for dependency on her antianxiety medication. She became very angry with me, another sign of her psychological distress, and reacted by declaring that she would quit all medication. At that point I knew I had only two options: hospitalize her for her own protection, or elicit Will's assistance. At my insistence Will and Carla came in for a joint session and Carla agreed to have Will monitor her meds.

Her daughter set the wedding date and Carla picked out a dress. The memories kept returning and wouldn't stop and then she reached her breaking point. Refusing to see me or even allowing Will to call me, she shut down. That is, she decided to stop living. With her weight already at a dangerous low, Will told me later, she quit taking any kind of nourishment and within two weeks she was dead. Will called me one morning in the spring of 1995 to tell me that she had died during the night.

CONCLUSIONS

The memories that Carla recovered first were hard to deal with, but she managed that and thought she was finished. Her physical symptoms were improving, her life was going smoothly and was closer to what would be considered more normal than ever before in her life. Then, when the second layer of memories began to manifest, she hadn't had sufficient time to develop the necessary psychological reserves to cope with them.

In my experience, abuse survivors can deal successfully with returning memories, even if it takes years. However, care needs to be taken to shelter the recovering person from unnecessary additional pressure, both distress and eustress, which can derail the healing process and stress the survivor beyond tolerance. In Carla's case, incest and abuse by her grandfather and father was proved beyond reasonable doubt with the corroboration of other family members. The second layer of memories was additional horror too soon, and Carla couldn't cope with the unrelenting flood, so she made the decision to die, and she did.

RITA————————————————————————

Rita is an obese, loud, 46-year-old woman who gives the impression of an angry bull. During our intake interview, she reported so many physical symptoms that they defied *Harrison's Internal Medicine Book*. Most of the symptoms weren't verifiable with any known scientific equipment or methodology.

Her unexplained fainting spells began at age 18, for which she was seen at a major medical center. Doctors' findings were inconclusive and her high school graduation had to be delayed. On occasion she has developed a persistent but unproductive cough associated with severe chest pains and a sore throat. She self-diagnosed and then tried to find a doctor to "give her an injection before it got worse." If the first physician wouldn't comply, she sought another and another until she found one she could bully.

Approximately nine years ago Rita had what were called "multiple paralysis attacks" that had no diagnosable physiological basis, yet she said she was unable to walk. An orthopedic surgeon placed her in a wheelchair and told her that she might never walk again. (I believe he was trying some reverse psychology on her, trying to make her angry enough to get psychological help, which, ultimately, she did.) However, undaunted for the moment, she went to a chiropractor who did a series of spinal adjustments, focusing on her lower back. She claimed that the chiropractor cured her, which wouldn't have been possible if the problem had been physical, and she made a point of returning to the orthopedist's office to announce his misdiagnosis in the hallway, letting bystanders hear.

Along with these more dramatic episodes, she had additional and frequent complaints: nausea, vomiting, headaches of every description, wide fluctuation of appetite causing weight loss or gain of around 70 pounds, low back pains, leg aches, periodic difficulty urinating without associated pain, and episodes of leg paralysis. She was a veritable walking encyclopedia of ailments and symptoms. Most of the problems I remedied with hypnotic suggestion, along with some bed rest.

At this point, the reader must not conclude that Rita was lying to get attention. Rita never, and I mean never lies! Because of betrayal by her ex-husband she is a stickler for the truth. She may be abrasive, but she is an ordinary, good, honest, countrywoman. Despite her hardships, she has never felt sorry for herself.

Rita cleaned house compulsively, even defiantly. She told rebelliously in one of our meetings with her husband present, for example, that she'd had a fall, although I could detect little damage, and then "defied" my orders and did her housework because if she didn't, no one else would, she said.

"But, dear," her husband protested quietly, "whenever I do anything for you before I go to work, you only do it all over again anyway."

"You don't do it right," she said.

After two private physicians told her that her complaints were psychosomatic, she dismissed them. Sometime after that she was admitted to a university hospital with a presenting complaint of a seizure. She reported that she was having as many as four spells a week. Her mother offered eyewitness verification of one of her spells, during which she fell unconscious, was limp, cold and clammy, had cyanotic lips and appeared dead. However, Rita's limbs didn't jerk, nor did she experience bowel or urine incontinence, as can be expected with seizures. (That was the case because she was having temporal lobe seizures.) The hospital did an electroencephalogram that revealed only borderline findings, but she was placed on antiseizure medication.

While she was in the hospital, they checked her out for bacterial endocarditis, because she had complained of spreading pain in her joints. They were in her ankles, she said, and spread to her lower back, elbows, wrists and fingers. In addition, they checked her for collagen disease, which usually attacks every system in the body, and for diabetes. After months of testing, they diagnosed her, without benefit of a psychiatrist, "inadequate personality with schizoid features."

Two years before she came to me she sought the help of a counselor and then a psychiatrist at the local community mental health center following the death of her son in a car accident. Rita was told that her son had taken the car without permission and went for a joy ride with his older sister and a friend. There was an accident in which the son was killed, but from which the other two occupants of the car emerged unhurt. Only years later did the daughter confess that they had lied about who was driving. In reality, the friend was driving. They thought that, since Rita's son was killed, it would keep the living out of trouble if they said the son had been driving. Rita's daughter suffered guilt for surviving an accident that had killed her brother, for her brother's death, and especially for the grief her family experienced. As for Rita, her psychiatric problems recurred.

She had a persistent nightmare, from which she awoke crying, in which she stood on a rise by the grave in which her son had been buried alive. He had clawed through the dirt with one hand, which he stretched out to her in supplication, but she couldn't move. The counselor at the community mental health center recommended that she go to her son's grave to say goodbye to him. Rita resisted his advice stubbornly, even to the point that she refused to return to his office.

Next she sought the help of a psychiatrist at the Center, and found that she liked and trusted her. During a sodium amytal interview, the psychiatrist uncovered a history of Rita's abusive first marriage that ended in divorce and a bitter custody battle over the children, as well as bits and pieces of her childhood in an extremely dysfunctional family. Under amytal Rita revealed that her son wasn't going joyriding, but to see his birth father, to tell him that he hated his abusive behavior toward the whole family, and he didn't want to see him ever again. These revelations are the first hint in Rita's record of the role of abuse in her history and the formation of her personality.

Later, during a hospitalization, a psychiatric nurse learned about episodes of incest with her father. That's when I was brought into Rita's case.

EARLY SEXUAL ABUSE

Her story begins in early childhood when her father began abusing her sexually, possibly beginning as early as age five and continuing into her teens, ending only two years before he died when she was 21. Thus, as a child, sexual abuse constituted a major part of her reality, affecting her sense of safety, identity and self-worth. She had four siblings, all brothers. One of them was her twin, with whom she was close in childhood and then grew apart in adulthood. She was never close with any of her other brothers.

Rita's mother worked nights and slept days, so the children's primary daytime caretaker was their father. Even so, Rita could never understand how her mother couldn't see evidence of the sexual abuse on the occasions that she did bathe her. Actually, it's not uncommon for the non-abusing parent to be blind to a problem to avoid having to deal with what is unacceptable and seemingly insurmountable. There had to be tissue damage, Rita reasoned, from intercourse between a five-year-old child and an adult male. However, if the penetration had been digital instead of penile, it could have caused the same severe pain for a small child, as Rita's body remembered.

While Rita was in therapy with me, she confronted her mother angrily about her apparent willful blindness to her daughter's violation. Her mother had no explanation. In fact she was speechless at the confrontation. Rita was refusing to play the manipulative game of codependency that her mother continues to play. Indeed, Rita's anger and refusal to play, empowered her to a point that she refused to bail her children out of their legal problems, but insisted that they take responsibility for their mistakes and learn from them.

At one time while Rita was in therapy with me and having a

particularly difficult time with her symptoms, her mother offered to come to stay with her to help. Rita refused. Considering the material she had retrieved, she didn't trust her mother and she didn't want her around. The fact that her mother came anyway, just arrived with her luggage on Rita's doorstep, is a clear indication of how mother put herself and her feelings first, and how little she regarded Rita's welfare.

One day during her stay, Rita confronted her mother furiously about how she had abandoned her as a child to her father's abuse. In an act of manipulative abandonment the mother telephoned one of Rita's brothers to come and pick her up, rescue her, deliver her from a difficult position. He came and mother used the opportunity to pit one of her children against the other. This predicament was familiar for them since she caused dissension habitually between her children, and between her children and their spouses.

MIXED MESSAGES

In her eyes, her father was a war hero. The metal plate implanted in his skull, clearly visible, was all the evidence she needed. He had returned from action in World War II a severely physically and psychologically damaged man, broken and unable to work. Too broken to function in the world, the role that fell to him was primary caregiver of the children, guiding, loving and nurturing them, a job that requires a psychologically whole person at the very least.

He was a practicing alcoholic who beat his boys, sparing only the youngest because he was frail, and Rita. She was his "darling little girl" who had the power to stop the beatings, something not even her mother could do, but had to endure sexual abuse. That abuse was their "special secret" which she mustn't reveal to anyone, especially her mother, or he would punish her unmercifully. While she had to carry the responsibility for most of the household chores, she wasn't allowed to attend social functions, such as ball games or parties, as her brothers were.

One day while Rita's brothers were at a ball game, her father's sexual abuse turned from manipulative to plain, violent rape. With that act, he changed the fiction that the sex between them was "something so special that he didn't even share it with her mother." As his health improved, he was able to return to work. However, when Rita was alone, he came home to have sex with her during the day.

He became sexually more demanding, coming home at night drunk and insisting on having sex. One night, in desperation, Rita took a short, extremely sharp knife from the kitchen, hid it under her mattress, and waited for the inevitable sound of her father stumbling toward her room. When he opened her door, she was sitting up in bed with the light from her bed lamp glinting off the knife she pointed at him. She said nothing. Her jaw was set. She stared into his eyes in defiance. He looked at her face, at the knife, then backed out of her room, closing the door.

That night, in her 15th year, she felt a measure of safety for the first time in her life. The next day she went to a friend's house and asked her parents if she could move in with them, earning her board and room by helping with the housework. She continued with high school and got a part time job besides. At last there was a real chance for stability and security in Rita's life.

It didn't last. Before long, her father found her and begged her to come home, promising never to hurt or molest her ever again. He cried. She wanted to believe that he was sincere and allowed herself to be persuaded. In reserve, her ace in the hole, she knew she had the knife. When she got home, she took the knife out of its hiding place and put it under her pillow.

She understood that his promises were as secure as a sandcastle at flood tide when she heard his footsteps coming down the hall toward her room. She sat up, turned on the light and, facing the door, held the knife out in front of her. It worked again, but she knew that her threat to hurt him wouldn't continue to work.

One night he came home drunk and determined and stomped into her bedroom. Without knowing what she was going to say, she grabbed the knife and turned it toward herself. "I'll kill myself if you don't leave me alone," she yelled at him so the whole house could hear. "Now get out of my room and don't ever come back. Go get your sex from your wife."

His eyes bulged in surprise and fury. He slammed her door and stomped back downstairs where immediately he began to pick a fight with his wife. Rita tried to ignore the noise. After all, he wasn't her responsibility. But the racket became alarming. She hurried downstairs in time to see him yank her mother up off the couch and fling her at the picture window. The window shattered, spraying glass over her mother.

In fear and fury, Rita waved the knife and shrieked at him to leave her mother alone or she'd stab him. He turned on her in a rage, grabbed her arms and flung her out the front door, yelling at her to go and never come back.

She was free, but she had no permanent place to go. She quit school, stayed with different friends and finally found a job. Soon, too soon, she met and married her first husband. Like her father he was a charming con artist and a violent, abusive, alcoholic man who abused her and their children verbally and physically. Like so many abused people, Rita had settled for what was normal for her and thus she was revictimized. He had made her feel special, like her father, and she thought this swaggering, chauvinistic male could stand up to her father and rescue her.

After their first child, a daughter, was born, her husband was involved in sexually molesting a mentally retarded girl in public, but he was never prosecuted for it. Her father, seeking to capitalize on the situation, told her she could come home, that he would take care of her and her daughter, but she was afraid to have her daughter alone with him. In her 21st year, her father died.

EFFECT ON THE CHILDREN

After 14 years, she divorced her husband. After the divorce, when she shared her own story of abuse with her daughter, her daughter told her that her own story was just like Rita's, her father had been sexually molesting her, too. Ironically, Rita and her daughter are images of one another physically and emotionally. The daughter even married a dysfunctional, drug-abusing man who abused her and her two sons physically and emotionally. For years these two women have had a poor relationship, which is improving more recently.

Rita's second son seemed to follow his father's pattern. He was in jail for almost a year for larceny, breaking and entering, and drug and alcohol charges. He is a high school dropout and a compulsive liar with an extremely poor employment record. Rita feels responsible for her children's failures because she stayed with her husband for so long. She should have got them out of that environment sooner, she says sadly.

She thinks of her son who was killed in the car accident. He had been loving, never in trouble with the law, exactly opposite of his younger brother. Would he have succumbed to the same destructive behavior if he had lived?

Her youngest child, a daughter, for a while seemed to be her last hope of absolution, of avoiding total failure as a mother. She lived with Rita and her second husband, a favored child, kind, thoughtful, loving and a good student. They spoiled her happily. She avoided the mistakes of her siblings, and assured her mother that she wouldn't follow her sister's footsteps. At age 18 she took the Air Force entrance exams, passing the written test and interview, but not the physical exam, due to bronchial asthma.

Her path took a turn, perhaps out of disappointment, and she eloped with her 15-year-old boyfriend when his parents tried to separate them because of their age difference. The marriage didn't take place and she came back and lived briefly with her father, then stayed with friends. After that she applied for legal emancipation from her parents so she could draw Social Security benefits.

RELAPSE

Rita was devastated. Her children had been her universe, and now she felt that her sun, moon and stars had winked out, her children were gone. She relapsed emotionally, going into deep depression and thinking of suicide. Once, she attempted to jump out of the family pickup truck while she and her husband were driving down the highway. She couldn't eat, sleep or work and wanted only to stay in bed all day. She argued and found fault with her husband constantly. She felt like a failure as a daughter, mother and wife, she said. She had nothing left to live for.

I admitted her to the hospital and started her on antidepressants. She lay in bed either crying or trying to hide in sleep, with her back turned to the door, or alternatively, expressing her anger at her parents, her ex-husband, her husband, her children, the nursing staff, God, everyone and everything. I don't know why I wasn't included in that anger.

Her second husband, whom I'll call "Pete," was 11 years older than Rita and had loved Rita since she was a little girl. Rita liked him, even loved him, but she concedes that she was never "in love" with him. All of the upsets in Rita's life and relationships took a heavy toll on him. He had developed a peptic ulcer and was taking medication for it. The small, unstable tool and die company where he worked was in financial trouble. Their savings were running out, there was no more medical insurance, Pete's little farm that had given them some stability would have to be sold to keep them afloat. More than anything, though, he wanted Rita to get over her depression.

Pete was an easygoing, unaffected, yet astute man who was unconditionally supportive of his wife, treating her like a doting father. His occasional use of inappropriate humor that seemed to make light of her therapy made him appear unaware or insensitive. During his service in the military his hearing was damaged, leaving him with a deafness that irritated Rita at times. She saw his deafness as willful, improving and worsening depending on the subject at hand.

Like a father, he soothed and placated her anger, agreeing to any demand for the sake of peace, but he didn't follow through. That was too much like Rita's father's behavior: while she was sick he was kind, patient, nurturing and thoughtful, acceding to her demands, only to exact payment in sex when she recovered. As Rita began to gain insight into the ground of her problems, not surprisingly she lost sexual interest in her husband.

"Little Girl," Pete called her, which is what her father called her. When she made the connection, she told him about it accusingly. When Pete came in with her for her therapy session, he told me with some consternation that he didn't mean to upset her; he was just being affectionate.

Rita's conscious and subconscious sense of helplessness and rage at her childhood victimization continued to dominate her and her victimization continued. For example, in her view her children got into trouble to get her attention, and then, because she **gave her attention to her children, she didn't have time to develop a healthy relationship with her husbands. Also, when her young**est son had gone to jail, she had adopted a runaway boy, who had later helped her daughter elope with her boyfriend. In short, everything was her fault, but everything was beyond her control. She was overwhelmed and furious.

Before she was my patient, during a family emergency she had dissociated and had become too dizzy to function, making it necessary for a neighbor or relative to stay with her while Pete was at work. During the time that I worked on her case, Pete called me often to say that she was having another violent outburst. She ran uncontrollably about the house, sobbing, flailing her arms, running into furniture, grabbing and smashing objects, banging her head against the walls, screaming, "No, no, Daddy! Don't do it! You're doing it again! I hate you! I hate you!" Just prior to these episodes she was glassy-eyed and oblivious to her environment. Afterwards she was tired, sweaty, confused, and had no memory of the event.

About that same time, on a trip to visit friends she became disoriented, delusional, insisting that she was going into the hospital for surgery. She became suicidal, tried to stab herself with a large knife, and to jump from the moving car while they were on the way to the local emergency room where he took her for treatment. When they returned home I hospitalized her. She still insisted that she was to have surgery, refused to eat and drank copious amounts of fluids. Her face was expressionless and she was having wide mood swings.

HER TREATMENT

Rita has tried every kind of therapy she has heard about and known to all of her doctors, friends and family. Truly, she tried them all. When she began working with me, my first line of treatment was, as always, a complete evaluation, including a complete history from the patient and his or her significant family and other associates. If a patient's state of mind is such that it is impossible to do effective psychotherapy, i.e., severe depression causing poor concentration and memory, insomnia, poor appetite, low energy, lack of motivation, severe anxiety and panic attacks, suicidal thoughts and plans, then I discuss medications with them. It's important to the patient and to me that his or her treatment is a team effort and that the patient is fully informed at all times.

An adequate trial of major and minor tranquilizers sedated Rita, but accomplished nothing else and when the sedation wore off she was back to where she began. Adequate trials of every existing antidepressant-tricyclics, bicyclic, tetracyclic, and MAO inhibitors were no more effective than the tranquilizers. Anticonvulsants Dilantin, Tegretol and Valproic Acid had only questionable effect. Beta blockers were as ineffective. Premarin Provera was given for menopause and various pain medications were prescribed for "whole body" aches and pains. When lithium, thyroid medications and Ritalin in combination with tricyclics and vitamins were applied along with behavior modification, she was non-compliant at home.

(Often patients come to me with a history of one or more therapies, and want to know if there is some kind of medication to help them function so they can continue psychological therapy.

Some patients come to see me for medications alone and want to continue their psychological therapy with their current therapist. I'm leery and very cautious in situations like that. There have been cases where a patient got medications from doctor #1, and continued treatment with therapist #2, then committed suicide and the patient's family sued doctor #1. I can understand the grief that drives such an action, but I'd rather put my energies where it will do patients the most long-term good.)

Rita was relieved when she understood why she reacted and felt as she did, and that many of her physical symptoms were caused by her body trying to compensate for long-term stress. She felt good that "psychosomatic" didn't mean imaginary, but rather that her body's effort to compensate for her very real mental conflict was being communicated as authentic disorders.

Unfortunately, her understanding caused her to decompensate, her feelings crashed and she became depressed. I talked with her at length about how much strength she had shown, the wonderful survival techniques she had used, the enormous changes she had wrought already, how her new role-model had already helped her children and soon the depression passed.

I believe that her depression was, in part, a healthy reaction to recognizing that she wasn't responsible for her abuse or for her children's behaviors. It really was out of her hands. As much as she wanted to take responsibility for it at some level and fix it, she couldn't. Psychologically, it was healthy, realistic and rational to be deeply discouraged in the face of major problems that she was helpless to fix, no matter how hard she tried. She hadn't abused her children, but provided choices and chances for them that she hadn't had as a child. Actually, she had nothing to be ashamed of under the circumstances.

Following that, physical therapy for aches and pains was fairly effective. Hypnotherapy was very effective and used often. She was non-compliant with relaxation therapy as well as with a program of proper diet and exercise. Combinations of medications and other therapies, including chiropractic treatment, were unsuccessful. She refused spiritual counseling, ACOA (Adult Children of Alcoholics), a support group and an incest survivor's group, but attended the mental health and occupational therapy program in the hospital.

Ultimately I continued marriage counseling and hypnotherapy, including teaching her to do autohypnosis, and her life stabilized. Her children and two grandchildren visited often and she and her husband got along better. At this writing she hasn't had a "spell" for over a year.

Though the problems that brought Rita to my office were psychosomatic in nature, in recent years her back pain, caused by a combination of physical abuse from her ex-husband and tension, recurred. Currently, she has temporal lobe seizures and osteoarthritis, plus chronic pain from a muscle disease called Polymyalgia Rheumatica.

Although Rita still sees me on occasion, these sessions are usually crisis-intervention sessions, such as supportive therapy when her husband had a heart attack. She took over her husband's duties most capably, nurtured him back to health, and had no psychological setbacks. I am truly impressed with Rita's ability to deal with the stresses that confront her, even now.

In therapy, even though survivors like Rita do well, there is a period of readjustment to a new normality and patients often are reluctant to leave what is familiar. As their relationships become safe and functional, it's not unusual for their inner rage to be unleashed inappropriately or incongruently, confusing everyone around them and themselves as well. Unconsciously they're trying to recreate the crisis-to-crisis living pattern that was their norm. That's why it's important that therapy doesn't stop as soon as they get out of their abusive relationships because they need reeducation and support while they're learning how to wear a new psychological wardrobe.

CONCLUSIONS

As with so many other survivors, Rita, through all of her physical and emotional ailments, was expressing a buried current of rage, an underlying explosive pain and anger caused by her abusive past. These feelings fueled her ailments, detonated and released during therapy, and subsided only after her rage and the source of her rage were acknowledged and treated in therapy.

My prognosis for Rita is excellent. In spite of the possibility of losing her husband to his heart ailment, he who is and has been the one stable element in her life and her tower of strength, she demonstrated calm and strength under stress. She has the strength and tools to handle well whatever the future brings.

CHAPTER SEVEN

GENERAL ANXIETY DISORDER

300.02 [DSM IV-R]

Generalized Anxiety Disorder is an unrealistic or excessive anxiety and worry (apprehensive expectation) about two or more life circumstances. For example, unfounded worry for six months or longer about a child's safety, or unfounded anxiety about finances, for a period of six months or longer, during which one has been troubled by these concerns more days than not. In children and adolescents, this may take the form of anxiety and worry about academic, athletic and social performance. At least six of the following 18 symptoms are present with the anxiety:

Motor tension
    Trembling, twitching or feeling shaky
    Muscle tension, aches or soreness
    Restlessness
    Easy fatigability
Autonomic hyperactivity
    Shortness of breath or smothering sensation
    Palpitations or accelerated heart rate (tachycardia)
    Sweating or cold, clammy hands
    Dry mouth
    Dizziness or light-headedness
    Nausea, diarrhea or other abdominal distress
    Flushing (hot flashes) or chills

Frequent urination
Trouble swallowing or "lump in throat"
Vigilance and scanning
Feeling on edge or keyed up
Exaggerated startle response
Difficulty concentrating or "mind going blank"
from anxiety
Trouble falling or staying asleep
Irritability

EILEEN

Eileen's doctor, a family practitioner, admitted her to the hospital because she was having what she called a "nervous breakdown." When I walked into her hospital room for the first time, I saw a 62-year-old, 5' 4", 90 pound, twitching, shaking, frightened, dried-up woman.

Making myself a quiet, calm, non-threatening presence, I sat in a chair a few feet away from her. She moved restlessly. Her eyes darted around the room, as if she anticipated an invasion. I began to feel apprehensive and glanced around the room myself. There was nothing alarming, we were in a room in a psychiatric unit. She licked her dry, chapped lips. I could hear the scrape of her tongue against her lips. She picked at the loose skin on her lips. Her hand shook.

"Can you tell me why you're here?" I asked her quietly. She jumped at the sound of my voice and then made what looked like a great effort to collect her thoughts.

"I hardly know where to begin," she replied in a soft voice. "I feel so overwhelmed." She spoke slowly, often groping for words and then apologizing for the delay. "My mind goes blank. That causes me a lot of trouble when I'm trying to work," she began.

EILEEN'S HISTORY

She was a widow, she told me, and earned her living as a house-keeper. It was hard to work since she had become ill, but she was afraid to quit because she was worried about her finances. But it was getting harder to work: she was so tired and irritable, and having trouble sleeping. (Later I learned that she had quite enough money to retire and to live comfortably, if she chose.)

Her family worried her, even though they were all grown and had families of their own. She was particularly concerned about the fourth of her five children, a daughter, who was going through a divorce from an alcoholic husband, had no job and two darling children. She had been helping her daughter financially, and the other children were jealous about it.

She wasn't on speaking terms with her second child, a daughter, who had married an African-American man, had a son with him and was now divorced. But she was in good financial condition, Eileen said. The daughter charged that Eileen was prejudiced against her son, and that she had never received encouragement from Eileen as a child, only criticism. She was close to her aunt, Eileen's sister, with whom Eileen was not on speaking terms, either. Eileen's youngest child was a son, an alcoholic and a philanderer who she feared would divorce his wife soon.

PHYSICAL SYMPTOMS

She told me she always felt tense. Her neck muscles, especially, felt tight all the time. Often, without warning, she felt that she was smothering, had chest pains, lightheadedness and a dry mouth. It scared her, because she was afraid she'd faint. Sometimes she thought she might have the flu because she got hot and flushed.

"I didn't feel like I could cope any more," she said, looking down at her lap, "so I went to my doctor. He said I should go to the hospital, so I did. After all, my doctor knows best." She looked relieved that someone knew what to do for her. She had been in the hospital for two weeks.

She had been having problems functioning at work for at least a year. She said she would have quit the job if it weren't for the financial security it gave her. I suggested that perhaps it would be a good idea to retire early for the sake of her health. She beamed at my suggestion, admitting that she had been toying with the idea, but wouldn't have done so if a doctor hadn't thought it was the best thing to do.

A DYSFUNCTIONAL FAMILY

Eileen clung unconsciously to the relationship patterns she learned as she grew up in the midst of a dysfunctional family. Her father was a practicing alcoholic who was verbally abusive to his passive wife and all but one of his ten children. He favored the oldest daughter and willed most of the family's substance to her, including the home and a parcel of land. When oil was discovered on that land, she became a very wealthy woman. It didn't surprise me to hear Eileen say that the sister shared nothing with her siblings.

When Eileen was six or seven, this same sister had molested her sexually and then threatened to hurt her if she told anyone. Probably Eileen wouldn't have told her parents, even if she hadn't been warned, because her mother was too ineffectual to surmount the father's partiality. The abuse was cut short, however, when the sister married and moved out and Eileen kept her secret until I asked her about it pointblank. She told me that she had never tried to address the problem with her sister, nor even tried to talk with her because her sister **was not trustworthy. Although some of the siblings have died, Eileen** has remained close with two of her remaining sisters. It's significant that these sisters dislike and distrust the oldest sister, although it's not clear if they also were molested.

Soon after graduating from high school Eileen continued the family pattern by marrying a practicing alcoholic who was abusive to her and their seven children. Two of their children died in a fire in their mobile home one evening when her mother was baby sitting for them, an event that Eileen still remembers with tears. At the time, she said she thought she would go crazy with grief, but she had the other children to take care of, so she had to cope, but their death continues to haunt her, she says.

Her husband was particularly abusive physically to their two boys, especially the oldest one. One night, in a fit of anger, he threw one of the boys out and wouldn't let him back in the house. In an uncharacteristically bold gesture of support, Eileen wordlessly left with her son and got a motel room for him for the night. This son, she told me with evident pleasure, had done quite well for himself and was now earning an excellent salary. In fact, she went on, one daughter was a nurse, another a social worker, another a well-paid secretary, and the youngest had graduated from high school and had a good job. Even though she expressed some misgivings about their long-term welfare, she said she felt she had done a pretty good job as a mother. Even though she didn't express it, her observation implied that she had felt, correctly or otherwise, quite alone as a parent.

THERAPY

We began our work together by resolving her employment dilemma. She decided to take an early retirement and go on disability. The decision made her happy, not only because I had validated her decision, but also because she felt she had worked all her life and had never taken time off to play. Now she was giving herself the opportunity to explore the playful side of her personality, to find out what fun was for her.

We discussed the emotional dynamics of her family of origin and her nuclear family. As we explored her past, she could begin to understand how she had contributed to maintaining her family in a chaotic state because that was the only state she knew.

It's not uncommon for children of alcoholics to marry alcoholics, often without seeing the relationship between the parent and spouse. Even if that marriage fails, they tend to marry another alcoholic and friends shake their heads and ask, why?

The answer is, because it's what they know. They repeat the pattern because they don't know *how* to live differently or even that they *can* live differently. Generation after generation they relive the dysfunctional patterns that they learned growing up with codependent behaviors. Generation after generation of alcoholic behavior (whether the person is a practicing alcoholic or simply on a dry drunk, which is every bit as destructive and keeps the pattern going), poor communication skills, inconsistent behavior, destructive relationship patterns, low self-esteem, mixed messages, enabling and then punishing, and so on.

All of these characteristics can be illustrated in an exchange that can take less than two hours. Wife says, "I don't want you to drink," yet buys liquor for a special occasion knowing full well that husband will drink (*mixed messages*). Then, when he does, she gets mad because she feels he has failed her, (*codependent behavior*), but gets aspirin for his hangover and makes excuses for his behavior (*enabling*). Then she keeps picking at him for letting her down, sighing and carping to the kids about Dad (*passing on the dysfunctional relationship pattern*). Or she bails him out of jail for drunk driving, but rubs in the guilt, provoking despair, lower self-esteem and another round of boozing. And round and round they go. It can be a man or a woman in either role. Both are good at it.

Another common problem involves a communication pattern. It's called *gunnysacking*, suppressing resentments, storing them up and letting them grow ripe, and never, but never letting them go. Then, one day, without warning, letting all the venom pour out from weeks, months and years past while the kids watch and learn. They become habituated to turmoil and repeat it just as anyone repeats any habit. It takes something to break the habit.

That's where groups such as Al-Anon, for family and friends of substance abusers, and ACOA, Adult Children of Alcoholics, are helpful in identifying the habituated behavior and some alternatives to intergenerational chaos.

To try to learn how to relate to her family in a more healthy way, Eileen began to attend a support group for children of dysfunctional families. She told me that she hoped that she could interest her children in attending also, so the dysfunctionality wouldn't be passed on to another generation. After a few months in the support group, she reconciled with one of her daughters and invited her son to spend a week with her to improve their relationship. Her two other daughters began to attend meetings of Adult Children of Alcoholics (ACOA), and soon the whole family was able to share their feelings in a more healthy way. As this happened, Eileen found that she was worrying less about her children and enjoying them more.

Early in this period I prescribed a mild dosage of antianxiety medication (Xanax) if her anxiety was uncontrollable. At the same time, I urged her strongly to use other methods of anxiety control, such as relaxation techniques, physical activity, stretching exercises and meditation. She used these techniques very successfully and used the Xanax only three months.

One of Eileen's therapeutic tasks was to grieve the losses that she never allowed herself to do. That included the loss of the two children who died in the fire; her mother; the loss of a healthy extended family relationship with her siblings due to the rift caused by their father's partiality; and the loss of a better life because she didn't know it was possible. That was actually how she expressed them to me.

As her treatment progressed, I encouraged her to recognize her strengths that had allowed her to survive all of the traumas in her life. I pointed out her successes, some that surprised and pleased her, and encouraged her to own them with pride. I helped her to see that her children had internalized some of her strengths and that she couldn't live their lives for them, nor protect them from their mistakes. Their mistakes would not destroy them, but would be opportunities for growth, I told her, and she smiled at the thought. In fact, she smiled more often and more easily as the weeks went by and the habit patterns of worry and anxiety were overcome.

EILEEN'S RAGE

Even though Eileen was a mild person, her rage erupted in our therapy sessions often, demonstrating her strength behind her reticence. She would begin a topic calmly enough, but then a memory would rise and launch her into an angry monologue. Furious words poured out along with tears as she related an event. Also, she had angry telephone confrontations with her sister, and later by letter. She had angry disputes with her daughter, the social worker who accused her of racial bias. At a family conference she had an angry clash with the son who wanted to regulate her life for her. At home when alone she would rage, beating her bed in fury until she was spent, then crying for hours afterward.

CONCLUSIONS

It was this inner rage that had created her depression and anxiety that finally was being expressed. The sexual molestation by her sister, coupled with the pattern of chaotic dysfunctionality in her family, combined in Eileen to create the severe anxiety that constricted her ability to grow emotionally. She felt revictimized by everything (her husband, her children, her supervisors at work) until she could cope no longer. Then the severe anxiety brought on by the gradually surfacing rage became the catalyst for change.

Eileen is a much happier woman now, totally independent, no longer taking on her children's problems. That in turn allows them to grow because she's not there to bail them out constantly. She travels with friends, continues in a woman's support group and ACOA. She babysits for her daughter on occasion, but she's not available to be dumped on and taken advantage of any more.

When Eileen terminated therapy with me, she smiled as she handed me a poem entitled "Let Go And Let God," from Alcoholics Anonymous. The poem was framed beautifully and we hung it in the waiting room with ceremony. She looked happy and strong as she walked out of my office.

CHAPTER EIGHT

POST-TRAUMATIC
STRESS DISORDER

PTSD 309.89 [DSM IV-R]

Post-Traumatic Stress Disorder (PTSD) is a reaction to an exceptionally distressing event. For example, threat of great bodily harm to one's self or loved ones, or the sudden destruction of one's home or community, or seeing someone being injured or killed in an accident or attack, or even graphic evidence of injuries from such an event.

In PTSD the traumatic event is re-experienced persistently in at least one of the following ways:

- Recurrent and intrusive memory, including fantasizing or re-enactment by young children, of the event.
- Recurrent distressing dreams of the event.
- Sudden gestures or feelings as though the event is happening again. Includes a sense of reliving the ordeal, illusions, hallucinations and dissociative episodes, and flashbacks. (The latter can happen upon first awakening or during intoxication.)
- Intense psychological distress at exposure to events that symbolize or resemble some part of the traumatic event, and on anniversaries of the original event.
- Persistent avoidance of stimuli associated with the trauma or numbing of general responsiveness, not present prior to the trauma, as indicated by at least three of the following:

- • Avoiding thoughts or feelings associated with trauma.
  - • Avoiding activities or situations that arouse memory of the trauma.
  - • Inability to recall an important part of the trauma (psychogenic amnesia).
  - • Marked loss of interest in significant activities. In young children, loss of recently learned developmental skills, such as toilet training or language skills.
  - • Feeling of detachment or estrangement from others.
  - • Restricted range of affect, e.g., unable to have loving feelings.
  - • Sense of foreshortened future, e.g., can't foresee a career, marriage, children or long life.
- • Persistent symptoms of increased arousal not present before the trauma, indicated by at least two of the following:
  - • Difficulty falling or staying asleep.
  - • Irritability or outbursts of anger.
  - • Difficulty concentrating.
  - • Hypervigilance.
  - • Exaggerated startle response.
- • Psychologic reaction when exposed to event that symbolizes or resembles any part of the traumatic event. For example, a woman who was raped in an elevator now breaks out in a sweat when entering any elevator.

SALly————————————————————————

Although ultimately Sally revealed that she had multiple personalities, she is included in this chapter under having PTSD because those were her presenting symptoms. Her case was referred to me following a suicide attempt and she was still in profound shock when I walked into her hospital room. The mind of this 33-year-old woman was being held captive by her most recent trauma. For the first two days she could think of nothing else.

I turned to her chart for information until she could talk. It revealed that she had come home two days earlier to find that her husband had taken their two daughters, who were her reason for living, and run away with them. She had telephoned her parents and cried as she told them what Darren had done, but after she'd hung up the phone, apparently she'd decided that she could absorb no more pain. She took a full bottle of aspirin out of the medicine cabinet, drove to a nearby motel, checked in, ingested all of the aspirin and lay down to wait for the release of death.

Later that day, when her parents had heard nothing more from her and she didn't answer her telephone, they drove over to her home to check on her. The house was empty. That wasn't like Sally at all, they thought. They called the police to report her missing, and then began to search for her. By the time they found her at the motel, she was unconscious. Whether they took her to the hospital or if they called an ambulance, the records didn't say, but from the emergency room she was sent to ICU for the next 72 hours. As soon as her vital signs stabilized she was transferred to the psychiatric unit where she was watched closely for her own safety.

A DIFFICULT MARRIAGE

When she could talk to me, she told me her most recent history. She was in a marriage that had turned sour within a year after the wedding. Her husband, she told me, was cruel, selfish and inconsiderate, but she stayed in the relationship because she believed in the sanctity of marriage, and because she was sure that if she just worked a little harder at making him happy, their union would improve.

Instead, it got worse. She discovered that he was a transvestite and that it excited him sexually to have sex with her while wearing her clothing. At first she tolerated it, hoping it would pass. It didn't. By the time both of their daughters were born, he was dressing up and going downtown. No one but she knew that the tall, slender, beautiful woman walking out their front door on gorgeous, long legs was actually her husband, Darren. She was confused, hurt and embarrassed by what had happened to her marriage, but she remained dependent on the relationship.

The harder she tried, the worse things got. Darren became more abusive mentally and then he got physically abusive. She could take the physical abuse, she told me, but she was afraid to be left alone. When he discovered that, he walked out of their house and disappeared for several days. She was frantic. She never knew what he was going to do, she said. Under the circumstances she felt she had no choice but to keep working to support her daughters and herself, and hope for the best. Then Darren left with the girls and her hope ran out.

THERAPY REVEALS A DEEPER HISTORY

After two days she began to talk with me more openly. She was trying not to think about Darren and the girls, but she was having nightmares about them. Hospital visiting hours were awful, she said. Seeing children coming to visit other patients hurt her, so she hid in her room during visiting hours.

Gradually she lost interest in everything. She felt indifferent toward everyone, including her parents who came to town to see her and visited daily. Sleep wouldn't come and if it did come, it wouldn't stay. She was irritable, disconnected and couldn't seem to piece events together into any kind of coherent order. Her life was in pieces. Even her past was gone. When I asked her about her past, she couldn't remember anything. We discussed a sodium amytal interview, and she agreed that it might help.

A MILESTONE INTERVIEW

The amytal interview marked a turning point in Sally's case. After the drug eased her stubborn dissociation, she began to retrieve the past that her mind had tried so hard to lose.

When she was six, her maternal grandfather died. He had been a gentle and loving man with whom she'd had a close and trusting relationship. His death was very hard on her. Sally's parents felt that Grandmother shouldn't be alone, so they sold their house and moved to Michigan to live with her. On the surface it appeared that the arrangement worked well for everyone, since mother worked nights and father drove trucks interstate and was gone for long periods of time.

A puzzling story emerged about her mother's only sibling, a brother, who had disappeared with his wife from their farm without a word, a trace or a clue. Lunch was still spread on the kitchen table. The livestock was untended. None of their possessions were missing or disturbed. Their car was in the garage and no money had been drawn out of their account at the bank. Sally's grandmother, who was the uncle's mother, didn't pursue the issue beyond a perfunctory search. Only later, as the rest of her story surfaced, would this story fit into the whole and make sense.

Grandmother took over Sally's and her older sister's daily care, feeding them, watching them, bathing them, disciplining them . . . and abused them sadistically. On one occasion she punished Sally's sister for some infraction by flinging her against the glass door in the kitchen. The door shattered. Later Grandma told that the sister had broken it by falling against it. When the girls protested, their mother shushed them to keep peace.

On another occasion, Grandmother ran Sally's hand into the wringer of an old washing machine and lied again, saying that Sally had done it accidentally. (When I met Sally, she still had scars on her hand.) Sally confronted her indignantly, and Grandmother promised that she would throw the whole family out onto the street if Sally told. Other times, Grandmother threatened to have the girls put in an orphanage if they told. To give her threat weight, she would pick up the phone and pretend to be talking to authorities at an orphanage. As a child, Sally believed that her grandmother had the power to do what she threatened, so she remained silent, absorbing the abuse and curbing her thriving fear of abandonment.

Long after Sally was old enough to bathe herself, Grandmother insisted on "helping" her, using the opportunity to manipulate Sally's genitals painfully. Although she knew what was happening was wrong, Sally was afraid to say anything. Bedtime was another nightmare, since Sally, as the smallest child, was chosen to share Grandmother's bed. In bed, Grandmother would lay her bulk on top of Sally, making it all but impossible for Sally to breathe. Worse, far worse, was Grandma's rank breath as she pushed her tongue into Sally's mouth, French kissing her. Sally was helpless.

The abuse escalated as time went by and Grandmother became intensely inventive and sadistic. She began to push a variety of objects into Sally's rectum. After a particularly bad episode, her mother took her in her arms and rocked her. While lying there, feeling safe, Sally was about to reveal what her Grandmother was doing, when she spied Grandmother standing behind Mother, glaring at her.

In time Sally developed diarrhea and severe abdominal pain, which a doctor diagnosed as irritable bowel syndrome. Predictably, the tissues lost their elasticity, and anoplasty was required to correct bowel incontinence.

Also, she remembered being involved in some kind of ritual in which she lay on a marble table with strange signs etched on it and a goat head above it. Grandmother presided at what appeared to be the head of the table and there were other people she didn't know surrounding the rest of the table.

Despite this cultish activity, and consistent with the behavior of other Satanic cult members, Grandmother attended church with the family, and behaved like a benign grandmother in public. Sometimes she even took the family out for ice cream, which Sally liked, but they always had to go home again.

Although Mother was submissive to Grandmother, Father and Grandmother didn't get along and kept their distance from each other. She liked it when he was home, because she felt safe then, and she loved it when Dad and Grandma argued because she knew he was stronger. Grandma bad-mouthed Dad behind his back, but Sally knew to keep her mouth shut at those times.

THE ABUSE STOPS

Four years after the first move to Michigan, Sally's family moved to Illinois for more than a year, leaving Grandma behind. After a year of freedom from abuse, when Sally was eleven, the family moved back to live with Grandmother. The sexual abuse stopped when Sally was 16; tall, beautiful and athletic Sally was too big for Grandma to abuse anymore. She played softball, basketball, was an excellent student, homecoming queen in her junior year, and very much in love with the boy she would marry after graduation. They had two beautiful daughters who Sally refused ever to leave alone with Grandma. Grandma died of congestive heart failure when Sally was 24.

Later, when Sally shared the revelations of her amytal interview with her parents, her mother was shocked and disbelieving, and then angry. (It's possible that Mother was angry at Sally for revealing a family secret, but she may also have felt a deeply repressed memory stuck in her own memory.) She told Sally that she had a hard time accepting what she told her, but that she had no reason not to believe her. Nonetheless, it was a year before Mother could discuss the issue with Sally again.

After Sally left the hospital, she was allowed to see her children only once because a long and costly divorce and custody hearing was underway that would not end for three years. During that time she encountered an old girlfriend who had divorced recently also. They found they were attracted to one another sexually and decided to live together. While that went against Mother's religious principles, Sally's father was supportive. During the next year, as both women worked through their individual problems, they developed a warm and supportive relationship, worked together and bought a house together.

ANOTHER AMYTAL INTERVIEW

For four more years Sally continued to have bouts of depression, panic attacks, dissociative episodes and thoughts of suicide that required brief periods of hospitalization. Then she began to hear voices in her mind. She thought she was going crazy, maybe because her daughters had turned their backs on her after she lost the custody battle and seemed to hate her now. More flashbacks from her past made her feel panicky. Could we do another amytal interview, she asked, to find out what was going on in her head? I agreed and asked if she'd mind if we video taped the session. She agreed, asking only that three others be allowed to attend: her friend, a nurse whom she liked and trusted, and her primary therapist (to whom I had referred her).

OTHER PERSONALITIES EMERGE

On the day of the interview, Sally was anxious because of the additional people present. However, when the amytal began to take effect and she started to feel drowsy, I was startled when another personality emerged.

Shelly told us she was six years old, which was the age Sally had been when she first encountered abuse from her grandmother. Indeed, Shelly told us that she remembered when the sexual, physical and emotional abuse began. Shelly was a charming and friendly child with a playful manner. She told us what school she attended and that she liked sugar cookies and ice cream. She remembered that the school nurse had given her ice cream.

"Who are these ladies?" she asked me in a shy aside.

I introduced her to Sally's therapist and her two friends.

"How old are you?" Sally asked the therapist.

"Thirty-three," he responded with a smile.

"Wow! That's old!" she responded with charming innocence.

"Shelly, are there others in there with you?" I asked her, to determine how many personalities Sally had developed. Shelly's emergence had been a surprise, but it had not been an unpleasant encounter because the Shelly personality was as soft spoken and diffident as Sally. Abruptly, Sally jumped to her feet and spun to face me, her face contorted and threatening. Slowly she raised a finger and pointed it at me, inches from my face. "I don't like what you're doing. Sally is mine!" she snarled.

I felt waves of evil coming from this personality and I was glad I wasn't alone in the room with it.

"What is your name," I asked in my best clinical manner, trying to hide my dry mouth and pretend that my heart wasn't thudding against my ribs.

"Cookies," she growled, glaring at me with lips drawn back from her teeth.

The name, which I have changed here, was that of Sally's abuser, her dead grandmother. Sally had internalized the personality of the person who had violated her young body and her innocent life. That's not unusual, but it's always distressing to see how the evil in one personality can insinuate itself into successive generations. To me, this alter felt particularly evil and it was apparent that it wanted to take control of the host personality.

I hadn't come into this session prepared to do an exorcism, but it appeared that was what I would have to do.

"Cookies, you can't have Sally. You are dead. Leave her. In the name of Jesus, I command you to leave this body right now," I directed firmly.

She made a quarter turn away from me to show her contempt, but she kept her eyes on me. "You can't make me go," she mocked.

Oh yes I can, I thought, rising to my full commanding height of five foot two and a half inches. I could feel my eyes snap.

"IN THE NAME OF JESUS, I COMMAND YOU TO LEAVE!" I said, my voice filling every corner of the room.

I saw a tiny flinch behind the glare in Cookies' eyes. Apparently the religious training in Sally's background carried more weight with her than either of us had realized.

"BY THE POWER OF THE BLOOD OF JESUS CHRIST, I

COMMAND YOU TO LEAVE SALLY'S BODY AND NEVER RETURN!"

With a parting hiss, Cookies' personality drained out of Sally's body. Sally sat down on the bed again and relaxed.

I felt shaken and a little embarrassed about my melodramatic performance, so I turned to the other therapist and asked him to continue the questioning seeking more alters. Besides, it was important that he be an active partner in this development for the sake of his future sessions with her. His questioning brought out Shelly Anne, a quiet and scholarly 16-year-old. She was the baby sitter for Shelly, she told us, but not a container of traumatic memories.

Further questioning uncovered no more personalities, so we wrapped up the interview. Later, when the effects of the amytal had worn off, Sally watched the video tape of her interview and then I discussed the findings with her. She was grief stricken to learn of her multiple personality disorder because it affirmed her worst fears, that she would never recover. For several days she would not be consoled.

One evening, I was sitting in her hospital room talking with her companion, Matty, about the impact on both of them of the new diagnosis. Abruptly, Sally went into what appeared to be a seizure. Her face was contorted and deeply flushed. She uttered unintelligible word-like sounds in a deep, hollow voice.

A presence of evil invaded the room and I could feel the hair on my arms rise in response. I reached for my Bible again and thought, here we go again. I placed the Bible against her forehead and began to pray the Lord's Prayer, and then I prayed for Sally's healing. Abruptly, her body arched painfully and she uttered long, tormented moans. Then her body relaxed and she lay quietly again. Later, when she regained consciousness, she had no memory of the incident, but she said she was hot and tired. Very tired. The next day she told me that she felt that the evil entity inside her was gone and, as a result, she had slept deeply and well.

While it isn't unusual for an abused person to internalize the abuser, the internalization can take a varying degree of forms. It might be as slight as adopting attitudes and personality traits, or as substantial as internalizing the entire identity of the abuser. In Sally's case, she had internalized both her grandmother and also, separately, an embodiment of her grandmother's evil. A double whammy.

My use of the name of Jesus in the first emergence of the grandmother personality, and the Bible in the second incident was fortuitous. It drew upon Sally's inner strength, a strength established by her earlier religious education.

A week after the video taping of the amytal interview another alter emerged while Sally was talking with her primary therapist in his office. This one was a tomboy, 16 years old, named Sandy. She was the alter who had been involved in all the sports in high school, and she was cheerful, upbeat and very interesting. Grandmother "had been sitting on her," she told us, which is why she couldn't come out earlier. Now she intended to take over the baby sitting from Shelly.

Next, Sandy introduced her belief that there were "seven angels" in her life, helping her to heal. Her concept was based on a chapter in the Bible's book of Revelations. She spent a full hour, pacing up and down the room, discussing her idea in great and interesting detail, and demonstrating that she possessed a very capable mind.

Another enigmatic alter emerged shyly and only part way during that first year. Ten year old John, the last member of the first family of alters, told us that he was hiding in the basement. Much of what we believe about him is assumption, because he would not communicate more than that. We assumed that he was hiding in the basement of the house in Illinois because he didn't want to return to the grandmother's in Michigan. We don't know the exact reason for his creation, but we can assume that it was the part of Sally that fought against return to her grandmother's.

It was almost another full year before the second family of alters began to appear. Sally began to feel hopeless because she had hoped that this business was all over, and obviously she had no control over her alters or their emergence. An incident triggered the appearance of the second family of alters.

While at work one day, Sally became confused and agitated without any apparent reason. Her supervisor took her to the office to calm her and called her therapist for an emergency appointment, and her therapist put her in the hospital. What the therapist learned was that the new alter, Leah, had just emerged, there in the factory where Sally worked. Leah had seen a machine that reminded her of an electric wood saw that ex-husband Darren had used to threatened her, which in turn reminded her of the wringer on the old-fashioned washing machine that Grandmother had used on her. Consequently, Sally decompensated, lost her psychological balance and fell apart. She got very depressed and unable to function at work or home and when she became suicidal again, she was admitted to the hospital again, where the rest of her alters came out, gradually this time, so she didn't feel so devastated.

After Leah came Jo, 28 years old and a precise businesswoman. Jo had been the one who ran Sally's and Darren's furniture business and made it successful. Then, when Darren decided to sell the business without bothering to share the decision with Sally, Jo left. The only reason she returned at that point is because Sally and Matty were thinking of starting their own business.

After the furniture business was sold and the family had moved to an isolated farmhouse in the country, the next alter to emerge was formed. If she had a name, I never learned it. She was a 30-year-old, soft spoken, bilingual personality whose primary language was German—a language Sally had learned as a child. This alter came out to assume care of the children when Sally couldn't. To entertain them, she taught them German and sign language. She's the one who was out when Darren left the family's pet cat out to freeze to death, and she's the one who shielded the children from their father's increasingly indiscreet adventures as a transvestite.

Finally, Connie emerged, the last alter. Her arrival was timed shortly after Sally's divorce from Darren was final and signaled her freedom from him and the start of a new committed relationship. Connie was a 34-year-old woman who was the happier, more pleasant side of Sally, much like Sandy but more conservative.

A MERGING PERSONALITY

Once all of the alters had emerged, we did another video taping. This time all of the seven angels that Sandy had talked about were present and Sally was aware of how they had helped in her healing process. She worked through her memories after claiming them from her alters and owning them as her own. She was experiencing co-consciousness with most of her alters and also feeling their pain. (Co-consciousness, you'll remember, is the ability of all the alters, including the host and birth personalities to have access to the collective memories.) Some parts of Sally's life were put on hold so she could put all of her energies into healing.

There were stressful distractions, divorce and illness in her family, but then, happily, Sally's mother began to accept Sally's relationship with Matty and even invited her to family gatherings. Then in a surprising move, Sally's mother threw out all the mementos and belongings of her mother as a signal of accepting the truth of Sally's story. She was able to express her anger at her mother and her support of Sally, which was healing for both of them.

CONCLUSIONS

As Sally's healing continues, she does repetitive work in a factory that doesn't begin to use her talents and capabilities, but it's a necessary income and provides benefits like hospitalization and sick leave. She continues to make progress in terms of co-consciousness, greater insight and more hope, improved relationships with her parents, and learning to let go of her children when they chose to stay with their father after a custody fight. She is still planning to start a business with Matty and is researching and projecting plans. That fact is significant because Darren's abusiveness had eroded her self-confidence.

She continues to work with her primary therapist, Dave, while I monitor her medications. Sadly, we had to terminate our therapeutic relationship because she owed me over $10,000 and Darren cheated her out of the money due her from the divorce. She declared bankruptcy and now is getting back on her feet, demonstrating great strength and fortitude. She hasn't been hospitalized for a long time and my last information about her was that integration was almost complete.

MANY PEOPLE ASK WHY?

Inevitably this case prompts certain questions.

Q. Why are some people such easy victims and some people so determined to victimize?

A. Let's take the first half of that question first. Obviously there are many reasons why some children are easy victims, but too often it is a lack of a protective adult. After that, the learned behavior may or may not be carried into adulthood, depending on individual circumstances.

In Sally's case it was clear to her that her grandmother had the most power in the household and used it with no conscience, threatening constantly to throw the family "into the streets" if her abuse was revealed. Children learn by example and Sally saw her mother defer to grandmother and always give her the benefit of the doubt. Clearly, the lesson here was that grandmother was all-powerful in that household. Father, who they might have turned to under other circumstances, was on the road and not available.

Q. And now the second half, why are some people so determined to victimize?

A. As discussed earlier, it's a fact that victimizers usually have been victims themselves and their unresolved history sets up a compulsion to abuse. In Sally's case there wasn't enough evidence to support my strong suspicion that Sally's mother was also a victim of the grandmother and she wouldn't or couldn't tell.

Several studies of adult incest victims show that the severity of incestuous abuse is greater in those who have been abused as children, and rape and other victim-claiming crimes is found in 20-46% of adults who had been sexual abuse victims as children. [20] One study was drawn from the first 20 participants in a 12-week incest victims' group for women who'd had at least one psychiatric hospitalization.

Anger was a significant factor in this representative group, either self- or other-directed:

- Eight had detailed plans to murder one of their incest perpetrators.
- Two described involvement in murders.
- Two with caretaking jobs described physical abuse of their charges.
- Several described violent actions that hadn't yet been detected.
- Fifteen of the 20 had eating disorders, four with Bulimia accompanied by obesity, one who had bypass surgery for obesity, fourteen were bulimic, one had an episode of anorexia, and five had normal weight. Most of these had flashbacks of being forced to have fellatio which precipitated their vomiting episodes.
- Eighteen had been raped in addition to the intrafamilial sexual abuse. Twelve of these were raped multiple times: five raped by caretakers, including two policemen, two physicians and one therapist.
- Many describe hearing their abuser(s) voice.

Q. What is it about some people that is so twisted that they victimize?

A. Based on my professional experience I believe that the massive inner rage of victims overpowers normal sensitivities that would prevent victimizing. Their experience of helplessness as children prompts them to choose victims who are helpless to fight them.

Q. How do *they* get that way?

A. It's the combination of reactions that I've discussed above. Their rage from being victims perpetuates their need to victimize others, which stems directly from their feelings of helplessness. That rage that is completely internal builds into hatred, and builds further and further as they are victimized repeatedly, increasing to a white hot fury too big to contain. It explodes, burning helpless victims in its path. Usually the victim is someone from whom they fear no retaliation.

Q. Specifically, how did Sally's Grandma get that way?

A. Sally's grandmother remains an enigma. Certainly there was a cause for her behavior. Everything has a cause; nothing arises *ex nihilo*—out of nothing. Perhaps, and I'm speculating here, she was abused in her childhood and then got involved in cult or cult-like activities, which gave her an outlet for her rage. At this point, we have no way of knowing, but if the possibility I've outlined above was the case, grandmother's behavior wouldn't be surprising. The combination of barely controlled inner rage and the mind-binding and mind-bending that characterizes cult-think certainly is a sufficiently volatile recipe to create an abuser.

Sally's mother was reluctant and afraid to say anything against her own mother at first, but then became very supportive and destroyed her mother's mementos in Sally's support. While she never remembered any abuse, she'd always been afraid of her mother.

Sally speculated about her memory of being in the middle of a circle surrounded by hooded figures, etc., as possible indication of Satanic cult involvement, but she had no further memories of cult abuse.

Q. Where does abuse come from?

A. Abuse rises from hoarded rage from the abuse. Or it can

come from pure evil, which writer M. Scott Peck in *People of the Lie (1983)* defines as the abuse of political power, the imposition of one's will on others by overt or covert coercion, in order to avoid spiritual growth. Then the abuser's lust for power increases as the abuse goes unchecked.

Q. Why does the abuse escalate?

A. Because it can, is the simple answer. Unchecked evil, like infection, escalates until the host is dead. In the case of sexual abuse of children, it escalates until the child dies or grows too old to abuse any longer, at which time he or she becomes an abuser. We are seeing something of the same dynamic happening right now in what was formerly the Soviet Union. Those who were repressed and abused politically were released at the breakup of the Union, and now they are trying their hand at being repressors. Further, evil, to use Peck's definition, gets more and more confident, severe and blatant as it goes unchecked.

Q. What can be done about it?

A. End the secrecy. The abuse can be stopped only as victims speak out about the abuse and tear the veil of secrecy. Victims of abuse must be enabled to release their anger, rather than turn it inward with predictably disastrous consequences. Therapeutic expression of anger is liberating and empowering. Expression of anger in a safe atmosphere, where empathic understanding fosters a genuine sense of security through meaningful interaction with a therapist who serves as a conduit, is ideal. Reality checking and validation also helps improve a damaged self-image. Eventually the victim emerges as a survivor and accelerates.

Part of the recovery process, therefore, involves the following steps:

- Breaking the silence and unveiling the abuse.
- Expressing anger in a therapeutic setting with an empathetic therapist.
- Validation of the survivor's feelings by the therapist and real-

ity checking to improve victim's self-esteem.

- Survivors are allowed to grieve their losses, encouraging a sense of connection with themselves through honest feelings of grief. Once grieved, losses lose their awful power.
- Victors begin to move forward with a sense of freedom to choose lives of fulfillment and pride, free of old feelings of helplessness and depression.

Q. What are the percentages of cure?

A. The effects of child sexual abuse, though devastating, are reversible with the right therapist-patient fit. The process of recovery can take years and patience because of the frustrations and high emotional content.

As far as "cure" is concerned, I avoid the word because it can be so misleading. "Cure" implies "new again," "as though never touched," and that's not possible. The patient will be different, changed, more effective and functional, will have healthier relationships and better physical health, will even be stronger. But, even though the abuse will no longer be the deciding factor, it will never be forgotten. The wounds will heal, but there will always be a scar on the healthy organism.

As to percentages of successful therapy, I don't know of a study, but I would venture that it would be at least 75%. I'm qualifying the word "successful" in the same way that I did "cure."

Q. From where does the evil arise?

A. The forces that result in victimizing behavior consist of a poorly understood set of factors including neurochemical or neurologic abnormalities and personality disorders.

Antisocial Personality Disorder is an example, with a higher rate of incidence in American males (3%) than females (less than 1%). It is also five times more common among first degree relatives of males with the disorder than among the general population. The risk to the first degree biologic relatives of females with the disorder is nearly ten times that of the general population.

They also carry a high risk of psychoactive substance abuse disorders, abuse of narcotic drugs, alcohol, other mind-altering drugs, and a gamut of psychotic and neurotic disorders.

There are some seizure disorders, such as Temporal Lobe Epilepsy, that can cause episodic violent acts of all kinds, and a frontal brain disorder called Kluver-Bucy Syndrome that can manifest itself with inappropriate sexual behaviors.

Researchers working with both animals and humans have implanted electrodes in the limbic area of the brain, often referred to as the seat of our emotions, and demonstrated that stimulation of the area called the amygdala could produce rages. However, not all people who have rages have limbic system dysfunction.

Several other mental illnesses, personality disorders like Borderline Personality Disorders, Bipolar Disorders, Schizophrenia, Obsessive-Compulsive Personality Disorder and others, or combinations of all of these, combined with the right environmental stresses, can trigger people to exhibit sick behavior.

Historically societies coped with people who demonstrate extreme unacceptable behavior by putting them in institutions like prisons, asylums, hospitals, and/or with a chemical straight jacket. Recently, however, this reaction to the treatment of sick behavior has been questioned. Alcoholism, for example, is now considered a physical disease with hereditary factors and not deviant behavior that calls for prison or an asylum. Alcoholism, it has been demonstrated, can provoke incidents of child abuse by impairing judgment.

It's apparent that the answer to what causes abusers to abuse children sexually is not a simple answer. However, although the causes are many, recovery is possible, and recovery of an individual, in most cases, is enough to put the brakes on generations of abuse in at least one family.

CHAPTER NINE

DYSTHYMIA,
OR DEPRESSIVE NEUROSIS

300.40 [DSM III-R]

Dysthymia is characterized in adults by a depressed mood or feeling that is present in and affects the life of an individual for most of most days, for at least two years. This can be either reported subjectively by the individual, or observed by others. In children or adolescents dysthymia can be identified by consistent irritability for at least one year. During this period a minimum of the following will be present:

- Poor appetite or overeating
- Insomnia or hypersomnia
- Low energy or fatigue
- Poor concentration or difficulty making decisions
- Feelings of hopelessness

BETTY————————————————————

As the youngest of three children (two sisters, five and ten years older) Betty felt like a mistake, a feeling that was validated by her mother's cold and distant manner toward her. Conversely, her father gave her mixed messages; he paid attention to her, but at a price. He took tender care of her when she was sick, making it clear that she was his favorite daughter. If she displeased him, he beat her. He began abusing her sexually when she reached puberty and allowed his homosexual partner to rape her while he watched. After that, he compelled her to watch while he and this same man had sex.

In spite of her burdensome home life, Betty was an honor roll student. The fact that she never felt hopeless as a child is a mark of her determination to triumph over her adversity. When she was 14, a 30-year-old man seduced and raped her and then threatened to report her if she refused to continue to meet him for sex. After almost a year of submitting to him, one day while she waited for him he was killed on the way to their meeting place. When he didn't come, she went home. Three days later, when she learned that he had been killed, she felt a mix of relief, guilt, pain and loneliness. She told me that she had felt that there was no way out of that relationship for either of them except through death and when her feelings became fact, she felt that she must have caused his death. She carried the guilt for years.

Also, she missed the attention that he gave her. In her subconscious mind he was connected with her father, who also had seduced and abused her. Since she married so soon afterward, at 17, sex with her father stopped too and both men merged in her mind. When her father died eight years later, she re-experienced both deaths and her freedom was complete.

In spite of the fact that both of her parents abused Betty, one passively by neglect and the other actively, she was most angry at her mother for her neglect. She says that the only mothering she had was caring, nurturing attention from her oldest sister. The anger she felt was acted out in truancy, suicide thoughts and threats and overeating.

At 17 she married and had four children in seven years. Her husband was a passive, unquestioning man who worked the seven to three shift and liked coming home to the settled security of a wife and children, meals on time, clean clothes and a clean house, no chores and his TV.

Predictably, Betty got weary of this routine. She was bored with the daily repetition, disappointed in the relationship, chronically depressed, increasingly overweight and fatigued. By 23 she was devoid of energy, had extremely low self-esteem and walked about with her head down, appearing to apologize to the world for her existence. The children were wonderful, a handful, and the only exception to a life that felt empty. Again she contemplated suicide.

Instead she tried getting more involved in activities in her church, and that helped for a while, but energy was always a problem. There was never enough time or energy to clean her messy house. It was a disaster area. Except the bathroom. At the time, she didn't know why the bathroom was an exception to the chaos. Then, when she was 25, her father died and a deep depression enveloped her. He had represented more than a father to her; he was her lover, her master, and her persecutor. On the other hand, while death had freed her again, she felt she wouldn't be free completely as long as she hid her dreadful secret. She knew there would be hell to pay when she uncovered the shameful secret. After all, her father had been a prominent, respected community leader. But she told and the repercussions were more than she anticipated.

The whole family turned on her, including her normally passive husband. Every last one of them refused to take part in a family meeting or a family therapy session. They blamed the person who was Betty's therapist at the time of putting ideas in Betty's head. While they didn't try to stop Betty from getting help, they did everything they could to make her feel guilty, telling her she was neglecting her home, her wifely duties, her kids, and indulging herself by dwelling on the past. Her pain was discredited entirely.

Abruptly her husband took the children and moved back home with his mother. He consented to attend two therapy sessions with her and then refused to come again, saying that the children would be taken away permanently if she continued what he called "this nonsense."

Betty persisted in her therapy, part of which was to improve her deficient hygiene. Like her house, she had neglected her body. She was grossly obese and her rotting teeth and inadequate bathing habits left her with a strong, repulsive personal odor.

INSIGHTS

Excerpts from a letter she wrote to her then-therapist demonstrate that she was gaining insight into her personal neglect.

> " . . . The truth is, my house is not just cluttered. It is a disaster. When the children were sleeping in the upstairs bedrooms it was all I could do to force myself to clean up there once a month. Things like dusting, sweeping, and making sure I had all the dirty laundry, particularly the socks. Bedding was a little easier.
>
> "One of my little quirks is that I like clean beds. I think I know why. When my father was finished with me, he would wipe himself off with the sheets and leave me there with the smell and the wet. There was nothing I could do. My mother wouldn't have washed them more often. I didn't even dare ask her. I was always afraid Daddy would find out and punish me.
>
> "As some of the abuse took place in our bathtub, it should not come as a surprise that the bathroom is a difficult place to be in. However, it does have the virtue of being the smallest room in my house, so it is the one cleaned most often.
>
> "As for my bedroom, it is and always has been a disaster. Anything I don't know what to do with is in my room . . . .The only thing really clean in my bedroom is my bed. I have never told anyone before but sometimes I change my sheets every day.
>
> [The bathroom was significant because most of the abuse happened there, and it was symbolic to Betty of cleans-

ing and ridding the body of filth. The rest of the house she considered safe.]

"When I was young, if my bedroom was a mess, I had a better chance of keeping things that were special to me. My writings, my drawings, my books, and everything else I didn't want him to take from me as a form of punishment.

"You see, I was never allowed stuffed animals on my bed. The dog I got for Christmas was soft and cuddly and somehow just holding it helped me feel better. I started sleeping with it. When my father discovered it during one of his visits, he was livid. He warned me not to ever let him catch me sleeping with it again. I tried to anyway. "Intelligent as I thought myself to be, I thought all I had to do was to hide it when I heard him coming up the stairs. One night I wasn't successful. I paid for it. He ripped it up and all the stuffing was on the floor. He made me pick it up on my hands and knees as he hit me with a belt.

"The kitchen isn't too bad, except for the dishes. It used to be only once in a while, but now it is more often that my dishes will sit there until there is no option but to do them. Very seldom anymore can I do the dishes and take care of them at the same time. [Washing] them is not the problem. It's the fact that it takes a long time and my mind is free to wander. Usually into my past and the times I should have said no, how maybe I could have said no more effectively and the times I did say no and failed.

"As for the living room. I spend most of my time there. It is the most cluttered part of the house. It is where the family gathers and no one picks up anything until it becomes absolutely necessary.

"Please understand how hard it is for me to admit these things to anyone. But I realize that I have to, if you're going to be able to help me."

In the hospital Betty was placed on a daily exercise program to help increase her physical stamina and to stimulate her endorphin output to combat her depression. Even though she balked, that essential inner spirit that kept her from feeling hopeless at 14 persuaded her to join in the stretching exercises. At the same time, she was put on a weight reduction diet to improve her appearance and her self-esteem.

Our first challenge when we began a personal hygiene regimen was to help Betty overcome her aversion to the bathroom and particularly the bathtub. The latter would take time, so she began by using the shower. She was helped to understand the necessity of frequent bathing, care of her hair and using deodorants, basic and fundamental things that normal parents teach their children as part of a caring rearing process, fundamentals that Betty never had. We urged her strongly to see a dentist and to begin taking care of her teeth properly. The thought of going to a dentist frightened her, so a staff member went with her as moral support for her first visit. After that she was able to go by herself, thanks in large part to the dentist she chose: a dentist who advertises himself as a "coward's" dentist, specializing in treating people who are afraid of dental work.

As Betty's therapy sessions continued, I discovered that she had deep-seated feelings of shame and guilt for what she considered her participation in the incest. I helped her understand that she couldn't have said no to her father and make it stick. She was a helpless child and so what happened was not her fault. She was a brave woman, I told her, for being strong enough to seek help and express her thoughts in spite of her family's lack of support.

Together we named and explored her strengths. They were her intelligence, her insight, her writing and artistic talent, her ability to articulate her thoughts and feelings and her ability to be a good mother to her children despite her depression.

In our therapy sessions Betty got in touch with her deeply buried pain and anger at the people in her life who had hurt her and continued to do so. As rational as her anger was, it had to be vented safely to remove its corrosive effects. She cried daily. Some days, when the rage rose to thundercloud height, she would pound on the walls with a plastic bat that we provided, and on her bed, the furniture, any place safe, and literally slam out her anger. She tore her expressive artwork into pieces and threw the pieces of disembodied memories on the floor. She wrote poetry and letters to those who had hurt her. Each venting reduced her store of rage and in the calm aftermath she could think more constructively. That was when reconstructive therapy could work most effectively to help her change herself and her life.

LOOKING AHEAD

Before Betty left the hospital, she and I sat down to discuss her future soberly and realistically. First, she had to continue therapy somewhere. If she couldn't afford private therapy, she could go to the Community Mental Health services. Second, if her husband refused to go into counseling, it could mean that they would be divorced, especially since he wasn't being supportive of her process. Third, if a divorce happened, she might lose the children because she would have no income. However, she might be able to solve that by negotiating with one of her sisters for babysitting help and she could apply to social services for financial aid until she got a job. Fourth, she needed to accept that her family's attitude was theirs and she couldn't change that. The only attitude she could change was hers.

Getting the problems and potential problems out in the open helped her to see that they were not insurmountable and she could look beyond them. She wanted, she decided, to go back to school and pursue a career. I supported her dream and pointed out that it would improve further her confidence and self-esteem. She decided she would learn to survive as a capable individual, learn to love herself and grow beyond her pain.

CONCLUSIONS

Betty's first psychiatrist, whom she had been seeing since she was 15, used now-oriented therapy because he didn't believe in recovering past memories and working through them. He felt it was necessary for Betty just to forget the past and deal only with the present. His method didn't work for Betty and he wouldn't change his mind. She was lucky that chance brought her together with someone, in this case me, who used a different approach because confronting and purging the past is imperative in cases of child sexual abuse survivors. Because of my professional experience I knew that. Betty worked well, confronted her issues and made excellent progress.

She was released from the hospital and went home. One day she came by my office to tell me about one of those happy twists that life is fond of making: she and her husband are living together and making their marriage work. That same day she gave me copies of two poems she wrote after our last visit in the hospital and before she returned home. They are, I think, expressive of the emotional transformation that takes place when the inner rage is being replaced with a sense of self-possession.

I WILL[21]

Somehow, I will defeat
  my pictures,
  my desperation,
  my reluctance to grow
    to understand
and heal the shattered pieces of my life.

Somehow, I will learn
  to handle my life,
  to accept the fear
  and make peace
      with God
      myself
and others.
So help me God.

UNTITLED

I feel isolated,
alone,
afraid,
Or maybe I feel abandoned,
rejected,
neglected.
Whatever the two, I am separate,
unloved,
ashamed.
From here, I need hope,
compassion,
trust.
Or maybe I need love,
understanding,
or to be held.
But in the end, will it be victory,
defeat,
death?
I want to feel like flowers,
laughter,
secure,

Or maybe I want to feel worthy,
proud,
graceful.
Yet, at this moment, that is clouded by dreams,
images,
pictures,
In the mirrors of my pain.

CHAPTER TEN

CONVERSION DISORDER

(HYSTERICAL NEUROSIS, CONVERSION TYPE)
300.11 [DSM III-R]

Simply stated, a Conversion Disorder is a physical disorder, such as a paralyzed hand, muteness, persistent cough, or any one of a variety of ailments that have no physical cause, but *do have* a psychological cause, although the patient is not conscious of producing the symptom. It differs from a Somatization Disorder in that usually only one prominent symptom is present.

VIVIAN————————————————————————

Vivian sat across from me, fidgeting in her chair, unable to get comfortable. She was slim, dressed in too-tight clothes and had prominent frown lines between her eyebrows that made her look older than her 53 years. She told me that she was divorced and remarried.

The reason she came to consult with me, she said, was a persistent, dry, non-productive cough that conventional medications were unable to control. She had been to every kind of specialist to have it checked, but nothing organic was found to justify the cough. It was precipitated by stress, she was sure of that, because she didn't smoke and she didn't work or live in a polluted atmosphere.

She had worked for the county in an administrative position, but recently had resigned due to conflict with a new supervisor who became difficult and unreasonable after her promotion. She had moved to a different job part time while completing a bachelor's degree in business administration, both of which she enjoyed. During this recital she stopped to cough for two full minutes. When the spasm had passed, she wiped away her tears and said, "See what I mean? The more I try to control it, the more I cough."

A couple of years earlier she had attended an Adult Children of Alcoholics (ACOA) meeting, and from that learned that her birth family had been dysfunctional, she said. Her father drank and her mother was a "typical co-dependent," she said. The information didn't seem to be particularly upsetting to her.

At one of the ACOA meetings, she said, another participant had shared memories of incest and the woman's words had jolted Vivian with a sudden, vivid mental image of her grandfather. That disturbed her because she had adored Grandpa and he was dead now. Besides, she had no memory of any incest. Nonetheless, it was after that meeting that she had begun to cough periodically. It was just a little cough, she thought, and dismissed it, but she couldn't dismiss the persistent feeling of unease.

First, she consulted a psychiatrist, an ear, nose and throat specialist, and an internist who specializes in pulmonary diseases. After that she consulted with a chemical dependency therapist and spent two hours discussing her problems. Afterwards, she didn't cough for two hours. Meditation helped, too. When she meditated before going to bed, she didn't cough all night.

Talking to her mother about the possibility of incest was something she didn't want to do, because she didn't want to upset her. When she talked with her step-brother, he said he didn't remember anything out of line. However, her sister called their grandfather a dirty old man who had tried to French kiss her when she was 14.

Vivian remembered him as a lovely man who brought tubs full of beautiful flowers when he came to their house and made animal pancakes for the children. She had a picture of herself kissing this handsome, gregarious man who loved to dance, date and drink, and who never remarried after his wife died when he was in his 40s. He had lived with them for many years and died in his 80s.

Her father was a drinker too and spent lots of time sitting in bars. He was rarely home and died from cancer when she was in her 20s.

Depression struck Vivian for the first time while she was still married to her first husband, an alcoholic. She found a psychiatrist and had four consultations with her. The psychiatrist conducted a sodium amytal interview that was inclusive about incest. During the amytal interview she remembered her grandfather hugging and kissing her but no other significant breakthrough was accomplished as far as she was concerned.

After that she consulted a chemical dependency counselor who helped her identify the issues she had as an adult child of an alcoholic and suggested that her children should seek counseling because of her husband's alcoholism. Vivian told me that her daughter is an alcoholic and her son has had problems with alcohol as well.

Following that, Vivian pursued several diagnostic avenues, again with no significant yield. She sought out another psychiatrist who did a sodium amytal interview, but no memories emerged. Neither did a hypnotist uncover anything. A lung specialist examined her and said that her airways were significantly irritated and put her on antihistamines for possible allergies, without benefit. Cough medicine with codeine worked, but she was afraid of becoming addicted, so she stopped using it. At that point, because her search for a cause for her cough seemed to be fruitless, she quit looking. Within a very short time she remarried, to a man who gave evidence and promise of being a thoughtful and supportive person. However, within six months he stopped being emotionally supportive, discouraged her from talking about her feelings, and was actively competing with her family for her attention.

To add to Vivian's sense of betrayal, her husband lost his job after their honeymoon and wasn't pursuing employment actively, so she had to support him. After the marriage there were several deaths among Vivian's family and friends that impacted her strongly. In spite of the multiple stresses, her husband, whom she said had never grieved the death of his own father, discouraged her from talking about her grief.

Then Vivian had a breakthrough memory. She remembered being molested, fondled and probed by his fingers, by her maternal grandfather from babyhood on. When she told me, she said her memory dates back to when she was about two, but she had some doubts about whether such memories can be trusted. Can a child of two really remember, she questioned. I assured her that, indeed, a child of two can. People, patients of mine, have had such memories, and when they check out their memories with those who can validate them, they learn that they are correct. Besides, there is no other way that they could have that specific information, except through memory.

Subsequently, she stopped taking the prescribed medications and put her therapy sessions on hold for financial reasons. Besides, she was doing so well, she said.

I agreed that she was doing well and told her that I needed to make sure she wasn't running from her problems by making a "flight into health." That's a common phenomenon when patients get better too abruptly to be true. What they've done is to make a decision to stop dealing with their problems and repress or suppress them so successfully that they really believe that they're cured.

In Vivian's case, she wasn't doing that, as the letter she wrote to herself testifies. She chose or created this unusual third-person format for herself simply because it worked for her. As you have seen, writing in some form is a normal and natural part of recovery. It is the patient who decides ultimately what form the writing will take. What I like particularly about Vivian's third-person format is the perspective it gives her.

My dear Vivian,

You have really tried to do the things Mark [her husband] is interested in. You've spent every weekend on the boat for two summers. You run around like a nut trying to do all your usual chores quickly so you could get out of the house by noon Saturday. Thursday was laundry, ironing, cleaning the bathroom, kitchen, refrigerator, doing the dishes. You do a little cooking. Not much. Mark is right when he says that you don't cook, but, girl, when do you have the time? You're not Superwoman! You're just you, the lovely person I've known all my life, who likes her house clean, loves needlework and reading, her cats, children and family.

You have a big family. They are all your friends. All these things and people take time. You can't do it all. This year you even let your flowers go. I know how much you love flowers, but you made a wise decision there. You knew it would only add to your mounting stress if you worked in them, cultivated them once and didn't even plant new ones. Vivian, that's the first time ever! [You will notice that her words reveal her obsessive-compulsive traits, which is common in abused people.]

I know it broke your heart when Mark wouldn't get your black dirt last summer. It meant a lot to you and you needed the help. You have been very sad and depressed for a year and a half because you realize that Mark is not what he led you to believe. I don't think he really meant to deceive you, but you think he did. When you were in the hospital [when she was sitting with her sister who was dying of cancer], he called every morning. He stopped in and took you to lunch. He showed that you were important to him. He was kind and caring. He really admired your going to college, too.

You were going to group therapy at the same time. You went a full year and then quit because it was so expensive. You could have gone to the ACOA group meetings that were free. You had asked Mark to go with you once in a while since the meetings lasted only an hour, and you even offered that he could go shopping while you were at the meeting. You felt very bad when he said that he wanted nothing to do with it. You would have liked for him to read a little about ACOA and go to a meeting or two so he'd know what you were talking about and could understand. Another big disappointment. He didn't even want you to discuss anything. He blamed others in group therapy for you being upset.

Vivian, I knew that the issues that upset you were your own issues, dealing with your inner self and feelings, not Gina's or Jean's. It seems that Mark cannot deal with real people and their experiences, such as your grief for Tony and Fran. You spent four years learning that you had feelings [signs of dissociation] and needs, and it is best to acknowledge them, to recognize that they exist so that the pain will dissipate and you can heal.

And then, you little dummy, you wanted his approval so much that you turned off your tears because he didn't approve of them. No wonder you're depressed! But it isn't working, is it? I see that you're not having fun. You do smile a little more. You're so serious, but you're doing much better. You couldn't even smile in December [five months previous]. I don't see you doing anything for fun. All you do is work. It preys on your mind that the garage is dirty, that you haven't cleaned windows for two years. Yeah, you and Laurie Jane [her daughter who is a lot like Vivian because she models herself after her] shared all the household duties for a long time. You never asked a boyfriend to do things for you. Sure, Ron carried a dresser in and another guy dropped by to fix the screen door, but you never took advantage of men. [Obviously, she has, but is rationalizing.]

You are a proud, independent lady. Enough men and women call you classy. [What appears to be narcissism is a facade for a deep-seated inferiority complex.] Remember Lucille telling you that one day at lunch about a lady friend who exclaimed, "Who's that beautiful woman?" as you came into the restaurant? I think she said that you had the gorgeous leather coat on and a new haircut.

That bastard, Rick, sure never did anything for you, did he? You could always wash shutters at his house. Never did he help you at your house. He sat all Sunday afternoon while you washed all the windows in your house. He was a prick, Vivian. I was so afraid you'd marry him, but you were too smart. I know you said you loved being able to rely on that big guy. Just lean against his chest and have him hold you and know that you're an okay person in all that you were trying to do for yourself.

It was another death, wasn't it, when you realized he wasn't really the person he pretended to be, that he led you on. I know how hurt you were and how you missed that person. But Vivian, my dear friend, he has shown you what he really is. He even told you that he felt no responsibility to do anything extra around the house, just because you had to study, because that was your choice.

Lady, listen to your own gut feelings! Mark isn't what you thought he was. You keep telling me that he is a dear person. I agree, but he's let you down. He won't change, and yes, he's very smart, but he lives in a dream world. He won't face up to the everyday hurts that you grieve about. You're my dearest friend. I know you better than anyone else, even Laurie Jane. I know you'd be happier without Mark. He isn't going to change. He doesn't have to. He's Mark and he's okay. Just not okay for you. I know you don't want to be alone [Like her mother, who was married twice and who survived both husbands and at 83 years would still get married if she could meet someone who is healthy enough to marry her so she can have a companion. Instead, she hires a companion during the day and often offers free board just

to have another woman stay in her house with her at night.]
But you'll be okay. Trust me. Trust yourself. I'm your best
friend. You can't go on being sick.

Following Vivian's writing that letter, she left Mark, had a brief affair with a married man whom she was loath to give up, but she did and then went back to Mark. He, on the other hand, now has a steady job and seems to have made some changes. He's more thoughtful and caring and does more fun activities with Vivian.

CONCLUSIONS

It's not surprising that Vivian felt angry and betrayed, nor that her cough continued. However, during our sessions together, when she was actively expressing her angry feelings, she didn't cough for periods of up to 30 minutes. I encouraged her to use stress reduction techniques, such as exercise, relaxation and meditation, as well as attending support groups that give her a place to vent her resentment. In addition, I administered 0.5 mg. daily of Klonopin, and together we worked through her feelings of grief and resentment. Jointly, these have served to alleviate her coughing.

Her retrieval of memories of her grandfather's molestation served to get her moving past her sticking point so she could confront and deal with relationship issues that were on hold.

ZELDA

Zelda was a 65 year old white female, originally from Eastern Europe, who had escaped from a Nazi concentration camp during World War Two. She had two children at the time. In the camp she was separated from her husband and oldest child and has never seen them again. Her baby died in her arms during the escape when, as she tried to still the baby's cries to avoid detection, she smothered it unintentionally. Because of that experience she couldn't or wouldn't utter a sound, nor communicate in writing. Zelda had built an impenetrable wall of silence around herself.

Long before I arrived on the scene Zelda was a resident patient of the state hospital where I did my residency training in psychiatry. Her record showed that no physical reason could be found for her muteness. Interpreters of several languages were called in case the problem was simply that no one spoke her language, but that was of no help either, so Zelda went her silent way. When I saw her in the halls, she appeared to be talking to herself. Her lips moved soundlessly. I never learned how she came to be in that particular place, but it was lucky for me that she was.

One day I was leaving the psychiatric unit after a distressing session with a difficult patient and I was distracted. My patient had tried to commit suicide by swallowing a straightened wire hanger and the wire had ripped through her esophagus and trachea. She had come very close to death and she was being watched closely. She requested grounds privileges, the right to walk around the grounds outdoors. I'd had to say no and she was furious with me.

New employees, students and residents are taught to take special precautions when unlocking the psychiatric unit door to enter or depart and never to turn their backs on a patient who may attack and try to escape. But I wasn't thinking about precautions. Instead I thought about my patient's history of severe sexual, physical and emotional abuse as a child, abuse so bad she couldn't tolerate even a foster care home. I thought about how pleasant and productive our sessions always were, about her request and that this was the first time I'd ever had to say no to her.

As I turned the key in the lock, I didn't know that my patient was right behind me. She put a hammer lock on my throat and began to squeeze. Then, although a hammer lock is a two-handed hold, she began to rake my face with her fingernails. I tried to fight her off, but she was much taller and stronger than I and held me up off the floor. I tried to scream, but my airway was closed off. Blood ran down my face and pounded in my ears, my tongue protruded from my mouth. I felt my eyes popping out of my head. I felt no pain because I was so profoundly shocked and I twisted, kicked and squirmed as best I could. Then off to one side I saw movement.

"Help! Help!" Zelda croaked in a rusty little voice that hadn't been used in decades. "Help! Help! Help!" She jumped up and down and waved her arms.

If I didn't do something to break this woman's hold on my throat, I knew that help, any help, would be too late. Zelda distracted her and she lowered me enough so my feet were on the floor. I reached back, grabbed a handful of my patient's hair, bent my knees, bent forward and yanked her over my shoulder and onto her back on the floor. In her shock, she lay still long enough for me to jump on her, grab her wrists and hang on for dear life. Because my ears were ringing, the commotion of two orderlies and two staff members running around the corner toward us was muted. They trussed up my patient and took her off to seclusion and I turned and looked up at Zelda from the floor. "Thank you," I croaked, my voice sounding like a seal with laryngitis. Self-conscious suddenly, Zelda turned and hurried away.

The next day the big news on the ward was not my patient's attack, but that Zelda had spoken for the first time in 30 years.

CONCLUSIONS

To jolt Zelda out of her prison of silence required something shocking enough to overcome the trauma that put her there. After 30 years of relatively quiet seclusion on psychiatric floors, seeing me attacked was sufficiently shocking to break her silence. She didn't begin to talk nonstop; she spoke only in brief sentences, and then never about what happened to her family. The last news I had of her was that she was placed in adult foster care and was happy there.

As for my assailant, she continued to act out her rage and couldn't seem to get past it. Before I was to be transferred to another division, I spent weeks preparing her for my departure. Nonetheless, after I left she tried suicide again, a behavior that continued up to the last news I had of her.

MAURA

Another example of converting a trauma, or a set of traumas in this case, into a physical symptom is Maura, who was born into an abusively dysfunctional family. Her father, an alcoholic, regularly beat their mother, Maura's two brothers and her. When she got pregnant in the ninth grade, she dropped out of school and married her husband, who was 20 at the time. It isn't surprising that he was a controlling and abusive man who allowed her no friends, wouldn't let her drive the car and controlled every penny she spent. They had three children who married early also and struggled constantly with dysfunctional patterns.

One day when Maura was 49 an incident set off a string of events. Her six-year-old granddaughter complained to her mother, Maura's daughter, that her own father "had made her lick his peepee and then had put his peepee inside her peepee." Maura and her daughter together took the granddaughter to the emergency room, but the findings were inconclusive. The case went to court and was dismissed.

That was enough to trigger Maura's repressed memory that the reason she had got pregnant so young was because her husband-to-be raped her when she was 15. She began to have vision problems and went to an ophthalmologist, who referred her to me with tunnel vision for which he could find no physical cause. After we talked I began to see the cause of her vision problem. She said she wanted to leave her husband but she had nowhere to go and no way to support herself. In short, she felt trapped, in a blind alley, couldn't see a way out, and her body, and specifically her eyes, were translating her feelings literally.

We talked at length. I offered several options that she could pursue rather than stay in her abusive situation, but she remained inconsolable and hopeless. Actually, she chose to remain inconsolable and hopeless because at that point she had alternatives. Sometimes fear makes us deadlock, but sometimes it's our subconscious quietly offering its own alternative. This was the case with Maura.

I urged her to make a healthy decision and stop her waffling and we ended that appointment. When she didn't return, I tried to telephone her home and learned her phone was disconnected. Later, when I saw her ophthalmologist at a meeting, I inquired about her. He shook his head and answered wryly. "You know, human nature never ceases to amaze me. Maura's vision hasn't improved, but now she doesn't seem to care."

"*La belle indifference*," I replied, and told him that, while her reaction would be inappropriate to a normal person, it's typical of people with Conversion Disorder, who are filtering their responses through an altered reality, to have this inappropriate complete indifference.

He nodded. "Do you know, I learned that her husband has responded by becoming more considerate and helpful around the house. He actually waits on her." He shook his head. "Incredible."

Not so incredible, I thought. Maura got her secondary gain: her "ill health," her vision problem, is getting her the attention and solicitude she couldn't get in health. *Voila*! She has no reason to get better.

CHAPTER ELEVEN

HISTRIONIC
PERSONALITY DISORDER

301.50 [DSM III-R]

An individual with Histrionic Personality Disorder demonstrates a pervasive pattern of excessive emotionalism and attention-seeking which begins by early adulthood and is present in a variety of contexts. It is indicated by at least four of the following:

- Constantly seeks or demands reassurance, approval or praise.
- Is inappropriately sexually seductive in appearance or behavior.
- Is excessively concerned with physical attractiveness.
- Expresses emotion with inappropriate exaggeration:
    - embraces casual acquaintances with excessive ardor,
    - uncontrollable sobbing on minor sentimental occasions,
    - has temper tantrums.
- Is uncomfortable in situations in which he or she is not the center of attention.
- Displays rapidly shifting and shallow expressions of emotion.
- Is self-centered, with actions directed toward immediate satisfaction and has no tolerance for delayed gratification.
- Has a style of speech that is excessively impressionistic, or subjective and lacking in objective detail.

JOLENE————————————————————

"I need to see you. I have a lot of stresses. My brother got in trouble and my son is having problems," Jolene said in a rush, smoothing her nurse's uniform down over her hips.

She had snagged me as we passed in the hospital hallway one summer evening as I was doing my rounds, and she would have continued this curbside consultation had I allowed it. "I'm sorry to hear that you're having problems," I interrupted her quietly. "If you call my office in the morning, I'll fit you into my schedule." I had seen Jolene around the hospital. She laughed often and loudly, both when she was embarrassed and when bantering coquettishly with the doctors. She favored jokes with sexual innuendo.

The next day she appeared for her appointment in an intricately detailed hairstyle, extravagant makeup and wearing a pair of abbreviated shorts and a sleeveless blouse. Her display of skin was appropriate for her backyard, but it stretched the bounds of propriety for a doctor's office of either gender. She said that she felt depressed but she didn't appear or sound depressed. She said that she had seen another psychiatrist briefly in another state shortly after her divorce and he had accused her of being seductive with him. She had argued the point with him, but the therapy didn't go anywhere anyway, she said, dismissing the subject.

Recently she had moved into her current residence, a nice townhouse, with her four children. The children missed their father who worked in another country and didn't even try to maintain contact with his children, even on their birthdays. Further, he intended to stay out of the country and had no intention of paying the court-ordered child support.

As a result of the lack of child support payments, she had to work a lot of overtime and had a sitter stay with the children. Sometimes the kids got out of hand, as kids will, she said, with a wave of her hand. Unfortunately, one of their neighbors had taken a dislike to her children, accused her of not supervising them and called the police to complain about the most trivial incidents.

Mark, her oldest son, she believes is rebelling against his father's lack of regard for him in particular and for the family as a whole. He had been to a child psychiatrist in their previous city and had spent some remedial time in a foster care home. For a while he straightened out, but recently he was having frequent temper outbursts, some of them violent, which she believed may have been precipitated by their move, his father's absence, the divorce and a new school. He had even threatened the younger children with a knife. He didn't mean it, she said. He wouldn't really do anything. Nonetheless, he was seeing another child psychiatrist who has started him on medications and has recommended a foster care home.

Jolene paused, sighed and looked down at the floor. Into the silence she said, "The psychiatrist's recommendation makes me feel like a failure. Besides, Mark doesn't want to go." Then she looked up, smiled and told of a hypnotherapist she had been seeing. She was attracted to psychic phenomena and the New Age Movement, and hypnotherapy seemed like a good idea. She had become infatuated with the therapist and began calling him, asking him out for a drink, for him to teach her photography and for therapy sessions with him. He declined the drink and teaching her photography, and accepted her as a therapy patient.

During the therapy sessions Jolene began to recall scattered incidents of sexual abuse from her father during her childhood. He would force her to have intercourse with him while her mother was at work, she remembered. The memories came slowly at first, then more and more. She remembered hiding in a closet, crying, while her father called and searched for her. When he found her, he pulled her out of the closet and raped her. In vain she begged him to stop.

When she got older and had a boyfriend, her father got angry and jealous, calling her a slut and a whore as she got ready to go out. On one occasion, as she prepared to leave the house, he grabbed her arm, threw her to the floor and raped her. When he was finished, he stood and stared down at her contemptuously, and threw dollar bills on her. Then he walked away and left her there, feeling used and worthless.

At 17 she left home to escape the sexual abuse. She couldn't talk to her mother about it because her father physically and emotionally abused her too. That's one of the reasons her mother worked, to get out of the house, and Jolene knew she was expected to stay home and do the chores when her mother was gone. At times Jolene was parentified, when her mother confided in her about the abuse and her desire for a divorce. It would never happen, Jolene sensed, long before she learned the word codependent.

She felt unworthy of her high school sweetheart who went on to medical school after high school, and after a long series of affairs she married her husband, more for his dark good looks than for love. The marriage soured after only a year, but she stayed because she hoped it would get better. Her husband, she told me, was self-centered, indifferent with the children, a lover who used her as a masturbation tool, satisfying his own requirements without any regard for her needs and feelings and then fell asleep. She began to fantasize about other men. The fantasy turned into affairs and soon she knew the marriage was finished.

After the divorce, coping with the children seemed to be beyond her and she went for counseling. Then, when her ex-husband left the country, they all felt abandoned and began acting out their feelings, each in his or her own way. Jolene's way was to drink heavily. About that time she found the hypnotherapist. When their sessions were finished, she told him she wanted a friendship with him, but he discouraged her gently by telling her that he had a girlfriend. One day her mother saw the therapist and his girlfriend together and she telephoned Jolene to tell her about this "extremely beautiful" woman and to say that Jolene had no chance with him at all. That's when she began to test her therapist with her telephone calls and invitations. Shortly after he declined her advances, she terminated their association saying that he didn't reciprocate her offer of friendship and she was tired of trying.

However, she continued her therapy with me and she was gaining insight, psychological balance and emotional strength. She was able to tell her mother of the incest incidents, but their relationship didn't change significantly. Jolene hadn't confronted her father recently and her relationship with him was unchanged.

After Jolene had talked with her mother about the incest history, her father was having chest pains and they feared a heart attack. Because her mother had to go to work, she called Jolene and asked her to come and stay with her father so he wouldn't have to be alone in case of an emergency. When Jolene arrived he was still in the living room and in front of her mother he asked to see Jolene's "tits." He said he hadn't seen them since her breast reduction surgery.

While Jolene's face flamed in embarrassment and shame, her mother said simply, "Shhhhhh."

"No, I won't," Jolene burst out in anger. "Go to bed and rest!"

"If you'll lie down with me and warm me up," he responded.

"I'll be outside if you need me." Jolene spun around and left the room.

Later, during one of our sessions, I asked why she didn't express her anger more assertively? She said that she was still afraid of him, that she didn't feel strong enough to confront him just yet and, besides, she was afraid to precipitate a heart attack.

AT THE PRESENT

Jolene changed a great deal in the following year. She lost weight, became more subtle in her dress and manner, and more peaceful and self-possessed. She married a quiet, tall, dark and good looking man who had never been married and with whom she shared interests. They work in the same hospital and he accepts her children.

She told me that she came to terms with her parents. The letter she wrote, but never mailed to her father may have something to do with that. In it she confronted his incestuous behavior during her childhood and expressed her anger at him for what his behavior did to her. He has made no further sexual advances or inappropriate remarks to her and her parents no longer live together. When her mother moved out, I believe that it was a significant gesture to Jolene that empowered her to move on in her own life. Among other things, it meant that she no longer needed to mother her mother.

All the changes have come as a result of her growing insight into her problems. She attended a weekend retreat with other people who had lost significant people in their lives and who came together to confront their grief and rage. The weekend, she said, renewed her.

The extended family issues no longer enmesh her and she is able to empathize and sympathize without needing to fix the problem. Even her children seem more secure with her new husband and their relationship and they aren't acting out any more.

At this point I believe that Jolene is on the right path, and both she and I are optimistic about her future.

ABOUT HISTRIONICS AND HPD

Histrionics are an exhausting, amusing, confusing and predictable part of adolescence. It's just one of the well-known stages, marked by excesses, narcissism and development of interpersonal skills that can be traced to normal hormone bombardment. Adolescents, bearers of normal histrionics, tend to travel in packs, apparently self-absorbed, actually highly self-conscious. The laughter, the speech, the music is too loud. The language is the current adolescent jargon, used to identify tribal members. The diet defies reason. The clothing and treatment of adults seem to attempt to defy any previously encountered standards. The affliction is temporary, however, in normal adolescents, as they learn the limits of their social power from consistently set boundaries.

Histrionic behavior in adults, on the other hand, is not normal and generally is less well tolerated. The behavior may be used voluntarily as an attention getter, or the individual may have a diagnosable case of Histrionic Personality Disorder.

One woman who was my patient briefly, who never finished any course of therapy that I heard of, indulged in histrionic behavior on occasion, but it wasn't her enduring pattern of conduct. Her husband had deserted her for another woman. After that, she devoted herself and her energies to raising her children, making sure they got the best education she could give them, and driving them to their sporting events, even after a 16 hour work day. At those events she seemed to experience a personality change, sobbing uncontrollably at losses, shrieking and flinging her arms around new acquaintances at victories.

It appeared that her goal was to get attention any way she knew because her behavior was inconsistent with her lack of self-esteem from the failure of her marriage. Making herself the center of her children's lives gave her a sense of success through their successes. Outside of her relationship with her children, she needed a lot of reassurance. Nonetheless, her histrionics could be put on and taken off like a sweater, which led me to conclude that it was not pathological, but an attention-getting device.

Histrionic Personality Disorder, on the other hand, takes over the whole personality and is treatable, if the patient wants to be treated. Julie, as it turned out, did not.

I was the on-call psychiatrist for the Emergency Room that raw day in late October when Julie came in to the ER, crying, shaking and talking suicide. She wore a tank top, no bra, a short, tight skirt and high heels with no stockings, clothing more appropriate to 80-degree weather. We drew blood to check for alcohol and drugs and found only trace levels of marijuana, nothing else. She continued to cry as we talked, smearing the clumps of sooty mascara that cut a ravine through the makeup on her thin, pale face.

She looked about 16, but she gave her age as 29. Her boyfriend had kicked her out after a fight, she said. She had nowhere to go and didn't know how to support herself. She combed her long fingernails through her long, blond hair. When she saw that I watched her gesture, she laughed and said, "Bottle blond," touching a trembling hand to the overstated ribbon-on-a-barrette that failed to tame the excess of curls. There was nothing subtle about Julie in manner or dress.

"I've been diagnosed as Manic Depressive, Borderline Personality Disorder, Schizophrenic, Schizophrenic Disorders, and drug and alcohol dependent," she told me brightly.

Her flip proficiency in rattling off the jargon directed my questions to determine if she had a history of psychiatric therapy. She had, she said, since she had been 12 and had run away from home and got involved in drugs and alcohol. She had run away from so many adolescent psychiatric units that she was put in a home for girls. When she reached her majority, she began living with one boyfriend after another, all of them older and willing to support her addiction until the cost became too great. The relationships usually ended with cruel beatings that required emergency room services, combined sometimes with psychiatric intervention and admission for drug detoxification.

Her last boyfriend had been little more than her pimp, regulating her contacts, locking her up, controlling her weight and forcing an exercise regimen. His latest fetish, one of several she found hard to tolerate, was for her to have sex with another man, naked, in a sailboat, while he watched. When she protested, he threw her out.

It wasn't until the next day that she told me that her father had abused her sexually as far back as she could remember, possibly as early as age four. When she told her mother, she was accused of lying and told that, if she didn't stop making up stories, her mother would "beat the tar out of her." Sexual activity with her father was daily and always generated gifts. Anything she wanted. She told me that she learned to tolerate the sex. It was her mother's hostility that she ran away from. When she ran away, it was her father, not her mother, who came looking for her. When she finally left home, the lesson she took with her was sex with men is profitable and women can be disregarded because they're hostile.

Her beauty and sexuality continued to earn favors and attention from men and habitually she turned on the seductive act when men were around. Particularly, she liked the challenge of married men. Since women were threatened by her behavior, female friendships didn't last. I asked her how she felt about that. "That's me!" she responded brightly, with a shrug, a smile and a flick of her hair.

The next day the unit nurse called to tell me that Julie's boyfriend had come to the hospital to take her home and Julie was demanding discharge, saying she was fine now. I talked to her briefly, trying to explain that she was taking a flight into health without resolving the cause of the problem. She cut me off midsentence, saying she would sign out against medical advice, a move apparently she was familiar with. She left. There was nothing I could do.

The shallowness of her rejoinders, the consistency of her behavior, her apparently genuine reach for help that ended prematurely when she got her boyfriend back, all reveal a pathological behavior that lacks authentic desire to resolve her problem. In spite of her very real distress and her awareness of what causes her dysfunctional lifestyle, she chose the familiar pain.

DEVELOPMENT AND SEXUAL ABUSE

While probably not all persons with HPD have been sexually abused, *all of my patients who have been diagnosed under HPD have had a history of child sexual abuse.* The behavior they displayed depends on the age they were when the abuse began, because the abuse causes arrest of development.

On one hand, children developing without abuse learn healthy boundaries and to accommodate other's feelings as they gain mastery over their own. On the other, abused youngsters learn they can control the abuse by controlling the abuser through their behavior. With their energies focused on abuse-related issues, their normal development fixates at that age. The three stages are oral, anal and genital.

Oral stage: If the trauma happened from infancy to about 18 months, before toilet training, fixation is oral. The symptoms are excessive eating, talking, drinking and smoking.

Anal stage: Fixation at the *anal stage*, when toilet training starts, causes a rigid adherence to schedule or inability to be prompt; perfectionism, obsession with details; anal retentiveness, meaning difficulty with constipation of feces and emotions; inability to have fun; extreme sense of morality and responsibility; and the classic symptom, compulsive hand washing.

Genital stage: In the third year, designated as the genital stage, children start to recognize gender differences and may explore their sex organs and those of other children. Traumatic experience then can cause such symptoms as sexually inappropriate behavior and using exploitive sexual behavior. Some go into prostitution. Often they don't enjoy sex, yet seem to have an insatiable need for it. Often survivors claim they are unorgasmic.

Theoretically, it should be easy to determine the age of abuse, but children who have been abused at a *pre-verbal age* have difficulty putting their feelings into words because their cognitive abilities at the time of their abuse affects how they process their trauma. My experience has been that children who were abused pre-verbally find it harder to recover their memories and usually question the veracity of those memories. These people have a general sense of shame, worthlessness, disturbances in attachments and inability to form intimate relationships. Their inner rage is often so diffuse that it gets mixed up and confused with a tremendous sense of need.

CHAPTER TWELVE

PEDOPHILIA

302.20 [DSM III-R]

The two essential features of this disorder are recurrent, intense sexual urges and sexually arousing fantasies of at least six months duration, involving sexual activity with prepubescent children. An active pedophile has acted on these urges or is markedly distressed by them, and is at least 16 years old and at least five years older than the child or children victimized.

GLEN————————————————————————

This suicidal 35-year-old clerk was referred to me by his therapist for emergency admission to the hospital psychiatric ward. His threat grew out of his depression that was precipitated by his wife's request for separation and divorce from their stormy 12-year marriage. His wife had sought counseling and this was her solution.

Glen began his story by telling me that he was a pathological liar and that he had fooled his minister and their congregation for years. He wanted to come across as a good guy, he said, and had tried to please everyone. With his wife he was a different man, he said, and he couldn't blame her for her decision because he had been a jealous and abusive husband.

CHILDHOOD ABUSE

His problems began in childhood, he believes. He and his fraternal twin brother are the oldest of five boys. Their father was a
remote, cold alcoholic who worked long hours, came home drunk
and physically abused his children. Their mother, who was no
more affectionate than their father, tried to shield her sons from
the abuse and, consequently, became the target instead. Glen
remembers hearing his parents' noisy arguments when his father
came home drunk and then through the thin walls he heard sounds
of his parents having sex. Glen's abuse ended only when he left
home at seventeen.

A neighbor and family friend, Uncle Ted, was the only person
in their experience who ever showed the boys any attention or
affection. He took them to his resort on weekends and gave them
expensive gifts. Also, he sexually molested all of them. Glen's memories of Ted masturbating him against his will began when he was
about ten years old and continued until he reached puberty and
was discarded in favor of a younger brother. Each of the brothers
received the same treatment in turn. Ted said "don't tell," and they
didn't. They didn't even discuss the abuse among themselves. Their
parents seemed pleased to have the boys off their hands and Glen
believes now that, even if they had told, they wouldn't have been
believed. Besides, they liked the attention and gifts.

MARRIAGE

Two years after his graduation from high school, where he was an
average student, he married. He was abusive toward his wife, following his father's example, which amounted to her revictimization
because it reactivated dormant problems from her childhood incest. In spite of four children, the rift between them grew and on
one occasion he broke one of her eardrums with a blow to the
head. Eventually, she was diagnosed with Dissociative Identity
Disorder in joint counseling sessions with Glen. Meanwhile, he

had noticed even before marriage that he was hypersexual, which became a problem between him and his wife. He suppressed his same-gender sexual attraction. He enjoyed sex with his wife, but it wasn't enough for him, so he masturbated secretly and compulsively, and worse.

HOSPITALIZATION

The joint therapy sessions with his wife, their therapist and me continued after Glen was first hospitalized for depression. During one session his wife confronted him with her memory of him molesting their children. Glen denied it vehemently at first. Later he went into a severe rage episode in which he shredded facial tissues, threw them about the room and then tore his room apart. We put him on one-to-one observation and when his rages continued and became disruptive to the whole unit, he was given intramuscular sedatives.

Again his wife confronted him about his sexual abuse of their children, and again he raged. But then he admitted his recollection of the abuse. He confessed that he remembered showering with his oldest son, who was then nine, and fondling him and putting his penis between his son's legs. He remembered masturbating his sons and rubbing his penis between his two-year-old son's legs. He remembered fondling his daughter's breasts. He told his children not to tell and they didn't. Also, he was physically abusive with his children, but they didn't tell about that either.

The primary therapist told Glen flatly that he would have to report Glen to the Child Protective Services and warned him that he probably would be arrested and jailed. Glen became frightened at first, but his fear turned to resignation and he hired a lawyer.

In the interim, his parents and siblings were invited for a family therapy session. His parents and one brother came, but nothing was accomplished because his parents and brother saw nothing abnormal about their family. Glen felt angry at their denial, which increased his feelings of frustration, which in turn increased his sense of internal pressure. As his feelings intensified, he isolated himself and refused to attend group therapy sessions because he wanted to stay away from other incest survivors. They might reject him, he thought.

One night he tried to strangle himself with a towel, but he was discovered and placed under acute suicide precautions. After that he became despondent and felt hopeless and powerless. It was clear that he would no longer be able to escape consequences for his sexual and physical abuse of his family. His anger grew to embrace his parents, his wife and particularly himself. It was only then that finally Glen became angry at Uncle Ted, probably seeing for the first time Ted's role in his troubles. He released his anger by ripping tissues, magazines, towels and punching a "Ted pillow."

Glen saw that he needed to deal with his homosexual feelings because they were causing him great problems. He was, he admitted, sexually attracted to his male nurse and male therapist, as well as to his own brother and son. Maybe he couldn't ever be around children again, he feared, because he might not be able to resist abusing them sexually. He admitted he was still masturbating compulsively which made him feel even more guilty and ashamed.

THERAPY

Therapy for Glen in the psychiatric unit included individual and group therapy sessions. There he uncovered the childhood trauma that led to his problems, described the details of his abuse by Ted and his father, as well as his abuse of his wife and children.

Breaking the secrecy of his own abuse allowed him to admit that he abused his own children. Honesty helped him gain self-esteem, a commodity he lacked sadly, and to develop the courage to face whatever consequences his behavior would bring. Although he was disappointed by his parents' and brothers' response to his honesty, he said it felt good to discuss his issues with them. Their discussion helped him work through and accept their realities, no matter how they differed from his.

Glen worked through his need to forgive himself and acknowledged that he was a long way from forgiving his perpetrators, Uncle Ted and his father. He was able to accept his homosexual feelings even though he has not and may never act on those urges with an adult.

An EEG (electroencephalogram) showed some abnormality. That led me to believe he might have temporal lobe epilepsy as indicated by his inability to remember details of his sexual abuse of his children in its early stages and of his hypersexuality. Later my suspicions were disproved by more in-depth studies done at a special clinic. He was treated with medication to help him with his anxiety and depression.

It is important to mention that co-therapy with a male therapist has been very helpful for Glen since that therapist and I used a confrontive, consistent and cohesive approach. Essentially we took on roles of caring-but-firm parent surrogates, yet we were never punitive and we involved him at all times in the course of his therapy.

We felt that despite his progress in the unit, it would be in his best interest if he spent some time at a specialized treatment center dealing with sexually deviant behavior. He spent six weeks at the John Hopkins Hospital. The diagnosis was bisexual pedophilia, history of depression, and histrionic traits. The laboratory examinations, CTScan, computerized tomography scan or X-ray of his brain to check for brain abnormalities like a brain tumor; EKG, a study of his heart; and chest X-rays all were normal, and psychological examinations didn't confirm a Temporal Lobe Syndrome. He was treated with a hormone medication, Depo-Provera, a female hormone that causes chemical, reversible castration to decrease his hypersexuality, and his anti-depressant medication was continued.

In court Glen pleaded guilty and ultimately was sentenced to 10-15 years. His wife has custody of the children and he may see them only under supervision. He continues receiving Depo-Provera and continues with his therapy.

AN OPINION

In my opinion imprisoning Glen was understandable given our thinking about punishing people who abuse children sexually, and it *is* the law. It was necessary in terms of getting him away from anyone he might abuse. In some respects, I agree, and would like to see the punishment go back generations to where the abuse began. However, punishing generations postmortem is neither practical nor possible.

What is far more important and germane than punishment is treatment, *effective* treatment during imprisonment. I can't emphasize the word effective too strongly because there are so many useless treatment programs for incarcerated sex offenders. Treatment programs for sex offenders are still in their infancy. To this point, not one singular therapy has succeeded. Too often, when offenders get out of prison, they commit the same kind of crime all over again, only this time more violently. In my opinion, imprisonment without effective and intensive therapy accomplishes nothing. Admittedly, my opinion may be biased because of my medical specialty, but my experience is that psychiatric treatment as part of the treatment team is the only dependably effective treatment available at this time. *In-depth psychiatric treatment of the perpetrators can stop the effects of abuse in its tracks, person by person, until it exists no more.* Anything less in hard-core offenders, and often even early offenders, doesn't do the job. Imprisoning offenders without effective treatment serves to do nothing more than pack more explosive into a waiting bomb; when they are released they will offend again, only with even more rage.

What needs to be treated and defused is their understandable rage stemming from their own sexual abuse that drives them to abuse others. The younger the sex offender is caught and the earlier treatment begins, the better the prognosis.

ELEMENTS OF TREATMENT

First and most important, treatment must be a team approach always including a psychiatrist because of the far-reaching complexities of the disorders involved. Anything less will fail to do the job, as they have been failing.

I can't stress too much a thorough history and physical examination at the beginning as the cornerstone of successful therapy. Psychological tests, such as personality inventories, Rorschach and other projective tests are valuable adjuncts to understand each individual. Other tests that are constructive diagnostic tools are brain mapping, PETScan, and the MMPI (Minnesota Multiphasic). Violence history, homicide-suicide profile, presence of mental illness, successful work history, and family history are all important factors to identify high risk cases.

Severely disturbed individuals whose impulse controls and reality testing are functioning poorly have to be assessed for pharmacological treatment after psychiatric, neurological and psychological testing are done. The current drugs of choice have been the female hormone Depo-provera, and Thioridazine, an anti-psychotic/major tranquilizer, used for improvement of reality testing, which has a side-effect of dampening sexual desire. Anti-depressant medications and mood-stabilizers such as Lithium Carbonate, and Valproic Acid and Tegretol, both anti-convulsants used for temporal lobe seizures, have been used with good result. Since a majority of sex offenders have addictive-compulsive behaviors, as I have pointed out elsewhere, Twelve Step programs built on the Alcoholics Anonymous model are useful but are insufficient alone to treat the problem. Also, incorporation of a behavioral modification program involving assertiveness training, anger expression and aversion techniques can be used effectively with other treatment modalities on an on-going basis, but are insufficient alone.

Obviously treatment is complex and requires a significant amount of time. My recommendation, based on my professional experience, is a minimum five-year prison term for the first offense, including from the first day, the treatment structure discussed above. From the prison facility the offender would go to a halfway house for two years, wearing electronic monitoring at all times, to continue treatment.

When re-entry into the community has been approved, community and family resources should be used during the probationary period if they're available, and both personal and group therapies should be continued as well. The offender's failure to comply with this regimen, or re-offense, would automatically dictate a return to prison. After the probationary period is over offenders must be required to sign an agreement to maintain therapy for another three years, at which time they would be re-evaluated again.

An offender who re-offends re-victimizes himself and retards his recovery and reinforces his compulsion. Should that happen, of course another re-evaluation must be done to see if something was missed previously. However, after a specific number of re-offenses, specified by state law, imprisonment for life is a definite option.

RANDY————————————————————————

Randy's story, told in his own words, further illustrates the abusive process that creates a sexual abuser. As painful as it is to read multiple stories of abuse, the stories are important to help us understand how complex the problem is and to give us insight into the etiology of child abuse in general and sexual abuse in particular. That understanding will help us to create effective treatment models. Randy's story:

HELL IS FOR CHILDREN

"I'm going to kill that s.o.b. if it's the last act in my life," I said
to my brother as I left home for one of my routine, three to
four day absences to escape the abuse. I was again at my

breaking point. Home means a haven to most people. A place where the family meets, eats and loves each other in a healthy, productive way. For me, home was another word for hell, where my story of my vicious and incestuous life began in my infancy.

As an infant I was kept in the crib day and night until the age of three. I was conceived by an alcoholic and drug-abusing mother who I believe was also schizophrenic. I believe I may have [been born with] Fetal Alcohol Syndrome since my mother drank all through her pregnancy with me.

My name is Randy, and I'm gay and a recovering alcoholic. It's important for you to know that I'm gay and that there are underlying reasons for my [sexual] orientation. I'm likewise emphasizing that I'm a recovering alcoholic, since recently I reached the end of my rope and tried to end my life with a bottle of narcotics and a fifth and a half of vodka. They pumped my stomach and did CPR all the way to the hospital. My blood alcohol was .385.

I feel lucky to be alive today, and I'm glad I am. I believe that God wants me here to tell my story and possibly to help other incest victims.

I was abused by both of my parents. The first time my father raped me, I was five years old. I was tied at the wrists and ankles, face down, spread eagle. The pain was worse than anything you can imagine. Try to imagine a butcher knife being shoved up your anus brutally and repeatedly. The mental pain was no less excruciating. To a little boy, the sight of a huge penis is truly frightening. Experiencing sex at that age brings a fear that goes right through and out your fingertips, and never goes away without professional help.

Restraints were a big part of my life from the time I was five years old until I was about 13 or 14. I'm still trying to recover memories that I've blocked out for years. I don't remember having one good day until I was 15 years old. [That was the day] when my mother died at the age of 42, brought on by her drug and alcohol addiction. After she died, my three sisters and I were taken to a foster home.

I remember after my father raped me, my mother untied me, cleaned me up, and put me to bed. I was never taken to a doctor. I could have bled to death that day, or any of the many days after when the sodomy was repeated, but I believe that God must have had a reason to keep me alive. Maybe I have a guardian angel. Mother was petrified to turn my father in. She was a petite woman, about 5' 4" and 120 pounds, whereas my father was 6' 2" and 250 pounds. He was quite abusive. He was a drug-abusing, power-tripper, alcoholic, hill-climber.

I looked forward to the weekends, as the house would be full of people who just adored me, but had no idea about the hell I was going through. The oddest thing was that, in spite of the severe mental, physical and sexual abuse, I seemed to bounce back as a happy-go-lucky Randy. The weekends gave me a couple of days of reprieve from the beatings.

By age six I was expected to clean the bathroom and do the dishes. My mother taught me to do these jobs, as well as scrub the floor. If it wasn't done exactly to her liking, I would be beaten with a belt. It was a ritual. My mother would gather all my sisters (I have three, two are older and one younger, and my older brother was never home) as her audience, and I was made to completely strip before them. Sometimes I was allowed to cover my penis with my hands, other times I would be slapped across the face with a belt. Then my mother would have me bend over a chair and [beat] me until she was worn out. I learned to endure the pain without crying because, if I did, there would be two more cracks with the belt.

I never knew when the beatings would come. My mother drank beer, abused drugs such as Valium or anything she could get her hands on, and her moods were affected by these substances. I might be ritually beaten for missing a spot on the floor, or for not using the right tone of voice when talking with her.

I was never allowed to go to friends' houses, or go out and play. When I did go outside, I was confined inside a locked six foot square fence. From there I would watch my brother and three sisters play with their friends on the swing set, or play the usual games children played. When I cried from hunger while my brother and sisters were fed lunch, I would be tied in my windowless bedroom for sometimes up to three or four days at a time. When I defecated or urinated, I got a beating for that as well.

I was a hyperkinetic child, so I was restrained. When I got up at night, using my free arm to untie the other, I'd play with my toys and wander around the house. After my mother woke up and caught me two or three times, the four-point restraints started, around both wrists and ankles. Sometimes the restraints around my ankles got so tight, my feet would go numb.

I was prescribed amphetamines and Ritalin to control my hyperactivity. During the days of restraints, I was given only my pills and a glass of milk to go with them.

When I was seven years of age, I walked in on my father having sexual intercourse with my oldest sister.

When I was ten years old, there was a party and for some reason I had to sleep with my mother. During that time I had a lot of blackouts. I didn't drink yet, but we were allowed to smoke marijuana and of course there was the Ritalin. Anyway, that night I woke up out of a blackout to find myself having sexual intercourse with my mother. Since I don't remember how [the incident] began, I have and will always call that incident incestuous rape.

About the same time, age ten, my father began to leave me alone, only to begin raping my sisters. He started from the oldest down to the youngest. Once he started, it became an ongoing nightmare every night. By this time my parents slept apart. My mother's bedroom was next to my two older sisters'. I slept in the farthest bedroom. My mother knew what went on but chose to drown her pain with liquor and pills. I resent her for that. She could have been stronger.

When I turned 12 they had my oldest sister sleep in my bedroom on the spare bed. Once again I was raped, by my own sister! This happened while my mother was sitting in the living room. Later, my father came in and sat on her bed. I remember my sister telling my father that she had "taught" me, and he seemed quite pleased with that. I had my back toward them because I felt dirty, ashamed and guilty. Then they began to [have sex] right in the bed beside me. My mother was in her bedroom drinking, as usual.

I have blanked out most of the next two years. I remember only bits and pieces of my school days, which were miserable. I had no friends and I fought with everyone. My grades were horrible. I got kicked out of kindergarten and flunked out and had to go back to pre-kindergarten school. I also got kicked out of second grade since I had to stay after school many times. Once, when I had to stay after school again, my teacher forgot me, so I missed the bus. She ended taking me home. Naturally, I got another beating, plus restrained in bed for the entire weekend.

In fourth grade I was kicked out again. I failed all my classes, so I didn't take my report card home and told my mother that we hadn't received [them] yet. She called my teacher to check it out and my teacher got very irate. He questioned me about lying to him and my mother. I wanted so much to tell him what was going on at home, but I was more fearful of the repercussions at home, so I lamely said, "I don't know." With that, he promptly jerked me out into the hall, along with my desk, and dumped the desk upside down so the contents spilled on the floor. He demanded that I find my report card, which I knew wasn't there. I went through the motions of looking for the non-existent card while the other classes went to lunch, laughing and jeering at me as they passed by.

When I got home, I received the worst beating of my life, stripped naked, with my sisters looking on as usual. I tried to roll around to avoid the blows, [and] this time I bled as my mother beat me furiously. I bear permanent scars on each of my hips and on my nose, between my eyes, which I sustained as she pushed me down and I hit the corner of the table, breaking both my glasses and my nose. Ironically, when my mother died from a massive heart attack, she hit her head as she fell, on the very same table.

After that beating, I blanked out almost everything. Memories of the fifth, sixth and seventh grades are spotty, and I recall nothing about the eighth grade. I do remember that my teacher came to my house once and my mother put on a great show, cleaned the house, brought out her best china. It worked. She was a very convincing con artist.

During my seventh grade year, they remodeled the garage, which was where my father first raped me, into a house, as my younger sister and I were going through puberty. [The advent of Randy's puberty and the remodeling of the garage, the place where his father first raped him, marked the physical change of two significant things—his body and the garage.] During my seventh grade year, my sister and I were going through puberty. We used to protect each other, but we had begun to argue at school and at home, as most teenaged siblings do from time to time. One day my mother was drunk and she had a couple of friends over. They decided to have my younger sister and I have a fistfight. We beat each other up pretty bad. A month after this we wound up in bed together. I tried to penetrate her, but I couldn't, so I quit. We never talked about it since, and we have never been close since then.

During my eighth grade year, my parents had a horrible fight over my oldest sister. My mother screamed [at my father], "It's bad enough to lose my husband, but I never thought I'd lose him to my own daughter."

My little sister and I had already planned to run away together to my aunt's. As the fight got worse and more hurtful things were said, we took off on a 15-mile hike. I was determined to make it, but my sister started to cry after we reached seven miles, because her feet hurt. So we had to go back home.

The incest continued between my oldest sister and my father, but now he also began to rape my second older sister as well as my youngest sister on a nightly basis. The screams and agonized crying that went on nightly is something that is permanently locked in my mind.

My mother started working at a store, but the punishments never quit. I was now 14. The form of punishment changed. I was made to sit for hours with my arms and legs straight out in front of me. Each time my arms or legs dropped, I was whacked with a belt anywhere on my body.

My parents had a married couple as drinking buddies when I was about seven or eight years old. They would bring their son over, and we slept in the same room. This was the first time that I knew I was a homosexual. We masturbated each other. He died from a heroin overdose eight years ago. [This sort of activity is not abnormal for children, especially sexually abused children. Even in children who haven't been abused, it can be only normal experimentation and not an accurate indicator of homosexuality. I will comment further on child sexuality below. L.C.] He was an incest victim, too. The second homosexual experience to which I willingly submitted was when I was 12. A lesbian friend of my mother came over with a cute young man in his 20s. I took him to my bedroom and initiated sex, which lasted two hours.

Another form of punishment my mother subjected us to when we were younger was, if we swore or screamed, she washed our mouths out with bar soap, dish soap or Comet cleanser. I had diarrhea from the dish soap and cleanser.

In 1969 my mother was admitted to a sanitarium. In 1976 she was in and out of hospitals for pancreatitis and stomach surgery from ulcers, brought on by her drinking and heavy drug use. As she got weaker, the mental abuse got worse. I was 15 then.

In 1979 I tried to kill her twice. I was still taking Ritalin, but now the effect on me was the opposite from when I was younger. I was also smoking pot daily and had begun a ten-year drinking spree. Once I put floor wax in her milk, stirring it well, but she smelled it and said the milk was sour. Another time I laced her roast with rat poison. She ate it, but it didn't do a thing to her. By then, my older brother and sister were out on their own. My brother had his own house and my sister was in the Army.

My father continued the incest with my two younger sisters. I tried to help them by giving them each a butcher knife to put under their pillows. They slept in the same room and feigned sleep. If my father came near either one, the other would cough. Once, when he was on top of the older sister, she pulled out the knife and wounded him in the leg. Then they both ran into my bedroom to hide. Mine was the only one with a lock on it. They stayed there the whole night. The next day we discovered that all the sharp knives were gone and only butter knives were left.

We even circled the number for Alcoholics Anonymous in red in the phone book and left the book open so our mother would take a hint, but it didn't work. Our second older sister was preparing to go into the Army, as well, so that would leave my youngest sister and me at home. Our only other alternative was to call the protective services, which we did. We were interviewed by a worker there, and removed from our home in December 1989. I was stoned at the time, which had become a daily occurrence. We were put in a police car and the police arrested my father on the spot. My mother was working at a nursing home then.

I spent Christmas, New Year's eve and day, and Easter at the foster care home. My brother got married on February 16, 1980, while my mother was in the hospital. I was allowed to visit her. I gave her a hug, and I could feel every rib and vertebrae in her back. I told my uncle that she's not long for this world. That was the last time I saw her. She died on March 18, 1980.

On April 2, two days after my 16th birthday, I was returned to that horrid house I called Burton's Concentration Camp. [The home of his birth father.] My coming home present was a quarter ounce of marijuana from my father. [Foster father.] From 1980 to 1987 I dropped out of school and tried to overdose on sleeping pills. I moved 15 times from 1980 to 1991, from city to city. I've had two drunk driving offenses and two misdemeanor charges for writing bad checks between 1982 and 1987.

In 1987 I began to build a small business as a rug weaver. My rugs have placed Grand Prize sweepstakes and first place at fairs. I have 30 customers now. I've learned to cater and catered my second sister's bridal shower and wedding, plus two other weddings. I've worked at two restaurants as assistant manager. I've also been in six different treatment centers for alcoholism and drug addiction. The first five times I developed no insight at all. The last time, though, my counselor, a very special lady, helped me be aware of my inner child. She only wanted to crack open the door of my memories. Instead, it flew wide open. Now I will be seeing a counselor twice a week. I'll also be attending as many self-help groups as possible.

Today I'm feeling pain, but I'm keeping it inside because of what was pounded into me as a child: don't let it show, don't cry out loud, hide your feelings. I feel, though, that in the very near future the cap will come off the volcano and I can truly begin to recover. I'll be truly free.

Today there are a few bright spots. Instead of seeing life in an unending gray mass, inch by inch I'm beginning to see life in bright colors. I have nothing to do with my father at all. I feel that God has put people in my life who will help me recover. It may well take years, but I'm on my way. There is a light at the end of the tunnel. Reach for it long enough, I believe and I'll get there.

COMMENTARY

Something that Randy doesn't mention is that among his efforts to cope over the years were suicide attempts, all but one attempted before he came into my care. At the time of his last attempt I received phone calls from his two older sisters. They confirmed, basically, everything that he has written. Both sisters seemed quite concerned about his poor judgement, manipulative behavior and the payee he chose, since this woman seems also to have emotional problems. His payee (a person chosen to handle his finances, pay bills, etc.) was appointed by the court since Randy was a recovering alcoholic. She is a motherly woman, a type Randy seemed to have an uncanny ability to find, who is unacceptable to Randy's sisters simply because she prevented them from getting their hands on his money.

However, Randy chooses to have no contact with his family. He continued to remember more about his parent's abusiveness, as well as other incidents. His father: taking him along to meet his lovers, beating his mother and breaking her arm, having sex with his wife's sister, selling guns illegally, being part of a motorcycle gang that destroyed the face of a man who cheated him. Those memories that have surfaced a bit at a time have helped him to see that he had, as a child, every right to be outraged and hurt, and every right to be the same now. Recognizing that right serves to help identify that he is very angry, enraged, in fact. That awareness, combined with his understanding of his hurt and frightened inner child, is helping Randy to heal.

He is still trying to deal with his older sister's incest with him and his own incest with his younger sister. He wrote to his younger sister a letter apologizing for his behavior and asking for her forgiveness, but he hasn't had the courage to mail it yet. I reminded him that he was still a child at the time that the incident happened. Also, his action was consistent with the sexual abuse and promiscuity that were overtly and covertly promoted in their sick environment. Further, his action had been modeled for him years earlier by his older sister, when she "taught" him and received their father's approval. Those factors are offered, not as an excuse, but to promote understanding and healing.

In his letter Randy says that the mutual masturbation incident when he was seven or eight confirmed to him that he was a homosexual. I explained to him that homosexual experimentation is not abnormal for children and it doesn't create or indicate a lifelong sexual orientation. However, Randy told me that he had always known he was a homosexual as far back as he could remember, but he didn't know there was a word for it. That homosexual experience at age 12 simply confirmed it for him.

AFFECTIONAL PREFERENCE AND SEXUAL ABUSE

The majority of men I've seen in therapy who have been sexually abused as children do have fears that they have latent homosexuality. Some therapists call it "homosexual panic." None of these men, however, have turned out to be homosexuals or chose to have homosexual lifestyles. They didn't have strong leanings toward the lifestyle in spite of their fears. Those who do choose the lifestyle have the desire on a lifelong basis. It is an in-born, physiological trait. These boys, relatives report, in spite of cultural conditioning, chose to play with toys that are generally considered feminine.

On the other hand, women who were sexually abused as children, who later chose to pursue a lesbian lifestyle, often do so as a reaction to the abuse. It is definitely an emotional choice as opposed to a physiological definition and the orientation can change, but I can remember only one incidence of it in my practice. A woman who was sexually abused as a child had a lesbian relationship with another woman for close to 20 years, but she had always been attracted to men, mostly younger men. During therapy she worked through her abuse issues and then recognized that she felt exploited and revictimized in her lesbian relationship. Still, she was hesitant to leave a comfortable relationship, even if it was dysfunctional.

She went back to school, got her Master's degree and is working on her doctorate. During that process she left the woman, met and married a man 19 years her junior, with whom she has a happy, healthy relationship. Her husband was also from a dysfunctional family and was abused emotionally. He had been in therapy and was also in graduate school.

It's obvious that whatever choices a dysfunctional or abusive childhood prompts us to make, we are never stuck with them.

MANIPULATION AND MAGICAL THINKING

Children who are being and have been abused go to extraordinarily creative lengths to cope. They adapt themselves, their surroundings, their responses. Adapt, adapt, adapt. Their bottom line is survival.

In Randy's case, adapt evolved into manipulation. Near the end of his letter, after telling how bad he had been treated, Randy puts a rosy glow on the progress he has made. In effect he's saying, "See how bad they were to me and what a good boy I am."

I believe that he is still trying to look and act like a good boy because he's arrested at a child's level and is looking for a mother figure in his therapists. He says he prefers female therapists. That comment caused me to wonder if this was because he felt he could tug at the hearts of women with his story and get nurturing from them, something he never got from his own mother. He asks often for a hug. He looks like a waif: short, cute, skinny, soft-spoken, melancholy eyes that can go puppy-dog at the drop of an inclination.

His use of "God" in the letter is an example of magical thinking. He's afraid to offend the most powerful male authority symbol in our culture, just as he fears all males because they symbolize the cruel, punitive father. By invoking God he feels he will be on his side. Magical thinking is not a conscious process, but in Randy's case, it's holding him back.

CONCLUSIONS

A colleague updated me on Randy's progress recently. He has accepted responsibility for his sexual behavior on a nationally broadcast radio program and says he recognizes there is no instant cure for his problems. He has committed no known further sexual crimes, has a different payee, has moved to a different apartment, continues to attend AA, continues to remain sober and is in a relationship with a man.

He still has a long way to go. He has yet to work through his rage, which I don't believe he is willing yet to recognize. In my opinion, he hasn't yet taken full responsibility for his actions, which keeps him from feeling truly good about his ability to succeed in his weaving business. He needs to gain insight into his behavior so he doesn't need to seek constantly for the parental love and nurturing he can't find. Only then can he move on.

PART III

REVICTIMIZATION

CHAPTER THIRTEEN

PERPETRATORS

WHERE DO THEY COME FROM?

Perpetrators of sexual crimes come from absolutely every sector and every profession in our society. That's a dismaying claim until you think about the fact that in the vast majority of cases perpetrators are made, not born, barring physical causes like Temporal Lobe Epilepsy, or a frontal brain disorder called Kluver-Bucy Syndrome. Perpetrators are products of the society in which they are reared. As children they absorb cultural attitudes and practices on a day-to-day minute-by-minute basis: who holds the power, and for or against whom is it used. Information pours in and the children absorb it. If they are sexually, physically or emotionally abused, if they are manipulated or neglected, if they see women objectified and used as sex objects, if they see power used opportunistically, the information is absorbed and stored.

In adulthood, then, these same people go into a variety of occupations where they apply the lessons learned early and uncritically. Unless by some gracious twist of fate these now-grown abused children find or make an opportunity to heal those early lessons, they become doctors, lawyers, ministers and priests, therapists, law enforcement officers, educators, musicians, technicians and parents, all with a high likelihood of being perpetrators of sexual abuse. The abuse may be against children, or against adults who were abused as children and who are as a result more susceptible to revictimization. It is, in either case, violation of trust and performance of a criminal act.

IDENTIFYING CHARACTERISTICS

Now that we know where they come from, how do we identify them? In the *Clinical Symposia* of January 1991, Dr. Daniel B. Kessler and Philip Hyden indicate that there is no classic profile for a sexual molester.[22] My experience verifies this, but I do find that there are certain factors common to them. Kessler and Hyden cite an article by D. Finklehor who proposes that there are four preconditions that are necessary for sexual abuse of children to occur:

1. Motivation for sexual abuse, including emotional congruence or comfortability, sexual arousal by children, and inability to have satisfactory interpersonal relationships with adults.

2. Absence of internal inhibitors such as morality and religion. [Substance abuse is a common way to overcome inhibition. L.C.]

3. Absence of external inhibitors, usually protective parents or caretakers. [When the caretaker consents to the abuse or is unavailable to protect the child, the perpetrator is free to abuse. L.C.]

4. Diminished resistance in the child. Chronically abused children may surrender and manifest symptoms of the child sexual abuse accommodation syndrome, which is exhibited in the following manner: helplessness when confronted with abuse; secrecy, accomplished by coercion, possibly in the form of a game or threats of harm to family members; entrapment into a vicious cycle of abuse; delayed or unconvincing disclosure; and retraction.

DIMINISHED RESISTANCE

Adults who were abused as children have less capacity to resist being sexually abused and sexually harassed, as well as lowered resistance to *becoming* abusers. I've seen them and treated them in my practice both as revictimized people and as victimizers (perpetrators). As victimizers, perpetrators are carrying out a life script just as they received it. To change that script and the psychological perceptions embedded in it, a course of psychological therapy is required, supported as required by appropriate pharmacology.

When those who were victimized as children are revictimized, usually they exhibit a delayed reaction. When confronted with abusive behavior, they're like a deer frozen in the headlights of an onrushing car and they may be so conditioned that they don't even recognize that they're being abused. Those who have lived all their lives with abuse (sexual, psychological or emotional) without the opportunity to work through the effects of it, actually will see nothing the least abnormal. Until, that is, they seek treatment for some other symptom that rises out of both past and present abuse. That therapy then, enables them to neutralize the past and overcome the present.

It's important to recognize that sexual abuse usually exists along a continuum of experience in a lifetime, from being the abused to being the abuser. If, that is, the abuse isn't dealt with therapeutically. The abuse in childhood may be subtle, covert, in which case the abuse in adulthood will lean to opportunism and denial of wrongdoing. This is the kind most often found among healers who turn abusers.

SEXUAL HARASSMENT

The issues involved in sexual harassment are the same as those involved in child sexual abuse: 1) exercise of unequal power, 2) manipulation of another person and 3) personal gratification. Malfeasance of this sort in Western culture is usually practiced by men against women, although it is possible for a woman to harass a man. The reason it's primarily a man's tool is because Western culture is male dominant. That's the same reason that American women rose up roaring in anger after the Anita Hill-Clarence Thomas debacle before the U.S. Senate confirmation committee hearing in 1991.[23]

Women have been sexually harassed in every place that women and men interact, in the boardroom, in the office, in the factory, in the doctor's office, in the church office, in the classroom, in the neighborhood. As a result, women knew the feeling of being the target of sexual harassment and then being made the pariah when they speak out.

SOME STATISTICAL DATA

Sexual harassment has been recognized only in the past ten years in both professional and popular literature as a problem requiring policy changes for prevention and correction. A Federal Merit System Protection Board study of federal employees bears out that sexual harassment is manipulation of (perceived) unequal power.[24] Of the people contacted, the report revealed that 42% of the women reported sexual harassment, compared to 15% of the men. Of these women, 51% were trainees, and 67% were between the ages of 16-19. Of the men, 68% were older than their victims and 40% were supervisors.[25]

An article in the New York Times, January 14, 1990, supports those findings, reporting that a medical school survey revealed that 50% of the female medical students said they had been subjected to sexual advances by their professors.[26] The same article reveals that 27% of women and 16% of men in the U.S. have been sexually and physically abused. Approximately 25% of sexual offenders were abused as children and of those, only a small percentage are hard-core offenders. What happens to the rest of them? They show up in the statistics that are still being assembled for sexual harassment. Child sexual abuse will, it's obvious, find an outlet, a voice, if you will, in adult behavior.

It's frightening to follow the statistics one step further to a study done by Maltz.[27] She says that the figures used commonly, one in six females and one in ten males are abused as children, *are conservative figures*, and the figures are rising yearly as reporting increases. *Of those sexual abuse victims, only 2% receive competent professional therapy.*[28]

ANOTHER CULTURAL CAUSE

Sex and violence in the media is a volatile combination for troubled youth, according to an article by Patrick Cody.[29] Three forensic psychiatrists and a former FBI special agent hypothesize that the growth of the "sexy violence industry" seems to be tied with the increase in serial killings and sexual violence, Cody said. Other factors they cited that aggravate the situation are extreme personal freedom, a violent culture and institutionalized selfishness. They all agreed that power is the motivation behind serial killing.[30]

CHILDREN AND SEXUAL HARASSMENT

Sexual harassment happens to children in school and it can get vicious between adolescents. In the case of younger children, the offenders are probably imitating adult behavior they've seen. Older children, adolescents, have been exposed to the cultural gift of sexy violence mentioned above. After all, observation and imitation are how children learn much of their behavior, and largely what they see is exercise and abuse of unequal power. Our culture is built on an unequal power relationship, which is built on the premise that possessing power must mean subordination of something or someone. We have lost natural access to the concept that power is something to be shared equally as a partnership. When we finally return to the partnership model, we will see an end to the abuse that comes from the abuse of unequal power, wherever it remains.[31]

As long as children are dominated and abused, they will grow up to dominate and abuse. And they will leave a trail of victims generation after generation.

SISTER MARY FRANCIS————————

A case in point is an elderly nun who was a victim of abusive children in her childhood, which left lifelong scars. She was referred to me by her internist for treatment of panic attacks. Her attacks started shortly after her motherhouse closed and she had to live with four other nuns in the community where they work. She responded well to a short-term therapy of an anti-panic medicine, Alprazolam, and later was maintained on a small dose of Nortripryline.

As she got better we began to discuss follow-up sessions. One day she mentioned casually that she felt intimidated by the men at the agency where she worked. They made snide and sexual comments when it was obvious that they knew she was there. Then they turned and apologized with a smirk, "Oh, sorry, Sister." She had got to a point, she said, that she felt a wave of dizziness and nausea when she was just walking up to the agency on the way to work.

As a child, she said, adults made sexually explicit remarks in her presence long before she understood what they meant. The impression she got was that sex was disgusting and painful and that it was women's lot to suffer as puppets of men. She was sure that those experiences influenced her decision to enter a religious order.

She remembered male cousins and their friends having a masturbating contest in her presence when she was six or seven. None of them had touched her, she felt sure of that, but she felt that she had been part of the repulsive episode. As a result, she felt a load of guilt that she had never confessed because she could never make herself use the language.

As she spoke to me she began to tremble and perspire, tears welled in her eyes and her voice got more and more faint. Her chest felt tight, she said and she felt nauseated. I took her hand in mine and encouraged her to go on. She continued to cry softly and then, abruptly, she stopped. She sat up straight, looked me straight in the eye and said loudly voice, "No, god damnit! I'm furious. Homicidally furious!"

She snatched her hand out of mine to pound her small fist in the palm of her other hand. "Look," she said in a strong, firm tone. She used the tone that makes schoolchildren sit up straight, and I felt my own back straighten in remembrance of my own Catholic childhood. "You might think I've absolutely lost my mind, but I think that my problems may be connected to what happened to me in the past, and I'm going to put a stop to it."

"How?" I asked, enthralled.

"Well, you're the doctor. I'm paying you to tell me how."

I fought the impulse to duck my head and say, "Yes, Sister."

Sister Mary Francis and I worked together for about six months, mainly on memory recovery and how the covert sexual abuse she had experienced as a child was tied to her panic attacks. Living in the motherhouse where she was safe among her peers and away from men had allowed her to feel safe. When she lost that safety, the comments of the men at the agency brought back her repressed childhood memories. Once those memories and the feelings they evoked were worked through, they lost their power.

Back at the agency, Sister became assertive. She chastised the men severely for their rude and vulgar remarks and told them that, if they continued, she'd report them for sexual harassment. They didn't continue and I'm sure their backs are straighter for the ex-perience.

On one other occasion she had a panic attack when she saw a man in the grocery store who looked like her long-dead cousin.

Intellectually, she knew it wasn't him, but she felt a primal shock of recognition until reason regained control.

She was assigned to another area and I lost track of her for a long time. Then one day when I was doing a hospital consult, I felt that I was being watched. When I looked over at the other bed, there lay Sister Mary Francis. She grinned broadly as I took the hand she held out in greeting. She was fine now, she told me. She had worked through the rage from her sexual abuse and now was off all medication. She was retired and lived in great peace with two old friends, also retired. Her hospitalization would be brief, she said. It was only gall bladder surgery.

CHILDREN WHO SEXUALLY ABUSE OTHER CHILDREN

Another highly disturbing issue that has been around for a long time and that is a significant social problem with very little attention paid to it is children molesting children sexually. Some parents are stunned when they learn about their child's involvement in such activity, either through their child's disclosure, or by witnessing sexual acts between their child and another child, a neighbor, a friend's child, a classmate, etc. Invariably they blame the other child and the child's parents.

Some of these parents come to me hoping that I will tell them it is mere age-appropriate sexual exploration, or a harmless game of playing doctor, or playing house. These parents are often horrified, and usually angry when I suggest that the best procedure to follow is to inform Child Protective Services and get them involved. When they refuse to comply, preferring to seek help through a private child psychiatrist or psychologist, I warn them that I will still need to report the incident to the Services. If the child's home environment has caused the problem, as is the case with incest victims, then the child will be removed from the home. In this country, teaching homes are available and provide a less threatening alternative to parents.

Teaching homes are alternatives to foster care homes. The children live with families and go to school, while counselors work with their teachers, both teaching-home and birth parents, and the parents are asked to participate in parenting programs. The children can go home on weekends if their behavior has been appropriate.

Barbara McClellan, a reporter for the Detroit News, equates confronting such a crisis, for parents, to walking into a dark, new world, with no laws or guidelines to help.[32] McClellan outlines a typical child sex offender, according to juvenile court studies: middle class, overweight male between 12 and 15 is under-socialized, choosing to hang out with younger children, and has a poor relationship with his father. [33]

Dr. Toni Johnson, Clinical Director of the Sexual Abuse Center at the Children's Institute International, a private, non-profit mental health facility in Los Angeles, advises parents to differentiate between overt sexual acts and the normal limits of childhood curiosity.

> "A normal child's actions might include telling jokes, masturbating, pulling up a little girl's dress, sticking a finger in a child's orifice or touching a penis. It wouldn't be repetitive and there would be no aggressive quality. In other words, there would be mutual consent, each child knowing they can stop anytime. There would probably be a lot of giggling. In contrast, a child who molests other children is angry, ashamed, guilty and lacks self-esteem. He will bribe the other child by promising to be his friend or threaten him not to tell."[34]

Dr. Johnson recommends that parents who suspect their child to be either a victim or a perpetrator of sexual abuse should consider:

1. What is the nature of the sexual behavior? Is it self-stimulation or with another child?

2. How frequent is the behavior? How long has it been going on?
3. What is the age difference between the children involved? Is trickery, bribery or coercion used?
4. How does the child perpetrator feel about the subject of sex. Uncomfortable? Anxious? [35]

In her studies, Johnson says, she has found that many child perpetrators come from dysfunctional families where the child suffers from emotional or sexual abuse. For example, I have seen situations in which the child-perpetrator's mother is a victim of domestic violence, or has sexual words hurled at her in anger. Also, the mother may be a prostitute, or may have been sexually abused herself. Or the household might be the scene of drug parties where everyone copulates. When children see and hear these kinds of things, it may confuse them, but it sticks in their minds and influences their perceptions, behavior, values and expectations. One consequence of growing up in such an environment is sibling incest and sexual abuse of other children.

(It is also possible that a child-perpetrator can have learned this behavior from an older child-perpetrator to whom he or she has already been a victim. Children do pick up behaviors from other children and a child who is emotionally abused at home will have the low esteem to make him or her especially vulnerable to victimization by a child-perpetrator.)

David Finkelhor, M.D., one of the country's foremost authorities on this subject and Co-director of the Family Laboratory at New Hampshire's University of Durham, concurs with Dr. Johnson, that a parent should report a child sexual offender to Child Protective Services, if for no other reason than that workers can recommend to the parents that the child get treatment.

"Parents didn't used to want to make a big deal over such occurrences. They feared that stigmatizing a child would have a negative effect on him. But clinical research proves it doesn't work to simply sweep [the behavior] under the rug. We now know the origins of adult sexual abusers can be traced to engaging in such behavior as children. They had to be victimized by someone else." [36]

Judge Randall Heckman of Kent County, Michigan Juvenile Court, says that child victims typically act out their frustration on at least seven other children by the time they reach the age of fourteen. He adds:

"Children who have been sexually victimized feel hurt, rage, fear, and a lack of control. To relieve that stress, they turn the tables on someone else. The pattern repeats itself. The perpetrator was usually victimized at the same age and in the same manner." [37]

Nicholas Groth, author of *Men Who Rape*, (Plenum, 1979) observed in the same article that among 348 men convicted of sexual assault, 31% had themselves been victimized as children, and that 41% of the sexual assault perpetrators were women.[38] Of those, 14% of the assaulters were female peers. Interestingly, the article cites a 1987 study based on data gathered by 44 treatment providers, that among girl perpetrators under the age or eleven, a full 100% had been victimized sexually. Of the female offenders between the ages of 11-17, 93% have been victimized sexually.[39]

Judge Heckman points out that the issue at hand with adolescent sex offenders is power and control over the victim, which is no different, in my opinion, from the issue driving adult sex offenders. For that reason, the Judge says, those who deal with the offenders must have power over them. To accomplish that, Kent County (Michigan) decided on court-mandated programs over private therapy, to oblige the juvenile offenders and their families to admit what they'd done and help them to accept responsibility for their actions. They have seen significant growth in these children who are in Kent County's combined individual, family, and group therapy sessions, and sometimes institutionalization when the offense has been severe.

The courts review each case every six months, requesting input from families and teachers. They are convinced by their data that they are seeing no problems repeated, which is in marked contrast to before the program began. While those involved in the County program are greatly encouraged, they recognize that they haven't found a panacea for a very old problem.[40]

RECIDIVISM

One of the most frustrating problems with a large number of adult sex offenders is recidivism, relapsing into former behavior. Unfortunately, statistics on the number of repeat sex offenders vary, since a significant number have not been caught or reported. Some people actually rationalize for the perpetrators, especially those coming from dysfunctional families, fearing imprisonment for the offenders and the shame it will bring to the family.

THE STORY OF ERIK SCHMID

The Detroit Free Press ran a long and very disturbing piece about a repeat sex offender.[41] Frank Bruni, the feature writer, based his story on interviews with the offender, his wife and children, parents of the victim and experts in the field of pedophilia.

The subject of the story was Erik Schmid, who was born in Munich, Germany, in 1942, and grew up among the bombs and rubble of World War Two and its aftermath. He didn't remember his father, who died on the Russian Front. His memories of his mother are bitter. She married an American GI and moved to Michigan, leaving five year old Erik behind with his grandmother for another five years.

He had been happy in Germany and he didn't know the

American language, except for the taunts of "Nazi" and "Jew killer." His parents worked at the Ford Motor Company and were undemonstrative people. He remembered his parents' wrath when they learned of his first adolescent crush at age 11 for a boy 14. They camped out in a back yard tent on hot nights, and they would touch, he said. Even after marriage and two children, Erik's passion was for boys.

One of his convictions was for attempted criminal sexual conduct, for which he was sentenced to two to five years in prison in Jackson, Michigan. He was out after 15 months for good conduct. He saw nothing criminal about the behavior that put him in prison, but he was filled with rage against a society that would put him with "all those lowlifes." He saw a therapist and a social worker once a month, since he could afford only $5 per visit. His therapist was a nice man who talked about Erik putting his life back together, but not about pedophilia.

Less than six years later Erik was back in prison, sentenced to 8-15 years. He could be out in five. Still he sees no perversion in his behavior, no criminal intent, and he is even more convinced that he is right and society is wrong. He is being punished unfairly for loving, he believes, and like most non-aggressive child molesters, he will be unchanged except for an increased fear of being caught again.

PRISON AS CURE

Nicholas Groth, a Florida psychologist who has studied approximately 2000 child molesters, says that these offenders are simply recycled, nothing more.[42] I agree that we need to do more than lock them up. We may be separating them from society for a while, but we're also subjecting them to loss of everything, including their homes and families, and degrading abuse in prison at the hands of the other inmates. They need psychiatric treatment, active, immediate and long lasting. Without treatment, we're accomplishing nothing but periodic separation from potential victims. That's not enough.

LINDA Y. CALLAGHAN

I believe that the problem for non-aggressive men like Erik is a compulsion and like any other kind of compulsion it may have its roots in genetic predisposition, like alcoholism, heart disease, diabetes, and so on. It may even be, as research is demonstrating, that homosexuality is a physiological condition based in the formation of certain brain cells and not an immoral decision at all. Nonetheless, in our society, homosexual acts with children are against the law. That very simple fact, for starters, must be understood and retained. It does not demean the offender; it's a simple black-on-white fact. Beyond that, psychiatric and pharmacologic therapy must be designed as dictated by the needs of the patient.

For abusive and brutal offenders, punishment is logical, but therapy is crucial. The current approach of the criminal justice system is ineffective in dealing with the complex etiology of the problem. Professionally, I am convinced that the therapeutic approach must be multi-faceted and include:

- A structured program, like the Twelve Step Program that offers guidelines for daily living, along with the comfort, safety and reinforcement in its predictability and camaraderie.
- Pharmacotherapy with a new anti-obsessive drug, Clomipramine.
- Strict attendance of support groups.
- Intensive individual psychotherapy to uncover and heal abuses of the past, to improve self-esteem, and to support healthier adult relationships.

In addition, we need to help the rest of our society understand how it is that child sexual abusers can hurt vulnerable, helpless children. We have to understand that the abusers were once vulnerable, helpless and abused children themselves, whose abuser was also once a vulnerable, helpless, abused child, and on back it goes. Unless we do everything we can to cure the illness, we are guilty of perpetuating the illness.

We can begin to end the cycle of this biopsychosocial problem

here and now through a collective community of helping professionals, educated law enforcement agencies, and educated and aware
citizens.

SEXUAL ABUSE BY CLERGY

People predisposed to committing sexual crimes enter the ministry, too. They are produced by exactly the same dynamics that
produce other perpetrators. However, sexual abuse and sexual harassment by clergy embraces an additional dimension of violation.
It violates the victim's faith in God.

All cultures hold special regard for their holy men and women
because they are felt to be closer to, or more like God. Or, as Ann-
Janine Morey, puts it, they are "freighted with a divine imprima-
tur."[43] So, they are elevated in our esteem and their instruction is
regarded as wise. Their injunctions and entreaties in God's name
are heeded and they are invested with a higher level of trust than
most other professions.

Then, when they assault those who trust them, and they do,
children and adults alike, denial sets in. There is no frame of reference for this level of betrayal. The victim denies that the minister
or priest made suggestive comments or a clear proposition of sexual
union, or put his hands in private places, or forced sexual contact.
Innocence and trust are stolen, leaving pain and diminished self-
esteem. Denial and pretense isn't sufficient to remove the memory
of the incident, and victims feel stained, soiled and isolated. They
blame themselves for letting it happen. They stop trusting, and
they begin to hate God for letting it happen.

Finally, they leave the church and often they repudiate God.
They are bereft. Hurting. Angry. Empty. Alone. Afraid.

STEPHEN————————————————————————

Stephen, a Protestant minister, was sent to me by his superior. He was 38 years old, married, with two children, and was in charge of a parish in a tiny, poor town in a north central state. Both his father and grandfather had been ministers and he followed their footsteps. His whole upbringing had been focused around religion, as was his brother's. Not surprisingly, his brother also was studying for the ministry.

When he was a boy, his father was gone most of the time, ministering to his congregation, so Stephen took on the duties of the man of the house as early as he could. His mother was sweet, he said. She told him to marry a woman who would understand his position as a minister. While she didn't talk about sex to him, he overheard her talking to her sister. He gathered that sex was a chore and she wished that her husband would leave her alone.

One day in his early teens, while reading a *Playboy* magazine, he became aroused and masturbated, ejaculating all over the sheets. He hid the magazine under his bed and tried to clean his sheets. Later he walked into his room and found his mother standing staring at the sheets. When she reached down and began to tear them off the bed, she discovered the hidden magazine. He froze. His mother bundled together the sheets and magazine and turned to leave. Her expression was hurt, not angry. She stuffed the sheets into the hamper and took the magazine out to the burning barrel. They never talked about it. He never felt any contrition, but he did feel chagrined that she had discovered his secret.

Soon thereafter his teacher asked him to stay after school to help her, as she did sometimes. She was attractive and nice to him, and he didn't mind. Besides, he was big for his age and could reach things that were too high for her. He liked that. They talked while they worked and she had told him that her husband traveled in his work and sometimes was gone for two or three days at a time.

He liked the way she dressed and he enjoyed watching her.

That day she wore a sheer blouse. She seemed to tease him pur-
posefully as she bent and stretched to reach things on the shelves.
He began to sweat as erection made a tent of his pants. "What's
the matter?" she asked, smiling at his fluster.

He thought she would be angry as his mother had been, but
instead she walked over to him and put her hand over his erection.
Then she unzipped his pants. He looked around wildly, expecting
to be caught, but everyone was gone, even the janitor. She helped
him have his first sexual experience and the relationship went on
for over a year until she left town suddenly. He assumed that her
husband had been transferred. After that there was sex with girls
his age, but it was never as good.

One weekend when he was 16, his father was out of town at a
church council meeting and his brother was visiting relatives.
Stephen had been invited and wanted to go with his brother, but
his mother insisted that she needed his help because she was three
months pregnant. She was standing up on a chair or a ladder washing cupboards when she lost her balance and fell to the floor. He
heard the thud and her call to come and help her. When he got to
the kitchen, he saw that she was bleeding heavily. He helped her
into the bathroom so she could change. She took off her clothes
seemingly without regard for her former modesty, but she was too
weak, she declared, to get dressed without help. Her nakedness
aroused him, but more than anything he was surprised when she
spread her legs and asked him to put a sanitary napkin on her. He
felt many feelings: confused, shocked, embarrassed, stimulated,
angry. Perhaps, he said thoughtfully, overwhelmed would be a good
word.

Afterwards, she behaved as though nothing had happened.
While the incident was never mentioned, she began to disparage
every girl he dated. Like a dutiful son, he absorbed her words and
stopped dating that person. But there was no end to her criti-
cisms, so eventually he quite mentioning his dates to her. After
graduation he went to the seminary and then was ordained. Soon
he met Marian. She was a calm, compliant, petite, average look-

ing, large-breasted schoolteacher with a brilliant smile who, not incidentally, reminded him of his seventh grade teacher. When he introduced her to his mother, she approved and they made plans for their marriage.

Soon after he was assigned to his first parish, he was called to minister to a 30-year-old parishioner who was dying of liver cancer. Stephen didn't approve of the way the dying man shouted at his wife and berated her without apparent provocation. She didn't respond, but simply provided what he demanded. When she raised her head, Stephen recognized her as a regular at services who never stayed for social hour. Other parishioners gossiped to him about her husband's alcoholism and how he beat her.

The man died very soon and Stephen called on the widow to comfort her because there was no family to help her. His wife sent small goodies with murmurs of "poor Marge." In the beginning he would pat her arm and put his arm around her shoulders when she cried. He wanted to kiss her. Where did she work? he asked her. She was a nurses' aide and a part-time maid at a motel, she said. What did she do for fun? he inquired. She liked to play the organ, she said. Where was her family? She told him how her family died in a fire shortly before she met her husband. Stephen called on her more often than necessary and he stopped telling his wife about the visits. Soon they were having sex together. Sex with her was more exciting than with his wife. His wife liked only the missionary position and Marge liked to try any position anywhere, in the church, the house, even outdoors.

When the elderly church organist died, Marge accepted Stephen's offer to be church organist. One day when Stephen was driving her home from the church, they became aroused and pulled off the road and walked into a place in the woods. That's where the police found them after investigating the empty car with its lights on. The police, Stephen told me, were more embarrassed than he was, and Marge was in tears. After the police left, he took Marge home and became very annoyed when she wouldn't resume sexual activity with him because she was too upset. Everything will be all right, he assured her.

Stephen didn't tell me how the community learned about the incident. Presumably it was from the police report. When the facts hit the fan, however, he quite simply stood back and did nothing. His wife went over to Marge's house, called her a whore and husband snatcher and slapped her. He took no responsibility. People in the congregation either shunned her or called her nasty names. They forgave Stephen. Marge's behavior was unforgivable and male parishioners made advances to her. Stephen's behavior was judged to be "normal for a healthy man." She stopped attending the church. He acted as if it had been all her fault, but also as if she had never existed.

FRUSTRATING THERAPY

When Stephen came for his first appointment with me, I began to gather information. "What do you expect to get out of treatment," I asked. It was a standard question.

He didn't need counseling, he told me smoothly. He was here only to satisfy his superior's recommendation, and to demonstrate to his wife and parishioners that he was contrite and willing to investigate any possible underlying problems.

After he told me about the childhood events related above, we discussed them together. I remarked that his teacher's actions constituted statutory rape.

Oh, no! She was just showing him the ropes. He was lucky. He wasn't abused, he insisted vehemently.

In subsequent sessions we discussed his relationship with his mother. "Looking back on the incident now," I said, "how do you feel about your mother allowing you, a pubescent boy, to see her naked, and how do you feel about your sexual arousal?"

Rather than face the specific question and the issues at hand, he intellectualized, launching into a long discourse of Freud's Oedipus complex. After only four visits he began to make excuses for canceling appointments. When I telephoned to find out what he wanted done with his other appointments, he said he felt no need for further counseling. He could work through his own problems, he insisted. Since even the best therapist can't force an unwilling client to have successful therapy, I had to let it go.

Several years later I met his superior at a business function. He took me aside and told me that Stephen had committed another malfeasance, this time with a teenager who pressed charges. His removal from the ministry was proposed and accepted. That should have been done years back, they agreed, when he had refused to continue his therapy. Stephen had said that he would have to live with the guilt of his second victim for the rest of his life.

While I pondered his continuing lack of remorse for his first malfeasance, I learned that Stephen was back in school to earn a degree in counseling.

CONCLUSIONS

Although Stephen was abused sexually as a child, overtly by his school teacher and covertly by his mother, he spurned any insight into his resulting problems. His defense mechanisms, rationalization and denial are so rigid that to break the barrier would require a major stressor. Unfortunately, such well-defended individuals have a poor prognosis in therapy.

WHOSE PROBLEM IS IT?

The Christian church, which until recently has been a bastion of male supremacy and *ex*clusivity, has a long history of protecting its own. It's not surprising, then, when another newspaper in another city reports another priest or minister accused of molesting altar boys, or parish children, or parish women. It's also not surprising, it's hardly even "news" anymore, that the priest is moved to another parish.[44] Or perhaps he is sent back to the same remote treatment facility for the third time, and *then* sent to another parish. Meanwhile, the bodies of his victims are stacked like cordwood in his past.

It has happened in every denomination of Christendom until the voices of anguished and angry laity grew too loud to be ignored. "There are," they cried, "pedophiles, rapists, molesters and abusers in your ranks, and either you face the problem and clean them out, or we'll sue your pockets empty and leave your membership in droves." Then the church began to listen.

Disclosures of formerly hidden data were issued and apologies were offered, commissions were formed.[45] Studies were made, experts consulted, guidelines issued. Between 1951 and 1991, one report revealed, 57 out of 2,252 priests of the Chicago Archdiocese were accused of sexual misconduct.[46]

Recently, former victims, now grown and still wounded from sexual abuse perpetrated against them in childhood, have raised their voices publicly, naming the guilty priests and ministers. At first they were ignored, denied, and the offending priest or minister was moved out of the parish.[47] Women who were sexually harassed found no support when they turned to their fellow parishioners for succor, but rather, the parish took sides against them. They were blamed for the priest's malfeasance against them and they have even been warned to leave the parish.[48] Thus they are victimized repeatedly.

Then late in the summer of 1992 a conference of people who had been abused by clergy was convened in the Midwest. Participants spoke out publicly, naming their pain and their perpetrators, demanding no more silence, no more denial. By the end of that summer, one ex-priest had been accused of sexual abuse by over 30 of his former charges in Massachusetts, Minnesota and New Mexico.[49]

Are these perpetrators any worse than any others? In one sense, yes, especially in the Christian tradition, because to steal one's faith in God is to steal, in effect, faith in everything that is solid, dependable and lasting.

ASSESSMENT OF OFFENDING PASTORS

Those who abuse or exploit their charges, pastors, therapists or other professionals who interact with troubled clients, can be assessed on a scale from one through six, according to Schoener and Gonsiorek.[50] The higher the number to the left, the poorer the risk the individual is for an occupation that puts clients at risk of malfeasance.

1. **Uninformed and naive.**
    - Trainees or professionals who have received substandard training.
    - Genuine lack of knowledge of standards in counseling and lack of understanding of professional boundaries.
    - Difficulty distinguishing personal from professional relationships.

    Conclusion: Some do not have ethical instincts or judgment necessary for professional counseling.

2. **Healthy or mildly neurotic.**
    - Sexual contact is quite limited or represents an isolated circumstance.
    - Aware of unethical behavior and remorseful.
    - Terminate inappropriate behavior on their own and often self-report, requesting help.
    - Situational stress often in evidence.

    Conclusion: Many, but not all, have a good prognosis for rehabilitation.

3. **Severely neurotic.**
    - Longstanding and significant emotional problems, especially depression, feelings of inadequacy, low self-esteem, and social isolation.
    - Work tends to be center of life; most of personal needs met in work setting.

    Conclusion: Rehabilitation is theoretically feasible but prognosis is guarded.

4. **Character disorders with impulse control problems.**
- Longstanding problems with impulse control; have often encountered legal difficulties.
- Rarely have true appreciation of the impact that their behavior has had on others; tend to deny or minimize harm they have caused.

Conclusion: In general, not candidates for rehabilitation.

5. **Sociopathic or narcissistic character disorders.**
- Some of the features of previous group, but tend to be far more deliberate and cunning in exploitation of clients.
- Typically cool, calculated, and detached; adept at manipulating others.

Conclusion: Not candidates for change.

6. **Psychotic or borderline personality disorders.**
- Poor social judgment and impaired reality testing.
- Variability in understanding of the impact of behavior on others and in level of remorsefulness.

Conclusion: Rehabilitation unlikely.

STAGES OF THE VICTIM IN SEXUAL ABUSE

Those who are sexually abused, exploited or harassed by members of the clergy go through the same emotional and experiential dynamics as any other victim of sexual abuse.

This is true whether the victim is a child or an adult who is being accosted for the first time, or someone who is being revictimized. The first injury, Courtois says, is the abuse itself. The second injury occurs when no assistance is forthcoming from parents, trusted adults, friends, the church congregation, hierarchy, counselors or agencies to which the victim turns for help and from whom she or he should rightfully expect to receive help.[51]

The second injury is experienced as four levels of betrayal:

1. The abuse itself and betrayal by the perpetrator.
2. Non-response by family or friends who know.
3. Non-response by professionals such as teachers, counselors, social workers, nurses and doctors.
4. Betrayal of the self, when the victim denies his or her own reality and experience in order to cope. The victim may blame him or herself for having caused the situation, since no other explanation is available. This can lead to the development of a shame-based identity.[52]

STAGES AND DYNAMICS OF ABUSE

Although Courtois is writing about child sexual abuse, as I am herein, it takes little imagination to apply her words to clergy sexual abuse of adults, as in Stephen's case, and the subsequent abandonment and blaming of the victim.

- *Engagement Phase:* Includes access and opportunity, relationship of participants and inducements.
- *Sexual Interaction Phase:* Escalation of inducements and progressively more intrusive sexual activities.
- *Secrecy Phase:* Concealment to eliminate accountability and allow for repetition and continuation of the activity. Sexual abuse has been described as an addiction or compulsion that provides reinforcing pleasure for the abuser. Here the authority and power of the abuser are motivators.
- *Disclosure Phase:* Usually accidental. The secret slips out, is discovered or reported in anger, or pregnancy occurs, precocious sexual activity is precipitated. Disclosure spurs divided loyalties and perpetrators usually react with denial, defensiveness and hostility toward the disclosing person.

- *Suppression Phase:* The victim's family and church members may attempt to suppress the report and to minimize the severity of abuse or victim's response to it. Under pressure, victim may recant allegations or refuse to cooperate with anyone attempting to intervene.

Finally, the Sexual Abuse Accommodation Syndrome activates: If victims are misunderstood, blamed, or if their report of abuse is rejected and their experience invalidated, they will adapt and accommodate in order to survive. Their experience will again become a secret, they will feel helpless, trapped, compromised. They may offer delayed, conflicting and unconvincing disclosures and then retract them if they are unsupported or challenged.[53] Suicidal thinking is not uncommon at this point since, as I said above, something basic and precious has been taken from the victims.

THE STAR IN THE PULPIT

Identified as a spiritual and moral leader of a congregation and often of the community, a minister is perceived as an interpreter for God. This person who regularly functions in a kind of spotlight, takes on a star role, according to G. Lloyd Rediger.[54] The role, allocated by virtue of the profession, is denied at first and then accepted with all the dynamics that accompany it.

> "The dynamics of the star factor . . . [that] contribute significantly to clergy sexual malfeasance by blinding [both] the performer and the admiring observer . . . are common knowledge. What does not seem to be common is the recognition that heightened sexual stimulation and the relaxing of controls, combined with the clergy's opportunities for privacy and intimate contact, inevitably will produce the significant increase in sexual malpractice and scandalous affairs that we now see in clergy circles."[55]

Responsibility for those dynamics is shared threefold, by the clergy, the congregation and the denomination, Rediger says.[56] He proposes that fully 10% of clergy, mostly males, have been engaged in what he calls "sexual malfeasance—the violation of expectation and the breaking of public trust."[57] Another 15% are only waiting for the opportunity.[58]

The dynamic that creates Rediger's "star factor" may be the same dynamic that causes what the American Psychiatric Association calls "undue familiarity." That is, incest at an unconscious level, which is symbolized by the transference of a parent-child relationship.

Glen O. Gabbard, M.D., Director of the Menninger Memorial Hospital in Topeka, Kansas, said of female therapist perpetrators:

> "A recurrent theme in female professionals who have become involved in unethical sexual conduct is a powerful fantasy that love is curative. The therapist will begin by trying to rescue the patient, eventually becoming involved in a love affair. A specific pattern observed in cases where the patient is male is that of the 'charming rogue,' whom the female clinician is attracted to with the unconscious fantasy of somehow influencing him to 'give up his wayward tendencies' and settle down. In my experience the male patients who are attractive to female therapists are typically boyish, immature and helpless, somehow evoking maternal instincts in these female therapists."[59]

A preponderance of the statistical data that I have tracked shows that between six and ten percent of male therapists and 3-8% of female therapists acknowledge being sexually involved with patients during treatment. The transference phenomenon is construed as unique in both the clergy-client-parishioner and therapist-patient relationship due to the self-disclosure involved which causes an asymmetric or unequal relationship.

The dynamic of a Star person holds valid for any professional who perpetrates sexual abuse on a client who trusts him or her. Any person, priest, doctor or therapist, may find him or herself corrupted by power and exercise it by inappropriate sexual behavior.

The church is in a fledgling stage of managing sexual abuse by clergy compared to the psychiatric and psychologic professions. The primary difference between the two is that, while the latter profession is now spending horrendous amounts of money protecting themselves from million-dollar lawsuits, the church is still repudiating the victim and slapping the offender on the wrist before sending him to another parish.

Neither system is better; the cost is staggering in both. Neither answer is correct. It is the system that creates the abusers that must be healed, and that can't be done until the problem is admitted and faced squarely.

IT'S INCEST

People in our culture are inclined to treat priests and ministers with a respect that borders on reverence, as well as trust as deep as they gave their parents. Because of that reverence and trust, any sexual abuse by clergy, whether it's sexual harassment or sexual manipulation or rape, becomes incest. It is betrayal of the greatest magnitude when a shepherd dons a predator's persona and attacks his sheep.

In my opinion, two things, at minimum, have to change. First, clergy has to be screened closer and more often and trusted less blindly. Two, parishioners need to discern their clergy as people who are in a particular occupation with a specialized education, nothing more. They are teachers, not gods, and no closer to God than doctors, psychiatrists, lawyers, journalists, plumbers, farmers, truck drivers, mechanics or politicians.

RECOVERY

Time and a loving therapist can bring healing to one on whom such trespass has been committed. "In time one learns just how hardy and independent one's eternal soul is. One learns that love and comfort do not reside in an institution. One learns that God is still very present, and without the intervention of the church, a relationship with God is very much cleaner and healthier. One learns that the church needs God; God doesn't need the church."[60]

A MODEL

One day my daughter was writing poetry. When she finished, she crumpled what she had written, threw it in the wastebasket and left the room. I looked at the basket, started to get up, and then sat down again. I had no right to look.

I stared at the basket, stood, then went over and picked up the crumpled paper and sat down again. I smoothed it on my knee and read what seems to me a good model of a healthy, safe, power-sharing relationship.

Daughter

wholesome, innocent

caring, considerate, protective, independent

hard-working, comforting, loving

truthful, trusting

Mother

CHAPTER FOURTEEN

REVICTIMIZATION

In the earlier edition of this book I touched on the subject of how susceptible survivors of sexual abuse are to being victimized repeatedly in a number of ways. Historically and contemporarily child sexual molestation is prevalent. Consequently, so is the revictimization that turns the wheel of history. It is, in fact, so common that we have become desensitized, accustomed to, even accepting of evidence of its aftereffects, attributing the psychological evidence in the victim's behavior to some lack of character or strength, or even to a criminal bent. It may seem like oversimplification to attribute so many ills to one cause, wholly or in part, but it is a sad fact that a great many of our interpersonal and social problems find their origin in child sexual abuse somewhere in history.

It's tempting to suggest that another flood of biblical proportions might wipe the slate clean of human cruelty. Unfortunately, human perversity has demonstrated great persistence. We're doing exactly the right thing by addressing that persistence case by case and by sharing the good news that the damage is reversible. I believe that the core, the essence of a human personality is goodness and that the goodness has greater power and strength than learned evil. Our task is to shuck off assimilated behaviors as we peel an ear of corn to access the nourishment of the kernels. Then we will throw those behaviors on the compost pile of education and cherish the sweetness and health that lies hidden beneath.

A POET'S VIEW

Parts of Emily Dickinson's various short works play out with exquisite delicacy and discernment the characteristics of survivors of child sexual abuse: their ambivalence about remembering, their adaptation to their pain, and their giving up on therapy before they reach a safe shore, the "Blue Peninsula." They feel that it's easier to stay in the painful known, than to venture into the unknown because it could be worse.

The Blue Peninsula

If recollecting were forgetting—
Then I remember not.   *(Ambivalence about remembering)*
And if forgetting, recollecting—
How near I had forgot.

And if to miss were merry—
And to mourn were gay—
How blithe the fingers that gathered this, Today!
Pain— has an element of blank—
It cannot recollect
When it began—or if there were
A time when it was not—
It has no future—but itself—
Its Infinite contain
Its Past—enlightened to perceive
New Periods—of Pain.

There is no Languor of the Life
More imminent than pain
'Tis Pain's Successor—When the Soul
Has suffered all it can.

How many Flowers fail in Wood—   *(Given up)*

Or perish from the Hill—
Without the privilege to know—

That they are Beautiful—   *(Adapted to the pain)*
How many cast a nameless Pod
Upon the nearest Breeze—
Unconscious of the Scarlet Freight—
It bear to Other Eyes—
It might be lonelier
Without the Loneliness—
I'm so accustomed to my Fate—
Perhaps the Other—Peace
Would interrupt the Dark—

I am not used to Hope—
It might intrude upon—   *(Avoid the frightening unknown)*
Its sweet parade—
Blaspheme the place—
Ordained to Suffering—
It might be easier
To fail—
With land in Sight—
Than gain—
My Blue Peninsula—
To perish of Delight—

SUSCEPTIBLE TO ABUSE

Abuse in childhood makes survivors predisposed to abuse, overt or
covert, in adulthood, as I showed in the previous chapter. The
earlier abuse leaves them with low self-esteem, which makes them
question the validity of their perceptions when their instincts tell
them something just doesn't feel right. Consequently, they bury
their feelings and decline to confront their abusers. It isn't surprising then that the people with whom they have significant rela-

tionships are usually just as abusive as their childhood abusers.
But they can't recognize it because of the low self-esteem and denial that makes them vulnerable to such a relationship to begin
with.

Ironically, when they do seek therapy, it's for reasons other
than the childhood abuse, but during the therapy the abuse memories begin to rise. At this point, when it seems that finally the fates
should be kind, we see that the very abuse that sent them into
therapy causes them to choose an abusive therapist. These therapists may exploit them sexually and/or tell them to forget the past
and get on with their lives. In either case, the repressed or dissociated abuse from childhood is on or close to the surface of accessible
memory and powerful enough to trigger old emotions from the
original abuse, which means that at that point the abused is carrying a double emotional load.

A CASE OF THERAPIST INCOMPETENCE

Recently a story in the *Detroit Free Press,* by staff writer Jack Kresnak,
told of a social worker who was charged with failing to report sexual
abuse of a girl whose family she was counseling. It is a clear case of
revictimization. Authorities said that the therapist told the child
to forgive her stepfather's abuse because he was "possessed by demons." Nancy Diehl, head of the child abuse unit in the Wayne
County Prosecutor's office, said that it was the first time that she
knew of that anyone had been charged under state laws that require teachers, social workers or other professionals to report child
abuse when they find it. The social worker was charged with a
misdemeanor, punishable by up to 90 days in jail.

Initially, the mother told a clergyman about her husband's
behavior. He referred the family to a psychiatrist, but the husband
refused to go, saying that the treatment was too expensive and he
was afraid to bill it through the company health insurance because
someone at work might find out. The family chose instead to work
with the social worker who charged $45 per session and promised

not to report the abuse even though she knew she was required to do so, and told the family so.

She told the daughter, who was by then 13, to forgive her stepfather. "It's not up to us to judge, just God," she was reported to have said to the girl. In addition, she urged the girl not to tell her mother, but to pray about the abuse. At one point she told the family that the stepfather was "possessed by demons," and performed a ceremony in which she put oil on the man and "spoke in tongues."

Later the girl confided to her aunt that her stepfather had resumed abusing her nine months later. The aunt told the girl's mother. Six months later the stepfather was charged with two counts of sexually abusing the child. At the time of the report he was a patient in a state hospital, judged mentally incompetent to stand trial.

REVICTIMIZING A DID PATIENT

It's not difficult to revictimize a DID patient, nor is it unusual, because they're so vulnerable. It is reprehensible, however, that revictimization often comes from the very places where patients should find safety. They seek comfort and community in a church and are told they are possessed by demons. They trust their pastors, are lured into a sexual relationship and then discredited and repudiated by the entire congregation. They are betrayed by their therapists, sexually victimized in mental hospitals, abandoned emotionally by their spouses, branded by their co-workers, and all while they are working hard to undo damage done by still others.

A LESSON FOR THERAPISTS

One day a patient came in for her appointment waving a poem that she had found that expressed how she felt about finally seeking help and then being revictimized by the helper. I'm sorry I can't credit the author, but the piece didn't carry a credit line. Nonetheless, its power is worth sharing.

I asked you to believe me
you said you did.
Then you connected me to a lie detector,
took me to court
where lawyers put me on trial
like I was a liar.
I can't help it if I can't remember the times or dates
Your questions got me confused.
My confusion got you suspicious.

I asked you for help
and you gave me a doctor
with a cold metal gadget
and cold hands.
Spread my legs and stared
just like my father.
You said it wouldn't hurt
just like my father.
You told me not to cry
You said I looked fine
Bad news for my case.

I asked you for confidentiality
and you let the newspaper get my story.
What does it matter that they left out my name,
they put in my father's
and our home address.
Even my best friend's mother
won't let her talk to me anymore.

I asked you for protection
and you gave me a social worker
who patted my head
and called me honey
because she couldn't remember my name.

She sent me to live with strangers in another place
and a different school.
I lost my part in a school play
and the science fair,
while he and all the others got to stay home.

Do you know what it's like
to live where there's a lock on a refrigerator?
where you have to ask permission to use the shampoo
or you can't use the phone to call your own friends?
You get used to hearing, "Hi, I'm your new social worker
this is your foster sister,
dorm mother,
group home."
You tiptoe around like a perpetual guest.
You don't even get to see your puppy grow up.

Do you know what it's like to know
more social workers than friends?
Do you know what it feels like
to be the one that everybody blames
for all the trouble
even when they were speaking to me,
all they talked about was lawyers, shrinks, fees,
whether or not they lose the mortgage.

Do you know what it's like
when your sisters hate you
and your brother calls you a liar?
My word against my own father's.
I'm 12 years old
he's the manager of a bank.
You say you believe me,
who cares
nobody else does.

I asked you for help
and you forced my mom to choose between us,
she chose him, of course.
She was scared
and had a lot to lose.
I've had a lot to lose, too.
The difference was you never told me how much.

I asked you to put an end to the abuse
you put an end to my whole family.
You took away my nights of hell
and gave me days of hell, instead.
You exchanged my private nightmare
for a very public one.

That twelve-year-old poet offers to all therapists a blueprint of what not to do when we try to help. Even though the help we offer serves the purpose we intend, we need to be sensitive to the fact that these children have more wisdom than we assume and may be able to give valuable input. But, at the same time, they are children and they may be confused and may not have kept a detailed diary to satisfy our legal need for details. And, for heaven's sake, when we take children out of the home for their safety, we can't treat them like puppies we're putting in a kennel. They are scarred and we mustn't scar them further.

Instead,

- *Do* advise the child that her father's transgressions have consequences for him, and that she is not to blame.
- *Do* tell her that she has a right to express her opinion about how the problem is handled and *do* solicit her ideas. If she says she doesn't know, tell her that's fine, that you know she's not an authority, but that you'll keep asking her in case she has some ideas.

- *Do* tell her that she has options, and then keep her informed about those options.
- *Do* tell her that you want to be discreet about her case, tell her what can go wrong. Tell her you don't want her to be revictimized in any way, and if she feels like that is happening, to tell you right away and you'll work together to remedy it. Remember, she has felt keenly her loss of control over her body and life as a result of the abuse, so allowing her control in her case will be therapeutic.
- *Do,* if possible, allow the child to choose a safe relative to stay with temporarily, if one is available, rather than putting her into a foster home.
- *Do* make every effort to keep her in a "normal" environment, the same school, same friends.
- *Do* conduct therapy always maintaining her self-respect and confidentiality.

UNDUE FAMILIARITY

One of the most sensationalized and hotly debated forms of revictimization is sexual intimacy between therapist and patient. The American Psychiatric Association labels this sexual intimacy "undue familiarity." I don't know of any classification of individuals who are more prone to have sex with their therapists than those who were sexually abused as children. It doesn't matter what the gender of the patient or therapist is, or who initiated the deed.

To date I've seen something like 25 patients who presented the same pattern: they were sexually abused as children, then they endured date rape and/or marital rape, and then were involved sexually with their therapists, which led to termination of their therapeutic alliance. Thrice victimized. When I first saw this correlation, I didn't know it would develop into a significant finding, so I didn't keep specific records. I haven't been able to uncover any study done on this phenomenon, but it is certainly a subject that begs a study because it happens far too often judging from what I have seen.

Among these patients, only one pressed charges against the therapist. Later, she withdrew the charges because she felt she must have consented to their sexual activities in some way, and therefore her claim couldn't be valid. Besides, she felt some strong emotional ties to him and didn't want to destroy his family and practice, she said. The rest of these patients didn't feel strong enough to face their therapist-betrayers in court and deal with the ensuing scandal.

Judd Marmor, M.D., former president of the American Psychiatric Association, commented that "such behavior between a patient and a therapist has all the elements of incest at an unconscious level and represents [on the part of the therapist] an equivalent dereliction of moral responsibilities."[61] Several other well-known therapists, psychiatrists and psychologists alike, have echoed Dr. Marmor's opinion, saying that it doesn't matter who initiated the seduction, the therapist is legally and morally obligated to know better.

Any debate that exists on this issue has been about what punishment is appropriate: a disciplinary proceeding by the ethics committee of the offender's professional association, a malpractice action, or a criminal prosecution. An argument favoring criminal prosecution says that because the sexual act in this case is the same as incest or rape and the patient's willing consent is due to the phenomenon called "transference," it means that the therapist has misused his or her power over the patient, and is therefore guilty of a misdemeanor.

Not all of my patients who have had sex with their previous therapists see it as a bad or negative experience and some have even said that they would have continued therapy with that therapist if the therapist hadn't terminated them. However, the majority, about two thirds, report a significant increase in their original psychiatric symptoms, such as increased rage, distrust, suicidal and homicidal thoughts, guilt and shame and more difficulty with intimacy in their personal relationships.

Several lawsuits have risen out of such betrayed therapeutic alliances. There was even a film about such a relationship, based on a real life alliance, called "Betrayal."[62] Unfortunately, the film exploited the melodrama instead of exploring the real issue, that sex between patient and therapist is an act of betrayal because it exacerbates the patient's illness and impedes healing.

Although historically therapists have been cited most often in this kind of perfidy, sexualization of therapy, increasingly voices are being raised against others in a veritable Greek chorus of protest. Being named are clergy, substance abuse counselors, lawyers, social workers, even physicians from non-psychiatric specialties.

One of my patients seems to have been raped or molested by just about everyone she has asked for help, and she isn't comfortable with me yet. I have allowed her to vent her collective anger at all those who abused her, but, at the same time, I've directed her attention to some of her behavior that can be seen as seductive or provocative.

For example, she asked me to examine her for what she believes are lumps in her breasts, or examine the mole in her pubic area that seems to be infected. She accused a former therapist, a woman, of molesting her. When she came to my office she would sit or lie on the floor in positions that exposed her breasts or genitals. I believe she was testing to see if I was safe. I told her gently to please sit on a chair and to sit so her private parts weren't exposed because it made me feel uncomfortable. At that, she got angry and silent or left her session early.

I believe that her behavior was learned: the sexual abuse destroyed her self-esteem and left her with the conviction that her only value was sexual and she had no other behavior ready to replace the old. That belief, I knew when I plotted the course of her therapy, would diminish as we worked together.

Even though I'm a physician and a woman, in cases like this I protect myself by requesting a consult from an internist or a surgeon, depending on the complaint. I warn those consultants about the existence of previous allegations of abuse by this patient so they can exercise caution themselves. For example, having a nurse present in the examination room and exercising proper decorum.

CONCLUSIONS

People who have been sexually abused as children are psychologically predisposed to be emotionally and sexually exploited. Those
of us who help them, all of us who help them, must absolutely-
without-failure be aware of their injury, their neediness, their need
to be respected and protected from exploitation and unthinking
missteps, and even from the system meant to help them. The purpose of therapy is to end the consequence of abuse once and for all,
and not to leave it in the psyche to surface in creative works, as
might have been the case with Emily Dickinson.

CHAPTER FIFTEEN

FALSE MEMORY SYNDROME: ANOTHER FORM OF REVICTIMIZATION?

"AMA Rules On Recovered Memories" the front page of the *Clinical Psychiatry News* announced.[63] The article said that the AMA had reaffirmed its policy about the use of recovered memories of childhood abuse, claiming it is "fraught with problems of potential misapplication." Therefore the AMA ruled that such memories are of "uncertain authenticity" and should be "subject to external verification."

Working with patients who are dealing with the aftereffects of child sexual abuse never has been anything but the most arduous kind of practice. Now the AMA's ruling, combined with the false memory backlash, promised to make it more formidable for patient and therapist alike. Although I understood the reasoning behind the AMA's ruling, as I stared at the headline, I grieved for the impact it would have on survivors.

ATTACKING MEMORIES, SURVIVORS AND PSYCHIATRY

In 1993 the concept of "false memory syndrome," a backlash against the increase of charges of child sexual abuse, was prominent in the news consistently, causing consternation among therapists and survivors of childhood sexual abuse. Assertions flourished that pop-psychology self-help books were creating the problem by convincing readers that sexual abuse during childhood was at the root of all their problems. In one case the news media reported an unprecedented $500,000 malpractice judgement against a California psychiatrist and a social worker. In another case a jury awarded damages to a man accused by his adult daughter of raping her when she was a child. His counter-suit charged that her therapist had planted the memories and that he was innocent of the charges.

In a professionally discouraging twist of circumstances, a therapist, Pamela Freyd, Ph.D., became the executive director of the False Memory Foundation. However, it's illuminating to read that "the foundation was established in 1992 by Pamela and Peter Freyd after their daughter Jennifer, now a professor of psychology at the University of Oregon, confronted them with accusations of abuse by her father, an allegation they have energetically disputed."[64] The foundation serves as an advocate for families who seek help to prove that accusations of sexual abuse against them are false. Often defendants claim that the memories were planted by the therapist and seek help to sue the therapist.

The timing of the "false memory" reaction isn't coincidence. Over a three-decade period the human rights movement had given increasing strength to the voices of survivors of different kinds of abuse. In particular, the women's movement had given strength to the voices of women who were survivors of child sexual abuse. They were being heard, and because they were being heard they were emboldened to speak their truth in increasing numbers. To the dismay of many, they were believed. Other voices rose. Yes! That happened to me too! Male survivors joined the chorus. Memories that formerly were vague and dismissed began to take on the resonance of fact and in a majority of cases were verified by family members. Survivors were standing up in increasing numbers saying, *J'accuse!* I accuse you! You raped me! You molested me! You hurt me! Patriarchy's mask of denial and silence was being ripped from its face and it had no defense ready. The cultural habit of abuse of power over children stood figuratively with its pants down.

To the degree that the entire cultural fabric was culpable, ever greater numbers of people hung their heads in shame. Their discomfort was extreme.

By the third decade, however, two things had happened. First, patriarchy in the form of conservatism was back on its well-heeled feet and eager to expunge its appearance of guilt with bluster and denial. Second, opportunists were using the recovered-memory phenomenon for financial gain. As a consequence, everyone who had worked long and hard to recover legitimate memories was suspected, patient and therapist alike, of being opportunistic liars with an axe to grind and sometimes they were charged outright.

In the rush to condemn, all claimants were viewed as opportunists and all therapists were assumed to be inept people who had arrived at their diagnoses carelessly or rashly. So it happened that survivors with legitimate claims and scrupulous therapists were sacrificed on the same altar of the denial movement. Psychiatry, a much-maligned and misunderstood medical specialty to begin with, was attacked with renewed fervor. In their book *Return Of The Furies: An Investigation into Recovered Memory Therapy*, authors Wakefield and Underwager mount what our culture deems the ultimate denial of legitimacy, that the recovery process is unscientific.

> Neither psychiatry nor social work are scientific disciplines. Psychiatry is an art or craft, not a science. The method of learning to be a psychiatrist is by serving an apprenticeship, called a residency . . . .There is no training in advanced statistics, research design and methods, philosophy of science, or related basic issues of human behavior . . . .The method of training is essentially the apprenticeship method of the craft unions . . . .Psychology is the only mental health profession that is also a scientific discipline.[65]

While psychiatry isn't the menacing, misbegotten offspring of the medical community that Wakefield and Underwager imply, their charge isn't entirely without merit. The psychiatric community, recognizing that it can make itself more effective, is responding with an unprecedented growth of scientific studies regarding the biological etiologies of psychiatric problems. These double blind and open studies document the chemical, genetic and sociological factors of various psychiatric illnesses. Thus we read about such studies as:

- "Childhood Abuse, Family Environment, and Outcome in Bulimia Nervosa"[66]
- "Clinical Research of Management of Extended Therapy for Depression"[67]
- "Effects of Sertraline on Mood and Immune Status in Patients With Major Depression and HIV Illness: An Open Trial"[68]
- "A Positron Emission Tomographic Study of Simple Phobic Symptom Provocation"[69]
- "Efficacy and Tolerability of Serotonin Transport Inhibitors in Obsessive-compulsive Disorder: A Meta-analysis"[70]

Impressive titles, and that's just a tip of a toe in a lake of recent clinical research from a responsive psychiatric community. A community, I might add, that is a distinct science and a legitimate part of general medicine.

MEMORY AND THE BRAIN

How can the veracity of a memory be determined by anyone, psychiatrist, psychologist or lay person? To answer that we must first review the human brain and understand the fundamentals of memory.

The central nervous system embraces higher and lower functions, as most readers know. *Higher functions* involve the more complex forms of coordination, such as the ability to reason and indulge in abstract thought. *Lower functions* include vegetative functions such as the sensations of hunger, touch, temperature control, respiration, functions of the digestive tract and control of the capacity to adjust movement. During the course of our development as human beings, our brain, which is our biggest organ at birth, grows forward to backward, cephalo-caudad.

Of importance in answering the question about validation of memories are the neuroglial cells which surround and support the nerve cells. The neuroglial, or simply glia, cells outnumber the nerve cells by ten to one. There are 10 billion nerve cells in the cerebrum and 100 billion glia, comprising about half the mass of the entire brain. In the past it was assumed that the glia cells serve only a supporting or subsidiary function. However, recent research gives evidence that glia are intimately concerned with memory function. Anatomists have demonstrated changes in the structure of these cells when conditions affect the cells significantly.

According to the Glial Theory, glial changes may increase facilitation of synapses. These are the spaces between cells where neurotransmitters, both inhibitory and excitatory, distribute information to the rest of the brain. This information creates emotional, intellectual and physical reactions that are important factors in the assimilation, enhancement and storage of memory. Any stimuli that provoke excitatory or inhibitory reactions, particularly when they are frequent or rapid, can cause synaptic fatigue, which in turn can cause depletion of stores of neurotransmitters which are stored in the synaptic knobs.

In addition, research chemists have demonstrated that the quantity and chemical composition of mucopolysaccharides, combinations of carbohydrates surrounding the synapses, change under different functional conditions. This finding has led to another theory of the formation of long term memory wherein the physical and chemical changes in the synaptic knobs facilitate transmission of impulses at the synapses. The facilitation of the synapses thus assists the thought circuit, which can be re-excited repeatedly by any signals from external sensory organs, thereby inducing stored memories. This circuit is called a memory engram, or memory trace.

COMPREHENSION AND MEMORY

Can we comprehend information, true or false, without believing it? Let's consider several psychological and physiological points that will inform the answer to that question.

A trio of researchers from the University of Texas, led by Daniel

T. Gilbert, Ph.D., says it's not possible because the process of comprehension automatically makes even false assertions believable. We are "instantly reprogrammed by the assertions [we] encounter . . . Scientists have long known that colors, memories and mental information is coded within patterns of tiny electrical impulses fired by groups of nerve cells."[71] In the same article William Calvin, a neurobiologist of the University of Washington, is cited as saying that the nerve clusters, roughly hexagonal in shape, form the basic unit of consciousness. Each contains a parcel of coded information and recruits neighboring hexagons through a process called *entrainment*. If successful, each hexagon multiplies into a vast mosaic through the cortex, and the larger the mosaic, the louder is the firing pattern. He speculates that our internal 'narrator' may simply be a string of the most dominant firing patterns.

Hexagons aren't permanent. Electric waves of neural inhibition flash periodically through the cortex, erasing hexagons. However, once a hexagon has been imprinted by a firing pattern, it will favor that pattern and even if erased it will respond to future stimuli in the same pattern until that pattern achieves dominance and becomes a conscious thought. Competition between hexagons may be how we compare different ideas or objects with the winning hexagon as the basis of our conclusions. When hexagons compete they try to recruit or entrain each other. This produces hybrid patterns, hybrid thoughts, which Calvin theorizes may explain how we "create novel thoughts, recognize novel or ambiguous patterns, and filter out the nonsense."[72]

In short, the entrainment process enables us to take the material we believe because we comprehend it, compare it, process it, evaluate it, and create a novel thought, a conclusion. So the answer is first yes and then no, if our mental processes are healthy. That's a big if.

PREFRONTAL LOBE FUNCTION
IN MEMORY AND ABUSE

The prefrontal areas of the frontal lobes, a part of the cortex, have always been considered the seat of human higher intellect even though attempts to prove it have been unsuccessful. In fact, destruction of the posterior temporal lobes and the angular gyrus region in the dominant hemisphere appears to affect the intellect more profoundly than destruction of the prefrontal areas. Previously, when prefrontal lobotomies were done on schizophrenic patients who were violent and unresponsive to medications and other methods of controlling their psychosis, they were still able to perform many intellectual tasks like simple arithmetic or simple problem solving. This demonstrated that the basic intellectual activities of the cerebral cortex were still present, even in the absence of the prefrontal areas.

These same patients, as well as laboratory animals that had been given prefrontal lobotomies, while retaining intellectual capacities, were uncommonly distractible, which affected their immediate memory. But when they were tested in non-distracting conditions, they showed an almost normal capability for immediate memory, but were incapable of long-term memory. Lobectomized patients had other problems. They were:

- Unable to code information, an essential requirement for memory storage, so they were unable to plan for the future;
- Unable to delay reaction to incoming sensory data so they could analyze their options;
- Incapable of recognizing consequences of their actions;
- Unable to solve complicated mathematical, legal or philosophical problems;
- Incapable of delayed gratification;
- Incapable of integrating signs and symptoms of grave medical importance for themselves;
- And unable to understand or control impulses in accordance with moral values.

Prefrontal lobotomies now are banned.

What does a prefrontal lobotomy or even injury to the prefrontal lobes have to do with child sexual abuse? My patients who have been seriously abused throughout childhood, though they have not been lobectomized, demonstrate many or most of the symptoms listed above. Can we say that child sexual abuse does such injury to the brain processes that it is like a lobotomy? Let's look at the evidence. Among my child sexual abuse patients, with or without ritual abuse, the population that suffered from Dissociative Identity Disorder, formerly called Multiple Personality Disorder, I found:

- Vindictive alters engaged in prostitution or promiscuous sexual behavior without payment. They saw but were unable without great prompting to project any future consequences for their sexual behavior.
- Many were involved in drug and alcohol abuse. The drugs were street or over-the-counter drugs, often in combination. Most weren't able to make significant connection between their physical ills and their chemical abuse.
- Impulsivity and self-abusive behavior triggered by seemingly trivial incidents demonstrated poor coping skills, further demonstrating that their learned defenses were pathological in nature.

Child abuse in many forms, including sexual, by any of an assortment of perpetrators and the effects on the survivors has been spotlighted increasingly in recent years. Awareness of the efficacy of treatment modalities, combinations of modalities, problems, special needs and complications has risen remarkably. One such particularly responsive institution has been the Menninger Foundation in Topeka, Kansas. One of their psychologists, Jon Allen, has noted that the issues of now-adult victims of child abuse are a particular mental health challenge, and specifically the issue of memory.

Allen has observed that some survivors have clear and continuous memories of their abuse, so false memory is not an issue for them. Others' memories are more cloudy, confusing, "'shades of gray' [occurring] along a spectrum, from totally true and accurate to utterly false, with many shades in between."[73] He has separated the gradations into seven groupings of those who:

1. Have continuous memory of their trauma and have corroboration by others, photographs or court records.

2. Have incomplete memories but have corroboration.

3. Have clear, continuous memories but feel no need for corroboration.

4. Have forgotten much of the traumatic experience, whose memory is hazy, who have no corroboration and feel "crazy" as a result.

5. Have highly distorted memories of their trauma.

6. Have not been sexually or otherwise traumatized but are expressing other illnesses through their claims (This could be, for example, a depressed or severely anxious woman who has heard that many persons with her symptoms have been abused as children, who then builds an image of abuse in her own childhood).

7. Have produced false memories in response to a therapist's inducement.[74]

In my practice I have seen mostly spotty memories with corroboration and fragmentary memories without corroboration (2 & 4). I have yet to see a classic example of therapist induced memories (7). Those individuals I've seen with the characteristics of 7 have come in with personality disorders that they were convinced were caused by external circumstances. Should a therapist validate their feelings, they feel relieved and may even elaborate on their alleged abuse with evident dramatic flair.

So, based on these seven shades of gray above, can we comprehend even false information without believing it? Dr. Gilbert showed that comprehension makes any assertion believable until another piece of information challenges that belief. To establish a memory, we saw, a thought is formed by comprehending sensory information, such as touching, smelling, feeling and/or hearing a car, a lawn mower, a horse, a baby or a dear friend. After the original experience with that object or person, further sensory contact serves to reinforce the original imprint in the hexagon.

A SMOKE SCREEN OF SYMPTOMS

That brings me back to the false memory syndrome controversy. An issue that the False Memory Syndrome Foundation doesn't address, when charging that recalled memories are therapist implanted, is why the patient sought psychiatric help in the first place? Memories of abuse that have been suppressed, denied or menaced out of conscious recall don't go away, but remain as part of the hexagons discussed above. The memories imprinted by the abuse hover beneath conscious thought like smoke from a fire hangs in the air, betraying the presence of the memory of the incident(s) in the form of symptoms. Symptoms that have been linked repeatedly with a history of childhood sexual abuse, as discussed in previous chapters, include alcoholism, substance abuse, anorexia nervosa, bulimarexia, phobic disorders, anxiety disorders, paraphilias, a spectrum of obsessive compulsive disorders, depressive disorders, and psychosomatic disorders that can run the gamut of irritable bowel disorder, bronchial asthma, gastric or duodenal ulcers, and so on.[75]

Another complicating factor is that abuse experienced as a child is perceived, not with an adult's understanding, but from a child's lack of understanding. Thus, when as adults the incidents are recalled, the events inevitably are distorted. After almost a decade of research on child sexual abuse, and even more years of psychiatric practice with these survivors, my impression of trying to sort out the essential information and symptoms from the non-essential is like trying to find one's way through unlit subterranean passageways that lead to tributaries and sub-tributaries, dead ends and false passages that lead back to the beginning. All delay one's arrival at truth. The False Memory Syndrome Foundation or movement is just one more false passage that only leads back to the beginning. It's another obstruction.

MORE MECHANICS OF MEMORY

Memory is a complex process whose neurobiology remains obscure, although science is revealing more each day.[76] It is the thread that binds us to our past, creates the experiences of the present and becomes the raw material for the future. *Declarative memory* can be described consciously and is recognizable consciously. *Nondeclarative memory* cannot be recalled consciously and is learned through classical conditioning.

Motor or procedural learning are habits acquired over time. *Procedural memory* is mediated by the basal ganglia. Learning is dependent on the integrity of the medial-hemispheric-hippocampal system, and access to learned information depends on the frontal-subcortical circuits. Amnesia, a disorder of impaired storage of new information, for example, is a disorder of declarative memory in which patients cannot recall or declare recent information, but have intact procedural memory, can learn new motor skills, and can respond to classical conditioning.

IMMEDIATE, RECENT
AND LONG-TERM MEMORY

Psychiatrists and psychologists test for three types of memory: immediate or sensory; recent, which is divided into short-term and primary; and long-term, which is divided into secondary memory and tertiary memory.

Sensory memory means the ability to retain sensory signals in the sensory areas of the brain for a short interval following the actual sensory experience, for example, seeing an unusually attractive individual walk by. The signal would be available for analysis for several hundred milliseconds, but in less than a second it would be replaced by new sensory signals. The instantaneous sensory information remains in the brain where further processing or scanning can be done to pick out significant details. This is the initial stage of the memory process.

Short-term memory or primary memory is the memory for a few facts, such as numbers, words or letters, as for example, a baby learning to say the names of persons or objects. It is retained for a few seconds, minutes or a little longer and is limited to about seven bits of data. When new bits of information are assimilated in the short-term storage, some of the older information is displaced. For example, if our baby sees a woman who looks like the woman she has learned to call "Mama," she may call the stranger "mama," but when her real mother comes into view, the other information is lost. The significant feature of the short-term memory is that the information is readily accessible so it doesn't take long to recall.

Long-term memory is stored in the brain and is recalled deliberately, or with intention. This type of memory has been referred to also as fixed memory, permanent memory and other terms. There are two subtypes. *Secondary*, also called recent memory, has a moderately strong memory trace, so it can take a few thoughtful minutes, hours, days or even years to recall a memory. For example, that common, embarrassing experience of meeting a colleague whose face is familiar, but whose name won't come to mind. Days later the name comes to mind through some external trigger. The second subtype, *tertiary memory*, is so well ingrained that it usually lasts a lifetime. This strong memory trace can bring up the desired information in a matter of seconds. For example, one's name, birth date, the alphabet, arithmetic formulas.

There are many theories by which memory can occur. Too many to discuss here. However, I want to emphasize that people who have been subjected to various kinds of abuse, sexual, verbal, physical, emotional, blatant and subtle, affects how their memories are consolidated. The use of drugs that change perceptions, physical injuries to the brain, inherited or acquired chemical imbalances, and various metabolic or nutritional or other systemic imbalances also play a role in the assimilation, interpretation and consolidation of memory. Thus, it's unprofessional, facile and self-serving to say, and just isn't possible to assume immediately that one's memories are absolutely true or false. As I've said above, a few do lie about recovering memories, but that simply can't be assumed *prima facie*, given the enormous incidence of child sexual abuse.

LONG-TERM MEMORY

Memory is created when experiences effect the strength of connections between brain nerve cells, or synapses. Animal studies have demonstrated that memory storage causes anatomical change. A passing experience creates less effect and creates a short-term memory. A stronger or repeated experience creates a greater effect, a stronger connection and an anatomical change in the brain.

Then there is implicit and explicit memory. *Implicit memory* handles unconscious motor or perceptual skills, or knowing *how*, and involves sensory pathways in the brain, the autonomic nervous system, and the amygdala and the cerebellum. *Explicit memory* is knowing *that*, facts, and is managed by the inside segments of the temporal lobes and the hippocampus. There is crosstalk or information exchange between the two when an experience is repeated, which is how habits are learned. We don't need to think about how to crochet a double crochet stitch or watch our hands, we just *know* what it feels like. That's a comfortable memory.

If someone whacked us on the head repeatedly when teaching us to make a double crochet stitch, the memory would be stored differently as a highly charged experience. That's because noradrenaline, a neurotransmitter, is released during fearful experiences. On the other hand, researchers have found that something different happens in our memory when an incident is traumatizing: our brain puts out endogenous opiates to dull the pain, and as a result the memory is stored less strongly. Studies demonstrate in laboratory rats that "weakly stored memory can be enhanced by injecting a stimulant drug like adrenaline."[77]

ENVIRONMENT AND MEMORY

To avoid confusion, we must keep in mind a basic fact: memory and consciousness are not synonymous. Remembering an experience depends on two main factors, one: the internal environment, the maturity of the central nervous system as well as its integrity; and two, the external environment, influenced by the type of event, and the impact of that event to the individual. These two factors are also referred to as *perception* and *apperception*. These phenomena begin in embryonic development, and later evolve into short-term and long-term memory. During the early development of the brain, both perception and apperception are among the foremost sensory motor roots synthesized. Later these will form the long-term and short-term memories—the foundation of future intellect.

When a baby is born, her environment is changed dramatically. If the birth is traumatic, the baby will react with intense hyperactivity of the autonomic nervous system, startle response, urination and defecation, prolonged crying and rapid movements of her extremities, etc. This experience of discomfort may be repeated over time, even if the factors that provoked the reaction originally are not the same, until the reaction becomes involuntary and the initial trigger isn't remembered consciously. The bodily responses are, in fact, tangible expressions of past experiences. Even intensive therapy with memory-enhancement techniques such as hypnosis may not give the individual a clue. If she is lucky, she may be able to glean information from someone who was present at her birth who remembers the traumatic situation and can help her integrate the material. Even so, some details are destined to be lost.

When two or more people share a significant experience, commonly they don't remember it the same; the core experience will be the same, but details will diverge. My own personal experience with this phenomenon was from an earthquake in my childhood home in Manila, Philippines, that registered seven on the Richter Scale. My family was seated around the dining room table at dinner when the pictures on the walls began to shake, then the table shook and water slopped out of the glasses. Glass smashed to the cement floor in the hot, humid, almost surreal silence. As the tremors intensified I wanted to scream. I don't know if I did.

Later, we compared notes. One sister couldn't stop her nervous giggling as tears streamed down her face. She remembered that we all looked silly, but she didn't recall any breaking glass. My mother had begun to shout what we'd learned in earlier earthquakes, "Head for the street. Everyone hurry. Hurry up. Come on, come on!" Another sister said she had just put some food into her mouth and felt stupid because she didn't know whether to spit out the food, or chew and swallow and then run out to the street.

Out in the street we stood through the aftershocks which, we agreed, seemed to go on forever, but which lasted maybe three to five minutes. After our initial disbelief that an earthquake was happening, rather than focus on the very real threat to our lives, we had all become aware of and focused on some detail. Mother said her mind went blank. She wasn't aware of shouting orders at us and she had no recollection of any other details of that day. One of my brothers told that an elderly neighbor woman, who had been ready to step into her bathtub when the quake hit, came out of her house onto the street naked. None of the rest of us remember that, but we didn't doubt that he saw it.

The point is that trauma distorts focus, fear impedes the brain's function, which colors recall, which can be further distorted by time. Sexual abuse is an analogous trauma.

SENSORY MEMORY

In addition to distorted perceptions, early and prolonged sexual abuse can cause memory repression, or amnesia of fragments or whole blocks of time during which the abuse occurred. Although the brain's voluntary recall system has been compromised, the "conditioned fear responses are stored as visual images or physical sensations in other brain regions," according to Bessel A. van der Kolk of Massachusetts General Hospital in Boston.[78] Moreover, van der Kolk says that "adult memories of confirmed childhood sexual abuse invariably appear first in perceptual fragments that get woven into a coherent story over weeks, months, or even years."[79]

Survivors have reported panic attacks, feelings of being smothered, and sensations of genital rubbing prior to remembering their actual molestation.[80] The prefrontal cortex, as discussed above, becomes involved because of its working memory system. When full memory is retrieved, depending on the pace and readiness of the individual, visual memories (occipital cortex), sensations (parietal cortex), sounds heard (temporal cortex), spatial sense (hippocampus), old motoric actions as well as associations of thoughts (frontal cortex), spoken words (language centers around the cortex such as Broca's area) activate part of the memory retrieval.

Old painful sensations from the body, commonly called body memories, which were stored in both implicit and explicit memory systems, are reactivated. The retrieval of traumatic memories is so painful that people prefer to repress them rather than deal with the pain. The patients' pain can be anguish for the therapist through countertransference. If the therapist doesn't deal with that pain consciously and promptly, it poses a boundary diffusion hazard due to the neediness of the survivor.[81] When this problem is brought to a survivor's attention, it's possible that he or she may respond with anger. Sometimes the reaction is retribution that takes the form of refusal to pay the therapist's bill or even threaten litigation. Usually after the first reaction most patients return to a more reasoning state of mind and resume their therapy. Those are the cases we *don't* hear about in the media.

NON-DECLARATIVE MEMORY, ENVIRONMENT AND ABUSE

Ronnie, one of my survivor patients, had memories that she tried to explain away as a product of her overactive imagination or something she read and then forgot. As an avid reader she thought it was possible that real life and fictional events had merged in her mind, that she'd gotten carried away, that there really wasn't any sexual abuse in her past. She had tried to talk to her mother about it but all she got was dismissal or inconsistent answers. But that kind of non-communication was consistent with her childhood experience of many words spoken, little inter-personal connection accomplished. For example, when at age nine Ronnie told her family that, when her uncle had raped her in her father's presence, her father had just told his brother, 16-year-old Jim, to "leave that child alone." Her telling made scarcely a ripple on her family's attention. After that she kept the knowledge to herself because apparently no one cared.

At her mother's funeral she was approached by her Aunt Louise, her mother's only sister and only living sibling. As they talked, Aunt Louise revealed that she had suspected that Ronnie was being abused by her uncle when she was a child. Then she told about an incident: one day she went to speak to her sister about a family gathering, but found Ronnie's parents weren't home. As she turned to leave, she heard eight-year-old Ronnie crying and screaming, "Stop it, Uncle Jim. Please, it hurts."

Aunt Louise turned back to the house and saw Jim dangle Ronnie out the second-floor window by one ankle, saying, "Shut up or I'll drop you!" Horrified, Louise didn't dare to move or make a sound for fear Jim would drop Ronnie. She held her breath until Jim pulled Ronnie back in the window, then yelled loudly, "Ronnie, are you all right?"

When Ronnie heard her aunt's story she was flooded by dizziness, nausea and soaring blood pressure that made her head pound and her ears close. As she reached for a chair to steady herself, she realized that what she thought had been a dream of a plump fairy godmother coming to rescue her hadn't been a dream at all, but her Aunt Louise. They'd been close when Ronnie was little and had fun doing things together, like nature walks. She hadn't understood why Louise had dropped out of her life so abruptly and had missed her. Now they compared notes and Ronnie could piece together past events and her suspect memories.

A few days after the window incident, just before Ronnie's ninth birthday, Louise had gone to talk to Ronnie's parents about Jim. They had gone into her parent's bedroom to talk in private. All Ronnie could hear was loud voices, and then Louise came out, red-faced and tearful, and left the house, never to return. Ronnie tried to question her parents, but they refused to answer. Louise told that she had gone over to Jim's and when she confronted him, he ran away. His father, Ronnie's grandfather, was furious and threatened to kill Louise. Ronnie's grandmother called Louise a lying bitch who deserved to die for trying to ruin a young man's life.

Louise's arrival at Ronnie's birthday party was greeted with anger. Ronnie's father slapped her face and said he'd kill her if she ever showed up again. Ronnie's mother pushed her out the door. Subsequently, Jim was welcomed back into the house. The sexual abuse, which was never mentioned, went on for another year until Jim drove drunk into a tree and killed himself just before his 17th birthday.

Ronnie and Louise talked well into the night, piecing together memories and crying. The memories Ronnie thought were dreams or overactive imagination were substantiated as fact, and she was able to release her rage, pain and fear and begin her healing.

MEMORY OVERVIEW

Memory is complex, but it is understandable,[82] and there is a wide range of lay and professional people who need to be purposeful about understanding memory, its workings and the forces that influence it. That range includes therapists, of course. But in addition it includes members of the legal process, judges, attorneys and jurors who deliberate the guilt or innocence of both perpetrators and therapists. Without this understanding, false memory as a definition becomes analogous to the temporary insanity plea, functioning to cloud the issue, not enlighten it. A further effect of advancing the false memory concept uncritically is to discount the credibility of psychiatry and psychology in the realm of hard science.

Most of all, survivors lose. Their memories are discounted, their experiences and pain are treated with skepticism and even contempt, therapists will become reluctant to undertake sexual abuse issues, sexual abusers will be free to continue, and child abuse will continue with our implied consent. It is an issue we must approach with intelligence, compassion and discernment.

PART IV

THERAPY ISSUES

CHAPTER SIXTEEN

THERAPY AND THERAPISTS

Little is written about the emotional, physical and financial impact of child sexual abuse on therapists. It can cause reactions like hives, nightmares, relationship issues, etc. Even if a particularly stalwart therapist doesn't have a strong reaction, it's impossible to be immune to the grief and suffering that is integral to survivors' recovery. Indeed, readers may even have felt a degree of such an impact from just reading these survivors' stories.

VERACITY

Invariably therapists will be nagged with skepticism. Do we really believe everything our abused patients tell us? How can we separate fantasy from reality? Is it better to suspend disbelief, or treat each story skeptically without devaluing our patients? It would be naive to treat every story concretely without recognizing that there may be another level or levels involved. In addition, even if the account is literal, some patients create a layer of their own interpretation of the abuse. Some add more and more outrageous information, perhaps testing our credulity. Then, if we appear or sound even slightly skeptical, they will interpret it as yet another rejection.

Discovery-recovery of memories is paramount to the healing process, even though tears are copious, the pain is excruciating and the horror is devastating to survivors and therapists alike. These moments of discovery are crucial to the success of therapy, but they can be dangerous to both parties. Thus, therapists need to maintain their boundaries and hang onto their own reality and not get sucked into the maelstrom of survivors' experiences.

Therapy sessions are supposed to last 50 minutes, but when discovery is in progress, sessions can last for hours. Some therapists advocate strict adherence to the hour time frame to maintain appropriate boundaries. However, because of the intensity of the suffering during discovery-recovery, often it's impossible to walk away from it between sessions without some kind of temporary psychological analgesia until the next therapy session.

Some therapists won't deal with cases of child sexual abuse and some can't. Its evil can be demoralizing as the intensity of the suffering spills out. We are trained to empathize, not sympathize; that's part of being a professional. With neurotic or depressed patients it's easier because we can see progress and healing relatively quickly. For the most part, their treatment is fulfilling.

However, in child sexual abuse cases, treatment is long, tedious and frustrating for the therapist. When the patient has a successful recovery, though, the rewards are great, and victims do heal. They move on to being functional people leading normal lives.

CASE LIMITING

It's best for a therapist to have only a few child sexual abuse cases at one time for the sake of his or her emotional and physical well being. But, because more and more cases of abuse are emerging each year, there is a growing shortage of qualified therapists to handle the need. I've found that a team approach serves the best interests of both clients and therapists, but even this resource needs to be expanded.

I offer this advice about limiting one's practice based on painful personal experience. I offer my story in Appendix V.

BOUNDARIES

What boundaries survivors of child sexual abuse have usually are few, poor and permeable because they were violated uncaringly during the time they needed to be learning. As a consequence, therapists need to set boundaries with patients early in the therapeutic process and reinforce them as needed in terms of both the patient's and therapist's rights and responsibilities.

Boundaries generated in a healthy environment will be woven serenely enough to admit new ideas and information to foster psychological growth, and firmly enough to thwart abusive or unacceptable behavior. Boundaries developed in a psychologically unhealthy climate of emotional, psychological, physical or sexual abuse can become flawed in two ways, or even a combination of these two ways. One, the boundary is constructed so poorly that it offers no defense or discernment of abusive behavior. Those with such boundaries commonly make poor choices in friends, life partners and actions, and are candidates for revictimization. Or two, the boundaries will be a defensive stone wall, keeping the hurt inner child safe from more hurt, but buffered from sensitivity and growth as well. The paradox of the stone-wall boundary is that typically it guards against *incoming* behavior, while permitting abusive *outgoing* behavior. Without conscious work on the issues that create the stone wall, the habitual wall gets thicker and tougher until it is a lonely and pain-filled prison.

Awareness and adaptability are primary to healthy boundary creation and maintenance throughout the therapeutic process.

BOUNDARIES AND
THE THERAPEUTIC RELATIONSHIP

Incest victims' poorly defined ego boundaries and distorted body boundaries cause them to demand inordinate amounts of attention from all of their relationships. Those relationships are often tumultuous, intense and short lived because their demands provoke such strong feelings of guilt. This behavior translates into constant demands on their therapists for emergency sessions and the conviction that they are entitled to whatever they demand. Their persistent and angry clamor for attention kindles counter-transference feelings in their therapists, which in turn can cause a stalemate in the therapy and even termination.

These patients often violate their therapists' boundaries by pry-ing into their personal lives, asking questions about the therapists' children, spouses, social plans, and so on. They assume that they are the least favorite patient and demand constant reassurance that they aren't unacceptable. Even with that reassurance they get jealous be-cause they believe their therapist is more interested in her other pa-tients. They bring generous gifts, which are often too extravagant to accept, and feel rejected when the gift is declined.

GIFT-GIVING

One experience involving gift-giving that is representative of many others is that of Donna, a 33-year-old single woman who is ex-traordinarily talented at arts and crafts. As a child, gift-giving was how she tried to forestall her mother's abuse. When an ominous silence fell, Donna knew another incident of violent rage would follow, so she tried to coax her out of it with a piece of pottery or a drawing. If it worked, her mother's rage would grumble away like a dying thunderstorm. Unappeased, there would be beatings with a wooden spoon, stinging slaps on the face and violent shaking, all accompanied by shrill curses.

During our third session Donna and I had a serious discussion about her penchant for arriving for her appointments 10 to 15 minutes late. She always had excuses; long, exhaustive tales. None-theless, her tardiness cut into the early part of her session, but then she stretched out the sessions at the other end with new memories that caused strong emotional reactions. She didn't need longer sessions, I told her, she needed to honor her appointment time and use the time wisely. She stormed out without a word.

She arrived for her next appointment on time, bearing apologies and an exquisite gift, a wire sculpture tree with leaves and fruit of quartz. Beside it stood a unicorn about to take flight. It looked very expensive. I told her that it was beautiful and I was honored but I couldn't accept it. Could she see, I asked her, a parallel between this gift-giving and the gifts she gave her mother to appease her rage?

She sat in hostile silence. I expected her to storm out again. When she spoke, she said sadly that she'd never understood why those to whom she gave gifts never seemed to appreciate them nor ever gave her gifts in return. She was always giving, she said. Gently, I told her that she didn't need to give me gifts. In fact, the best thing she could do for me was give me her commitment to therapy. She did.

Years later, on my birthday, she came with a beautifully wrapped box. She held it out to me saying, "Surely you're not going to refuse this gift since the occasion is your birthday and my rebirth into a new life." Then she turned over her left hand to display a diamond engagement ring. "Leo asked me to marry him."

Today Donna is a happy mother of two lovely girls and has a daycare program in her home which she enjoys thoroughly. Last Christmas she sent me a family picture card that said simply, "Thank you for allowing me to express my rage, my pain and my grief. That will always be the greatest Christmas gift in my life."

THERAPIST MALFEASANCE

One of the most talked about breaches of boundaries is sexual involvement between therapists and their patients. Some professionals say that when therapists misread patients' need for love and nurture, and then violate professional boundaries by having sex with their vulnerable patients, it is analogous to violating the original sexual boundary in childhood. While reenactment of their sexual abuse is felt to be a repetition compulsion on the patients' part, the therapists' exploitation of the patients is a grave breach of ethics. The two most recent notorious sexual misconduct cases involved two otherwise competent and professionally respected psychiatrists.

The first involves Dr. Jules Masserman, an internationally prominent figure and past president of several psychiatric associations.[83] In her book, Barbara Noel, a former patient of some 18 years accused the then 81-year-old doctor of raping her while she was unconscious during a sodium amytal interview.[84] Noel alleges that Dr. Masserman used sodium amytal frequently during her 18 years with him and caused her to become addicted to it, as well as alcohol. The incident was brought to national attention when advice columnist Ann Landers devoted her column to the subject on September 13, 1992.

Legal resolution of the case was complicated by two factors. One, the American Psychiatric Association felt that Masserman's suspension was complicated by lack of physical evidence, such as indication of rape and signs of ejaculation, and he avowed his innocence resolutely. Two, Masserman was already 81 years old, there was a large backlog of court cases and the case had a history of hearing postponements, so it was highly possible that he could die before a hearing date was even set. While Noel wanted Masserman punished and expelled from the psychiatric community publicly, due to circumstances he was only suspended. Noel settled out of court and Ann Landers accused the APA of "taking care of their own." Two other former patients brought suits against Dr. Masserman. Both were settled out of court.

The second case of sexual misconduct by a psychiatrist involved Dr. Margaret Bean-Bayog, a clinical assistant professor at Harvard Medical School with a reputation as a gifted lecturer and a dedicated researcher into substance abuse. Dr. Bean-Bayog voluntarily surrendered her medical license after being accused of seducing a patient, Paul Lozano, a medical student, and driving him to commit suicide with a lethal dose of cocaine.[85] Lozano's family alleged that Dr. Bean-Bayog brainwashed him to regard her as a loving mother, then discarded him when he could no longer pay for psychotherapy. Bean-Bayog conceded that while her therapy was unconventional, she did not have sex with Lozano

and that he was suicidal chronically due to his horrendous childhood abuse. Her voluntary and unconditional resignation was to
spare her family and patients the trauma of public assault.[86]

Although there will always be unanswered questions and doubts
about these two incidents between therapists and patients, and
possibly thousands more, I believe that the public will always judge
therapists culpable. It's almost inevitable because psychiatrists are
portrayed in extremes. In books and films they're depicted crazier
than their patients, evil beyond belief, or sagacious saints. Such
depiction is no service to the already fragile trust of incest survivors, nor to the community of psychiatrists who work hard and
honestly and see themselves as unremarkable.

I'm not a proponent for or against physical contact with patients in general, but I'm careful. Very careful. Incest survivors
become either physically distant and distrustful about any physical touching, or they are always asking for hugs or some kind of
evidence of caring. In my practice I permit safe hugging. That
means an unprolonged, non-sexual, non-exploitive touching in
selected cases where boundaries have been defined clearly.

The psychodynamics of sexual boundary violations must be
understood by therapists and their origins identified in sex abuse
survivors so sexual exploitation can be prevented. There are complex dynamics involved in therapist-patient relationships, but some
researchers claim that the most common factors noted in therapists who abuse are:

- Psychopathic exploitation where the therapist has a superego
  lacuna, a hole in the superego or conscience, who lacks moral
  conscience due to poor development. They bond sadistically
  with their patients through the exercise of power and destructiveness. These therapists may have had sexual involvement
  with many patients. Also, they may have been profoundly
  abused as children.

- Another postulate is that of "lovesick therapists." One survey
  claimed that as many as 65% of those who were sexually involved with their patients believe that they are actually in love

with them. These therapists may succumb to lovesickness and such patient violation because they are inexperienced and may be having problems in their personal love life. Many therapists believe that the transference-countertransference dimension of the relationship is symbolically incestuous. Patients may see their relationship with their therapists as appropriate.

- Another theory is that therapists confuse their needs with those of the patients. Some mental health professionals say, and we've even seen it portrayed in the popular media, that love in and of itself is curative. Those professionals who feel they were insufficiently loved as children may attempt to rectify their perceived loss through therapeutic zeal with their patients. There is an unspoken hope that by meeting their patients' needs, their needs are met also; by rescuing their patients, they rescue themselves.

There are characteristics shared by victims of therapist sexual boundary violation. They include a history of sexual abuse; Borderline Personality Disorder diagnosis, many of whom have been sexually abused and a majority have been abused generally; bonding disorders, where individuals had no nurturing as children for a variety of reasons; and other elements of vulnerability such as Masochistic Personality Disorder, low self-esteem, dependent traits, women with a history of being close to their fathers and had difficult relationships with their mothers, who saw sex with their therapists as special and a validation of their self-worth. These latter victims often litigate when the relationship ceases, even though the relationship lasts for years.

Whatever the dynamics, in the end therapists must recognize that they, and they alone will be held culpable.

DEMANDING PATIENTS

One evening after a particularly grueling session with a patient I sat down with a magazine, sighed and opened it at random. My eyes fell on the title of an article, and I felt a shock of recognition as I read, "Even The Best Psychotherapist Cannot Be All Things To All Patients."[87] I had told myself almost the exact same thing that afternoon after a patient terminated therapy with me. I read on. I needed to hear this. "Many patients in psychotherapy do well with virtually any competent therapist, but some who need a lot of patience, tolerance and sensitivity to their injury can only work with a few."

The patient who had terminated had seen several therapists before me and had castigated them all during our sessions. Most therapists know that's a danger sign, a red flag that usually I heed and get wary. But I didn't this time for some reason. I rushed right in and took her on as my patient.

She told me that several of her friends who had worked with me in the past recommended me highly. She said she had a history of sexual abuse as a child and had been given at least six diagnoses. Four of them were Personality Disorders. All belonged to the same cluster in DSM-IV-R: Borderline Personality Disorder, Narcissistic Personality Disorder, Antisocial Personality Disorder and Histrionic Personality Disorder. The other two were Post-Traumatic Stress Disorder and Dissociative Identity Disorder.

We worked together for a year. In the very beginning we discussed carefully healthy therapeutic boundaries so our process together would do the maximum good and had a minimum potential to harm either one of us. At that time she told me about incidents of serious boundary violations by more than one of her previous therapists. By the end of that year, which had been uncomfortable all the time and unproductive most of the time despite my caution and training, she left. To my great relief, I might add.

Her behavior toward me was abusive, manipulative and mercurial. One moment she idealized me and the next she criticized me. During our sessions she asked questions about my health, and then moments later turned the conversation against me and castigated me for what she called "inappropriate disclosure." She asked hidden-agenda questions about my husband or children, then use the information as a weapon. She left in the middle of appointments in a rage and then telephoned later and ranted at me. She wrote blistering letters. She expected me to be available to her 24 hours a day without notice, showed up at my door and then got furious when I was unavailable.

As I said, it had been a miserable year. But what surprises me most when I look back at it is how much her behavior distressed me, how vulnerable I was. As a psychiatric resident I had gone through in-depth psychoanalysis and a group therapy course called group process. In addition, like every other psychiatric resident, I had a preceptor, a staff member who serves as an advisor or counselor.

Sure, I had issues, but I dealt with them, or I thought I had. But this patient hooked me. She had transference issues, and I had counter-transference issues, and the result was a sandpaper relationship instead of a therapeutic alliance. I discussed the effect that these dynamics had on her healing and suggested that I refer her to another competent therapist. She accused me of abandoning her. I told her that we both needed to pay close attention to our boundaries to be sure they're strong and healthy and repair them where necessary, and she needed to decide who her therapist would be in order to end our mutual misery. I discussed our dilemma with colleagues who sympathized but offered no better solution that the one I proposed to my patient.

Who was to blame? Both of us. But I accept that the healer in a relationship with one who seeks healing bears the greatest responsibility to recognize that a relationship isn't going to work for any reason and terminate the relationship for the good of both. Although I've said it before, it can't be said too often: a therapist can't be all things to all people. Therapists are human and fallible and have limits and there are some patients with whom they simply can't work.

Sometimes it's a matter of personality and sometimes a matter of style. Some therapists work inside the patient's process and are actively involved, while others stay outside and remain objective.

Some therapists can vary their style according to the needs of the patient, most can't. That's why it's necessary for both patients and therapists to be alert to a good fit between style and needs. When a fit isn't right, it's best to acknowledge the fact and move on before damage is done to either party.

One day, during a particularly manipulative, unproductive and angry session with this patient, she pulled down the corners of her mouth, turned her head to one side and peered down her cheekbones at me. She didn't think, she said, hauteur dripping from every word, that we could ever form a therapeutic alliance. Clearly, she was dismissing me, telling me that I was less than adequate. She was as surprised at my response as I was. Normally, if a patient feels she must terminate with me, I feel deep regret that I have failed her. That day, however, I felt a thrill of relief, and I asked her how I could facilitate her decision. Understandably, she felt thwarted and furious. She stood abruptly, jammed her hands in her jacket pockets, rapped out "No!" and stalked out.

I realized that in time she would recast the scene into me deserting her, but frankly I didn't care. My health, my family life and my marriage had all been taking a beating because I had allowed my patients to drain me. In fact, at that point, I had no choice but to take some time to vacate my stress and recreate myself as a whole, healthy woman. As I grew into my individuation as a therapist, I found that my patients are more comfortable and get to work on their issues faster if I appear healthy. A therapist's apparent ill health makes patients feel insecure and threatened.

DEFENSE MECHANISMS

Those who work with survivors of child sexual abuse need to weigh the extreme complexity of treatment and recovery because one must deal with the defense mechanisms that slow progress. It's possible to take years of therapy to break through the mechanism of denial alone, it can be so massive. Repression of memories, an unconscious way of forgetting the trauma, which once helped the client become a survivor can, in therapy, hinder uncovering memories of the abuse. This defense mechanism often has been strengthened by the abuser's admonition not to tell, or even his insistence that it never happened.

There are six commonly used defense mechanisms. As you read them, remember that *all defense mechanisms are unconscious,* no matter how stubbornly employed:

- *Denial:* Incest victims reject external reality and replace it with wish-fulfilling fantasy or behavior.
- *Repression:* Pushing memories down, down into the unconscious. The layers of consciousness are:

Conscious, always available;

Subconscious, accessible with a little effort; and

Unconscious, accessible only with the greatest effort, and often only with outside or professional help. Memories of events too traumatic to deal with, that are unintentionally forgotten, go here. That's how we might forget painful events and remember only happy ones.

- *Rationalization:* Giving a plausible explanation for a behavior or perceived failure to prevent the devastation of one's ego. For example, an athlete who blames his failure to win on the poor condition of the field or bias of the referee.
- *Dissociation:* Unconsciously blocking out one's environment to escape a painful situation. For example, walking on hot coals and being oblivious of the pain. Or carrying on a seemingly normal conversation while severely stressed and having no memory of it later.
- *Depersonalization:* Feeling that one's mind and body are unconnected. The body responds

robotically, while the mind is numb, without emotion.

- *Intellectualization:* Being argumentative during therapy sessions, attempting to blur boundaries, and deflecting necessary psychological intrusion of her boundaries by the therapist. At the same time the survivor may try to enmesh the therapist in her problems and tries to learn everything personal about the therapist.

UNWELCOME MEMORIES

When memories start to surface, perhaps from psychiatry, massage therapy that awakens a body memory, a smell, an incident that breaks the hold of the defense mechanism, there will be a mighty effort to push it back under, but memories won't go back. Anxiety builds. The patient might seek relief through therapy, with compulsive exercise, with overwork, over-the-counter drugs, street drugs, alcohol, sleep, anorexia, bulimia, heavy gambling, fanatical cleaning, partying, religion, self-help books, support groups. Some activities take up time. Some take lives.

Fear of reprisal can strengthen the will to forget even further in survivors whose abusers demonstrated the potency of their threats by committing acts of extreme brutality. For example, by killing the victim's pet before her eyes, or torturing and murdering infant siblings while forcing the child to watch. These are both practices of ritual abuse, but they are not limited to cult members. Cults have killed viciously those who have betrayed or tried to leave the cult, forcing the ritually abused to watch as a warning.

It's not surprising in view of the malevolence of abusers that survivors often express feelings of hopelessness and helplessness, leading them to a sense of fatalism and distrust that they can ever overcome their trauma. Often they become involved in dysfunctional relationships which repeat the pattern of revictimization and the experience confirms their worst fears.

They are masters at defending their repression of their memories because to reclaim the memories means they must confront also the fiction that their parents were loving and caring. Even worse, if they allow the memories into recall, that hateful treatment also will confirm their deeply held fear that they are bad, evil, unlovable and therefore deserved the abuse they received. After all, their abuser(s) said they did!

DEFENSIVE REACTIONS

Sexual abuse victims usually have trouble expressing anger, even in the face of severe abuse and humiliation. On the other hand, a few become exceedingly angry, abusive people and become sexual abusers themselves. Most often, though, they have become passive, accepting. Their posture is usually, but not necessarily, hunched, as though they are ready to roll into a defensive ball like a hedgehog, and, truly, they are. As children they learned that they had no defense and there would be no rescue. They were powerless in every sense. Their only option seemed to be to become a tiny invulnerable ball and, if that failed, to go deep inside their minds and hide and forget.

Even their voices tend to reflect that hiding. Survivors are often mumblers because no one ever heard their pleas; they were voiceless children. So, they became, in essence, mute. Now there seems to be no energy in their bodies to push out their words because all their energy went into surviving. It still does.

These survivors who are still mumbling and even some of those who have regained their voices, especially those who have not had psychiatric treatment, are still in many ways living an escape mode. For example, encounters with other people are tolerated better if the mood is very low key. Enthusiasm and energy, mental or physical, cause these survivors to feel overwhelmed and they are inclined to run away in fear. This behavior decreases as their healing progresses.

WHAT VICTIMS DO
WITH THEIR MEMORIES

Just to survive, most victims of sexual abuse bury their memories deep and lock them up tight against recall with such defense mechanisms as denial, repression, rationalization, dissociation, depersonalization and intellectualization, as I discussed above. But the memories don't go away. They are locked in the minds and muscles of the victims, festering, causing physical, mental and relationship problems.

When they seek treatment, their presenting symptoms can cover a gamut of psychiatric disorders:

- Bipolar Disorder, Manic form, Depressed form, or even a Rapid Cycling form;
- Various personality disorders, particularly Borderline Personality Disorders from their self-abusive behavior;
- Recurrent suicide thoughts or attempts;
- Splitting, all things are seen as good or bad, black or white;
- Sexual Dysfunction, which is often difficult to treat if the sexual abuse of one or both members of the couple is not uncovered;
- Eating Disorders, which also has been linked to child sexual abuse;
- Post-Traumatic Disorder
- Substance Abuse, reports vary from 65-90% of substance abusers have been sexually abused.

When a patient comes to a therapist presenting one or more of the above conditions, the process begins to release their deeply buried memories and begin the healing process. It's important not to force the memories or oblige the memory to give up its secrets before the patient is capable of dealing with them.

Sometimes, however, some of the deepest and most traumatic

memories may be triggered quite by accident. Perhaps by a gesture or movement of another person, certain words, a smell or a
touch, or even in a dream. It's not unusual for a body memory, a
memory stored in the body's muscles and tissues, to be released
while a patient is receiving a massage, a chiropractic treatment or
some kind of deep muscle therapy, like Rolfing. It's not uncommon for the patient to denounce the memory as implausible and
probably the figment of an over-fertile imagination. However, once
the memories begin, there is no stopping them. Familiar defense
mechanisms no longer work. That's often when survivors who have
resisted therapy will finally seek it.

My approach to new patients varies depending on their presenting symptoms. For example, if my schedule is full so I can't see
a patient right away, I may recommend medication for the patient
who has become insomniac due to fear of recurrent nightmares, or
possibly has panic attacks, depression, severe anxiety or even ago-
raphobia. Once we begin therapy together, though, I honor each
patient's rhythm and pace. Their memories will come in the
patient's own time and I will not impose my convenience on that
timetable.

TAILORING A TREATMENT PLAN

A new patient, a schoolteacher, began having flashbacks of her
abuse in response to an argument with her husband about his
form of sexual overtures. It was just prior to the beginning of the
school season. Soon she was having flashbacks of her grandmother
bathing her and the flashbacks caused her to have panic attacks
when she took a shower. She told me she didn't want to pursue her
memories too vigorously because it would interfere with her teaching.

Together we worked out a plan to meet once a week on a regular basis, but if she felt the need she was welcome to see me more
often. She told me she would get support from her prayer group
who prayed collectively for the special needs of members when

asked to. I encouraged her to journal daily. Nothing lengthy or taxing, just support for the returning memories and what triggered them, as well as recording her dreams as soon as she woke.

She had a good friend who was also a sexual abuse survivor and was well into her recovery. This friend offered to listen to her when she needed to ventilate. She was fortunate to have this friend because her husband wasn't willing or able to listen to her talk about her emerging memories, although he didn't discredit her. Her friend listened without trying to be a therapist and offered to walk or do crafts with her when she became distraught. If these options didn't work, I recommended judicious and short-term use of an anti-anxiety medication, warning her of the possibility of psychological dependence.

I taught her how to do relaxation techniques using deep, even breathing, while listening to soothing music. Let your thoughts flow freely, I told her, and don't try to suppress anything that comes to mind. In your mind hold a picture of yourself surrounded by a soft, warm light that protects you from harm. Even though your emerging memories are painful, allow them to surface and write them down. Eventually the pain will decrease to a level that you can tolerate.

BEING SPECIFIC

As a doctor and a therapist I am familiar and comfortable with the specifics of body parts. I have found that it helps victims become survivors if during our sessions the words they use about their trauma can be direct, explicit and anatomically correct. It helps relieve their shame and revulsion.

Sometimes, when their memories are overpowering, a five-minute telephone consultation with me can help them over a hard place. If that isn't enough and they are overwhelmed and unable to function in concert with the emerging memories, I offer them a brief hospitalization. In the hospital they have the safety of the availability of 24-hour staff when they need to talk and I can see them daily.

PATIENT VULNERABILITY

Past experience has made them vulnerable to all kinds of abusive situations, even to being unable to recognize and accept indications that a new relationship has strong potential to be physically or emotionally abusive. This includes vulnerability to sexual or emotional abuse from their priests or ministers. I have had patients who passively and even willingly have submitted to sexual abuse from past therapists, rationalizing or justifying the abuse, and then were devastated when the therapist terminated treatment with them.

Survivors get inordinately anxious and frightened when their confronter gets the least bit assertive. If I forget myself and raise the volume of my voice to emphasize a point in a therapy session with a survivor, even though my tone isn't angry, the patient will probably become uncomfortable and, reflexively, begin to take a defensive posture, as though expecting a blow.

Creating a therapeutic alliance with these patients usually takes a long time because they are operating out of such a deep insecurity. They may demand constant reassurance that they are worthy of my attention, or they may be so submissive that their therapy makes poor progress. Indeed, survivors can be submissive to authority figures, while at the same time being overbearing and abusive to their spouses, constantly testing their spouse's loyalty.

These patients usually put me through a testing period. During this time they may provoke my patience by constant requests of emergency services, or they may prolong their therapy sessions beyond their normal hour with dramatic revelations of new memories at the end of the hour, or they may test or question my loyalty to their treatment.

SETTING LIMITS

Setting limits and boundaries in our relationship is difficult for, at minimum, two reasons: often patients have an insatiable need to "fuse" with their therapist and they feel essentially untouchable and unlovable. Thus, I feel it is essential for me to be willing to give patients reassuring touches and hugs while helping them to learn to respect themselves and me.

Some of my patients call me Doctor Mom, and want to be hugged and reassured that each is my favorite patient. This is acceptable in the earliest stages of treatment, while patients develop their own internal strengths and a growing sense of emotional proficiency. But I help them understand that their work is for themselves, not to please me as a substitute parent. Their need to please, their fear of provoking, their terror of abandonment and rejection all must be addressed in therapy and converted to inner strength.

HOSPITAL DEPENDENCY

Judicious use of hospitalization often is necessary when thoughts of suicide and self-destructive behavior become a threat to their survival. Hospital dependency is a threat and patients need to be monitored carefully. In the therapeutic milieu of the hospital, the predictable and dependable schedule, the unconditional acceptance of the staff and daily visits from the therapist can allow patients feel nurtured and validated, safe for possibly the first time in their lives, and unwilling to leave. There is a point during these hospitalizations at which, with sensitivity, the therapist can see that the patient feels this safety and will be able to identify and replicate it internally at a future date, but before he or she is dependent on the hospital. That is the point at which the therapist must end the hospitalization.

Cult victims who develop Dissociative Identity Disorder are the most difficult to diagnose and treat, and may require frequent and longer periods of hospitalization. Their thoughts of suicide have been programmed intensely to rise often and powerfully should they attempt escape or recall, so they literally are bombarded with thoughts of self-destruction. These patients are highly volatile and easily triggered into re-experiencing their trauma afresh. Their behavior may be perfectly appropriate and rational one moment and within minutes they can become extremely agitated and even combative.

THE HEALING POWER OF TOUCH

One of my DID patients gave me a lesson in humility. I was talking to one of the adult alters, and we were both laughing about a joke she had shared with one of the staff earlier that day. Suddenly she became rigid and hostile. She moved away from me into a corner of the room where she stared at me. "So you think that's funny." Her tone was menacing. "You're like all the rest. You only like me when I'm entertaining. Well, I'm not going to stand on my head any more and act like a monkey. Not for my fucking mother or my father, and certainly not for you."

I sat stunned by this abrupt shift in her behavior and tried to think what might have provoked it.

Before I could say anything, she switched into a much younger alter who sat down on the floor and began to weep. "I want my mamma. Papa's hurting me."

Then she shrieked, "NO! NO! NO!" and pressed against the side of the bed, trembling.

I, who had always prided myself at my ability to handle crisis situations, felt totally helpless and inadequate. Instinctively I reached out to touch her. She didn't pull away, so slowly I slid down to the floor to sit with her. She clung to me, sobbing. I put my arms around her, and her body relaxed against me. As she relaxed, sighing one enormous sigh, she became quiet and I began to rock her as I rocked my own children when they were upset or hurt.

We sat quietly and rocked for quite a while. I don't really know how long it was. When my legs began to cramp, I helped her to her feet and led her over to the bed, where she lay down and closed her eyes. I sat in the chair watching her, trying to decide what to do.

Abruptly her eyes flew open and she smiled at me. "Thank you. Becky needed that. You see, our mom never hugged us when we hurt." It was the adult alter I had been speaking to when Becky came out.

At that moment I realized the truth of what one therapist who worked with DIDs had said: Healing is always in the present tense and that appropriate touching at the appropriate time is healing also; words are not necessary. With experiences such as that, I have realized how much my patients teach me that books cannot.

EMPATHY

An important part of the healing process is the therapist's empathy with the victim. However, it's important to distinguish here between empathy and sympathy. Empathy means understanding what the patient feels and validating those feelings as real. Sympathy, on the other hand, means being so affected by the patient's feelings that the therapist feels the same thing. That identification robs the therapist of his or her perspective and robs the patient of an objective therapist.

Empathy involves the ability to be in contact with the patients' states, to understand their feelings by attuning oneself to their perspective. It involves being patiently receptive to the nuances of their behavior and verbalizations. It involves listening to what they may not be capable of saying, and then clarifying what they are saying. It involves self-understanding so that one's own moral or ethical values or experiences aren't projected onto the patient. Therefore, as a therapist one promotes greater awareness for one's patients by allowing them to discover their own realities.

As a therapist, I have always felt enriched by my patients' insights. As they grow in understanding, so do I. I have been careful not to say, I understand, when they tell me how they hurt and that they feel that no one understands, for I truly never can fathom the depths of their despair, shame and self-hate. I can understand only in the context of my own life experiences.

INTERACTIVE THERAPY

I have found that interactive therapy with sexually abused victims seems to be the most conducive to their getting in touch with their feelings. Interactive therapy means that the therapist and patient are mutually active in expressing their feelings and responses to each other's interactions. When patients come from dysfunctional families in which severe physical, emotional and/or sexual abuse created maladaptive ways of communicating, a *tabula rasa*, or blank screen, approach, where the therapist gives the patient no indication of his or her thoughts or feelings, does not work well. These patients tend to assume the therapist's thoughts and feelings, and the assumption is usually negative, based on how their abusive parents or authority figures responded to them.

A therapist's emotional honesty is therapeutic for the patient, offering them a sense of validation of their feelings. It gives them the sense of being truly accepted as an equal by the therapist, who sees their feelings as appropriate, given the circumstances that provoked them. The apparent unconditional, non-judgmental and genuine need to understand them allows them feelings of power and control because they are treated as adults and not as helpless children.

SELF-DISCLOSURE

I have used self-disclosure only in very selected cases. In my training as a psychiatrist there was never a rigid admonition against self-disclosure. It was to be avoided only when revealing my feelings would be destructive or obstructive by removing the focus of therapy from the patient's psychopathology. Even when self-disclosure promotes emotional growth for the patient, the therapist must be vigilant that boundaries are not violated.

One of my patients, who had been sexually abused by her father and discounted by her mother, vowed to be a good mother by putting her children's needs above all others, including her own. Clearly she was overcompensating for her feelings of rejection and powerlessness as a child. In spite of devoting her entire life to the service of her children, they turned out bad in her opinion. She felt like a failure, and she asked me how I raised my children while having a full-time career.

Self-disclosure in that instance was a two-edged sword. If I told her that my children had turned out "bad," she would attribute it to my dual role as mother and doctor. If they turned out "good," it would confirm her failure, in her eyes, as a mother.

Instead, I responded by acknowledging her disappointment in her children. She had done the best she could, however, considering the circumstances of her childhood, and under the same circumstances, I probably wouldn't have coped as well. Her children hadn't been subjected to the harsh conditions that she had, I pointed out. Instead, they had grown up in a safe and protected environment. Further, they had the capacity to make choices, and she couldn't take responsibility for the ones they made. Then I pointed out that I, too, had failed to get her children involved in her therapy, and that two of them had refused several of my attempts.

She had listened quietly to my response, and then sat back and began to process it. Ultimately, she was able to let go of her guilt and stopped trying to bail out her children every time they got into trouble.

EMOTIONAL AFFECT

Allowing some of my patients to see my honest emotional response to their pain has helped them. However, I have always been careful to reassure them that I didn't assimilate their pain, I hadn't internalized it, and therefore I had maintained my role as a therapist and they were still secure. That allowed them to feel emotionally interactive with me without burdening them with the responsibility for rescuing me from injury by their pain.

I had been working with a severely abused DID patient whom I had never seen cry, nor showed any inclination to cry. Her affect was flat and unemotional all the time. She appeared unable to empathize or sympathize with her peers who had been similarly victimized. Even as she related horrible events of human torture, repeated rapes, murder and cannibalism, she showed no emotion. One day, as she told of a gruesome event in which she was forced by the cult to kill her own baby in a cult sacrifice ceremony, I felt tears come to my own eyes. They were spontaneous and I made no effort to hide them.

Apparently surprised at my emotional reaction, she looked at me wordlessly for a full minute, and then, slow as a glacier, she began to cry. Tears formed, puddled and overflowed. A small sob started somewhere under the ice. Then, one after the other, the sobs rose from deep within her soul, wracking her body. Her face wore the look of a small child in profound grief as she rose and walked across the few feet that separated us, holding her arms out like a child seeking comfort. I stood, opened my arms, and then held her while she cried. Previously her hugs had been wooden. This embrace was real. We stood like that for what felt like a long time, both of us crying, each for our own reason. Finally her tears slacked and she drew back. Her eyes searched my face briefly and then she smiled. "You do understand," she said quietly.

After that she became more animated, her eye contact was much better, and she was no longer wooden and mechanical when she told of her sufferings.

REVICTIMIZATION IN THERAPY

I have had many requests from sexual abuse victims asking that I take them into my service because they feel their own therapists didn't hear them. They felt retraumatized by their therapist's discounting behavior and remote tone of voice, all carrying the subtle implication that their sufferings are no big deal. They tell me that when they share these feelings with the therapist, they've been told that their perception was probably exaggerated and they were just feeling sorry for themselves.

That's crazy-making treatment, to be told that you don't feel what you know you feel, to be told that what you know full well happened didn't happen. It's a cruel and none too subtle form of abuse that usually is part of a power struggle in a relationship between spouses or parents and children. When it happens between a counselor and a counselee, however, I *hope* that it is only a form of ignorance that will be corrected as soon as the error is recognized.

Children are vulnerable in their innocence, lack of physical power to defend themselves and dependency on adults for survival. If they're abused during this vulnerable period, not only is it the worst kind of boundary violation, but it can foster a deep-seated feeling of powerlessness. Then, when they reach physical development and feel confident of wielding physical power, it isn't surprising when formerly abused people display repetition compulsion.

Those victimized aren't necessarily only children, but can be any person or group of people they see as easy prey. Something the abuser doesn't realize, however, is that as the abused abuser abuses, he or she continues to abuse himself by keeping the victimization fresh.

When the abused carry a double load due to re-abuse from a therapist, their original reason for seeing the therapist, such as depression or anxiety attacks, gets worse. When a crisis arises, as surely it will, they can feel that something is very wrong and end treatment. *Except*, and here's the rub, if the therapist has masked the abuse with *pseudo* caring. Then it can take years for the survivor to see what's happening and get out of the situation. And with that observation, we are right back at the need for healthy boundaries and the need to establish limits without being rigid or inflexible.

Trying to work therapeutically with a therapist who is rigid in his or her approach can be an abusive experience for patients because no one method is right for all circumstances. In my opinion, the rigidity that some therapists practice routinely grows out of their particular training. Nevertheless, the indiscriminate application of that training to all patients may only confuse the patient and retard his or her progress, but also it can do great psychological damage and leave the patient afraid to trust all therapists.

Life is dynamic, fluid. When it becomes rigid or stagnates, it no longer can adapt to its environment and that is the beginning of its death. When we apply that to the field of therapy, we can see that therapists must be able to be intuitive and flexible with their patients. If one approach doesn't work, try another, and always with great sensitivity.

One patient told me of her distressing experience with a previous therapist, who told her that no amount of talking would help her; only medication would alleviate her symptoms of alienation. Her husband, who happened to be with her during that session, listened, but didn't comment. She went home feeling confused. Not only were her perceptions false, she concluded, but she had some kind of physical defect that promoted these false perceptions. Her already low self-esteem dropped further. She began to question all of her perceptions and became increasingly unable to make decisions. Her anxiety and panic attacks escalated in spite of the medications.

From some inner place of self-preservation rose the determination that she needed to change therapists for the sake of her own mental health. She discussed her decision with her husband, who validated her perception that the therapist was revictimizing her by discounting her perceptions. With her new therapist, her self-esteem improved. As therapy continued, she became more assertive, more self-assured and less anxious.

I encourage my patients to express their feelings and opinions and to challenge my opinions or recommendations, if they are so moved. After all, I tell them, I'm not infallible and therapy is definitely a cooperative endeavor.

VIDEOTAPING SESSIONS

The technology of videotaping has provided a helpful tool in treating sexual abuse survivors because the way they assume they present themselves to others, the way they think they appear on the outside, is often at total variance with what the camera captures. When they view the videotape, they can see why people react to them as they do. After that, forging an alliance between their external and internal realities helps them to stay grounded.

DID patients benefit from viewing videotapes of their sessions, in part because it allows the different alters to get acquainted with each other and with the dominant personality. Often, though, they can't relate to the images they see. While they recognize the physical similarities, in the beginning they feel no connection. Recognition and identification develops with time and patience, and it helps them to integrate. It's important, however, to begin videotaping only after the therapeutic alliance is made between therapist and client because some victims have been subjected to pornographic videotaping.

Watching video playbacks offers patients several benefits. It helps them to feel they are on an equal footing with their therapist in reinforcing the therapeutic alliance and gives them the sense that they bear equal responsibility in their recovery. Observing and analyzing their own behavior empowers patients in their therapeutic process. After some time has passed and they can watch a series of videos, they are encouraged to see for themselves the changes and progress they have made. Finally, when they can see and understand how they come across to other people, they can eliminate maladaptive patterns of behavior.

SODIUM AMYTAL

Sodium amytal has both clinical and therapeutic applications. Its clinical applications are:

Catatonia, which is characterized by a wide range of symptoms including mutism, negativism, waxy flexibility, posturing, stereotypy (involuntary repetition of words just spoken by another person), echopraxia (involuntary repetition of movements made by another person), and stupor. In many cases, catatonic symptoms improve dramatically after intravenous administration of sodium amytal.

Unexplained muteness There are times when a patient is fully alert, able to follow commands, but inexplicably mute, making no attempt to communicate. Sodium amytal has demonstrated the capability to overcome this muteness.

Stupor is a state of decreased reactivity to stimuli, but it doesn't always imply disturbed consciousness. Stupor may be hysterical, depressive, schizophrenic, or organic in origin. The amytal interview can be helpful in differentiating these conditions.

The therapeutic applications are most useful in those disorders where the psychological defense mechanisms of repression and dissociation are operative. Three specific applications of the amytal interview have been identified.

Post-Traumatic Stress Disorder: Amytal lowers patient defenses against an anxiety-provoking event, promotes the release of repressed emotions, and assists in reintegrating dissociated ideas and mood states.

Psychogenic Amnesia and Fugue: Psychogenic amnesia is a disorder characterized by extensive memory loss for a specific period of time. Psychogenic fugue is a similar disorder in which there is also loss of identity. The amytal interview has proved to have a higher success rate in treating these than conventional methods, including hypnosis.

Conversion Disorder refers to physical symptoms for which there is no demonstrable evidence of organic etiology. It is indicated by:

1. A history of similar symptoms having the characteristics of conversion disorder, such as paralysis and amnesia.
2. A history of other neurotic symptoms such as anxiety, depression, obsessions and phobias.
3. A history of sexual disturbances, especially frigidity.
4. The presence of "la belle indifference," the patient's complete apathy for what seems to be very serious symptoms.
5. Recent loss of a significant person or some other disturbance in personal relationships preceding the onset of symptoms.

The sodium amytal interview has been an excellent tool in the therapy of child sexual abuse victims. It seems most useful in those disorders where the psychological defense mechanisms of repression and dissociation are operative. Using amytal lowers the patient's defenses against an anxiety-provoking event, promotes the release of repressed emotions, and assists in reintegrating dissociated ideas and mood states. However, use must be selective and it must be administered only by a trained and qualified physician.

ADMINISTERING THE AMYTAL INTERVIEW

A physician *always* does patient preparation, with the patient arriving at least two hours before the interview is scheduled to begin. Place the patient in a reclining position in a quiet, dimly lit room and explain that the medication should make the patient relax and feel like talking. Then insert a narrow bore scalp-vein butterfly needle into a dorsal hand vein or antecubital vein.

Medication: Slowly begin injecting a solution of sodium amytal (1 gram of sodium amytal dissolved in 20cc of sterile water) at a rate no faster than 1cc/min. (50mg/min.) to avoid sleep or sudden respiratory depression. The sedation threshold is usually reached between 150mg (3cc) and 350mg (7cc) but can be less in elderly or organically impaired patients. The level of narcosis is maintained by infusing the amytal at a rate of about 50mg (1cc) every 5 minutes.

Continue infusion until sustained rapid lateral nystagmus is present or drowsiness is noted. At this point the patient can be prompted to talk. Although his or her speech may be slurred, the interview can begin, starting with neutral or non-threatening subjects and moving in an organized fashion toward areas of trauma, guilt or repression. These particular areas should be gone over several times to help the patient recall forgotten memories and feelings.

The interview should continue for 20 or 30 minutes, or until therapeutic goals have been achieved. If a patient gets agitated during an interview, it may be necessary to terminate the procedure. In that case, an extra 50 to 100mg. of amytal can be given for sedation and to promote prolonged sleep. If the interview concludes well, the patient should remain prone for at least 30 minutes and then helped to walk until after-effects are gone.

POSSIBLE DISADVANTAGES

Sodium amytal has some disadvantages when used on ritual abuse victims. During their years of abuse many of these people were given mind-altering drugs to interfere with their rational interpretation of events and to brainwash them during torture sessions. The drugs may have induced hallucinations so that, at the time, they believed that Satan was truly present, and in the present they may question their own memories of traumatic experiences.

Brainwashing sessions commonly are repeated often and it's not unusual for several different forms of brainwashing to be used on a victim. The cumulative effect covers any number of situations from continued cult participation, to conceiving babies for cult sacrifice, to believing that their families are in mortal danger or self-destruction if the victim ever is inclined to spill her or his cult secrets.

For those reasons it takes time, patience and prolonged therapy before cult survivors begin to trust enough to even consider the use of sodium amytal. Even then, the invasive procedure of injecting the sodium amytal or nembutal may, in the mind of the abused, make the doctor no different from the abusers. Patient trust, as I said earlier, is essential before this procedure is initiated. Even then, it's helpful to allow the patient to have a person they feel safe with to be in the room with them and to audio- or videotape the event. Later, after the interview, the patient can listen to or watch the tape and feel more in control and a partner in the recovery process.

One patient, a 34-year-old woman, actually ran away from the hospital in sheer terror when she remembered the time she had tried to run away from her abusers and she was caught by "council members" and dragged back. For her punishment she was forced to watch while her friend was locked in a metal cage over a roaring fire and burned. The stench of burning flesh and her friends screams were too much to bear, but the council members kept beating her to force her to watch.

Before the girl could die she was taken from the cage. Her hair was burned off and her skin was a mass of bullae—Holly called them bubbles—and laid on the altar in front of Holly. There Holly was raped repeatedly. Then she was handed the sacrificial knife and told to do the "cutting ceremony."

Becky turned her ravaged face to her and pleaded with her eyes to be spared. "No, Holly, please."

Holly made one deep cut along Becky's neck, as she had been taught, and the blood squirted all over her. In her memory Holly can still hear Becky's screaming as cult members ate her burned flesh, then forced her to do the same.

Holly felt that Becky was still inside her and that she had to die in order to let Becky out and she could be at peace. Holly had written letters and drawn pictures of Becky, and even refused to eat meat, without relief.

It took three staff members to get Holly back and reassure her that Becky is in heaven and that she is forgiven for what she was forced to do. During the days following the amytal interview, there was no more mention of Becky, and Holly seemed more at peace. There remained a multitude of memories to be processed, not to mention de-programming her from all of the childhood cult programming which was very deep-seated. Finally Holly took a big step by participating with another ritual abuse survivor and me in a local investigative television report exposing cult activities that still continued in her area. After that she functioned medication-free as a homemaker and mother and began writing a book about her cult experiences.

HYPNOSIS

Dissociation is a common defense mechanism that sexually abused children use. Since one of the ways to repress memories is through self-hypnosis at the time of the event, these children have practice, even though they don't know it, and they are excellent subjects.

Many of my patients abreact, release emotional tension by

recalling repressed traumatic experience, during both the sodium amytal interviews and while under hypnosis, re-experiencing their torture afresh. That can be dangerous to both patient and doctor alike, so it's vital that the room is free of anything that could be used as a weapon and that there are no glass doors or windows that the patient might try to use to escape. It's important to keep reassuring the patient that one or more persons they trust are close by and that it's safe to express the rage they feel. Even though the rage is fresh and the pain feels fresh, I remind them that what is causing the pain is but a memory at this point.

Scream! I tell them. Revile your attackers. Call them all the names you want. Tell them they aren't powerful any more. Now you are the powerful one. They can't hurt you any more.

THE CHALLENGE OF DID PATIENTS

DID patients are the most difficult to treat, particularly those who were ritually abused for a long time. Even after fusion or co-consciousness has been achieved, new and overwhelming stresses can cause another disintegration and formation of new alters to deal with new stresses. A patient can have internal stresses between alters who differ about how to resolve conflict. This can lead to internal power struggles between alters about who is in charge. In the struggle, the more aggressive and impulsive alters force themselves out and create new crises.

Problems in therapy can arise despite a good therapeutic alliance and transferences can resurface when an alter who is accustomed to taking on and acting out all the collective fury and rage reemerges to act out. At that point, homicidal and suicidal behavior can happen. As the therapist, one must be vigilant constantly to note a patient's sudden changes in mood, affect and non-compliance with the established program, be it not taking medication or appointment cancellations.

These patients might expect more therapist loyalty than is possible. They might demand time available on demand, which isn't possible. It helps, I've found, to have others involved in a team effort, such as other therapists, a group of safe friends and relatives, and clergy who have experience with this kind of patient, so when I'm out of town, acting out is minimized.

In spite of all of these precautions, it's impossible to avert catastrophic reactions. A few of my patients have made near successful suicide attempts while I was out of town or out for the evening. In their extreme dependency, with their unresolved feelings of abandonment by previous therapists, as well as feelings left from rejection and abuse from their parents or parent figures, they had fastened on me. When I was absent when they wanted me, it confirmed their worst suspicion, that no one in the world could be trusted. In their desolation, they turned on themselves. Later, they turned on me.

THERAPIST EGO STRENGTH

It takes a lot of ego strength not to feel discouraged by constant accusations of lying about being available, or being uncaring, or incompetent for prescribing too much or too little medication, and so on. It's hard not to take the abuse to heart, especially when the therapist is new at treating DIDs.

Often these patients come into treatment labeled Borderline Personality Disorders. They use up a lot of therapists with their constant self-abuse and self-destructive behaviors. Reluctantly I have had to terminate treatment with a few of these patients when I couldn't work through their negative transference and my own counter-transference issues.

For example, if a patient is resisting therapy because she has projected onto me her anger at a figure in their past, perhaps because something I do reminds her of that person. Then I get frustrated because I can't help her and that creates another barrier. At that point, not because of anything she says or does but because she needs to stop spinning her wheels, I refer her to another therapist who I hope will have better results.

This has happened on occasion. Even after I've worked through the circumstances intellectually, I've still had a very human period of self-accusation and regret for what felt like my failure. I've gone over and over the case, trying to understand what else I could have done to prevent it ending that way. Ultimately, my consolation was that I discussed the termination process thoroughly with the patient to ease the transition and that I did everything I know how to help her. I put her first.

A NEW CHALLENGE

Prior to my professional involvement with adults with histories of sexual abuse as children, I admit that I paid scant attention to books on the subject, self-help or otherwise. The subject of Satanic ritual abuse I treated with a lot of skepticism and attributed its reputation to media sensationalism. At the time theaters were so saturated with films on the subject that even children movie-goers perceived them as fiction and became jaded. However, I screamed with shock at what I saw on the theater screen, embarrassing my children so much that they refused to accompany my husband and me to such films.

Little did I know that soon I would be treating adults who had been abused in ways as bad and worse than anything on the screens. Yet, once I began, I felt committed to continue, even after I developed "sympathetic hives," tension headaches and deeply frightening nightmares. Working with these patients has taken such an enormous toll on me that several times my husband has asked me to consider terminating these particular patients, quit practice altogether, or cut down on treating patients with such histories. Or, at the very least, to take a couple of weeks off to heal myself. The most I could do was take a brief vacation. I can't abandon these patients, and others like them, because they have so few resources and few psychiatrists and psychotherapists who can and will treat them competently.

THE CONTROVERSIAL DID PATIENT

The subject of dissociative disorders, particularly DID, is still a highly controversial and hotly argued diagnosis that has the power to divide psychiatrists and other mental health professionals. Divisions aside, I am convinced of the authenticity of the Dissociative Identity Disorder and feel that doubters' bias is the reason it goes undiagnosed. I think it helped that my training was in an eclectic program that included biological, pharmacological and behavioral methods. At that time DID as a psychiatric diagnosis was struggling to be born, even though the condition is one of the oldest of clinical psychiatric syndromes.

Most of my DID patients were highly intelligent, even brilliant people, although DID can be found at all IQ levels. One of my DID patients had an IQ that fell between Borderline and Mild Mental Retardation, and the intelligence of his three alters was commensurate. One usually came out during a drinking bout, got quarrelsome and got thrown in jail for assault and battery. Another was a meek laborer who picked up the pieces after the others make a mess. The third was a combination of the other two, and an assertive, thoughtful, moral, religious, loving family man. This DID, I found out after he dropped out of therapy, had wives in three states.

While intelligence is not a factor, it remains a fact that the vast majority are among the brighter. Some of them are professionals who graduated magna cum laude. They are multi-talented people and therefore skilled in employing the most sophisticated defense mechanisms to allow them to survive and function. This very wit and talent also works against them. As they become professionally involved in their fields and their responsibilities increase, the additional stress overtaxes their emotional reserve, and they find they must seek psychotherapy. In recovery they tend to be dedicated, compassionate and highly successful.

A number of sex abuse survivors who have attained self-actualization have decided to help others who have been similarly abused, and they're very good at it. One such woman was a heavy drug and alcohol abuser when I first saw her in therapy. She had passed her nursing exams while intoxicated. After she had worked through her sexual abuse from her father in therapy with me, she went on to get her Ph.D. in psychology and then her M.D. She has written several articles to help people recognize child sexual abuse.

NEW ATTENTION TO AN OLD PROBLEM

With the increasing willingness, however guarded, to acknowledge that child sexual abuse and Satanic ritual abuse have been and are still being committed daily, a cry has arisen from all segments of our society to protect our children. Public figures have come forth with their stories of a childhood scarred by sexual abuse: Oprah Winfrey, a charismatic television personality; Roseanne Barr, the wise cracking comedian; LaToya Jackson, the rock singer and sister of Michael Jackson, whose parents still deny her claims; Miss USA of 1958, Marilyn VanDerbur, whose storybook family life would seem to have been protection from such ugliness, and on and on. None of these people had anything to gain from their disclosures, but they serve to strengthen those among us who are still hiding their pain in a dark inner closet.

It's encouraging to know that 12 states besides Michigan, the state I live in, have addressed the statute of limitations in child sexual abuse cases in favor of the victim-survivors. Some attorneys, too, are beginning to specialize in representing survivors who decide to sue their abusers after the memories begin to return, sometimes for punishment, sometimes to recoup the cost of their therapy.

In the December 1990 issue of the *Michigan Lawyers Weekly*, attorney Richard Dumas writes that under a new ruling from the U.S. District Court for the Western District of Michigan, "each specific event of [child abuse] now has a limitation of its own." The article cites a case of a 31-year-old woman who was sexually abused by her father between 1962 and 1972. Fourteen years later, in 1986, the plaintiff began treatment for acute anxiety, depression, and other complaints. In March 1987 the plaintiff began to recall her abuse. She wrote to her father about the incidents. His return letters admitted they took place. In February 1990 she filed suit against her father, claiming negligence, willful and wanton misconduct, intentional acts and conduct, intentional infliction of emotional distress, assault and battery.

The father/defendant moved for summary disposition, saying his daughter's claims were time-barred. However, Judge Gibson denied the defendant's motion to dismiss, noting that the plaintiff's cause of action was based on a claim of personal injury. The Michigan statute of limitations in personal injury cases [MCL 600.5851] is three years, and more than three years had passed since the alleged abuse happened. Notwithstanding, the court declared that "Michigan also recognizes that a cause of action for sexual abuse may be tolled by a plaintiff's disability." Under Michigan law, insanity is defined as "a condition of mental derangement such as to prevent the sufferer from comprehending rights he or she is otherwise bound to know."

Further, the plaintiff continued to remember additional abusive episodes within ten days of filing the suit. Until she was aware of the later-recalled episodes, she could not have complained about them. Judge Gibson concluded that the plaintiff had one year from the date of remembering *each* incident of child sexual abuse in which to file.

March Walker, a board certified diplomat in social work and an expert witness in many child sexual abuse cases, says in the same article that child sexual abuse is not a crime of sex, but of power and control. It may, she said, take a long time for the victim to view her or himself as powerful enough to confront their attacker in court. She indicated that victims often blame themselves, even if they were only three or four years old at the time of the abuse. Threats from their attackers tend to instill in the victim a non-specific fear of dealing with the matter, even years later, she concluded.

Sadly enough, this is still quite true and sometimes it takes the death of the perpetrator for the victims to even begin to recall the abuse.

AVOIDING THERAPIST BURNOUT

Dealing with sexually abused victims causes powerful feelings in therapists and it's vital not to lose objectivity, as I've already said. Because that's so, personal and professional boundaries are often difficult to maintain in therapy sessions. That's especially true when patients have borderline traits, but don't have the full spectrum of a true Borderline Personality Disorder and have lost their support systems. That tends to happen because these people are demanding, tend to idealize and then depreciate their therapists, friends and relatives.

Although I allow acutely distressed and suicidal patients to telephone me, I discourage abuse of this practice for less emergent problems. Then I define, with painstaking care for clarity, what that means to me as opposed to what it means to them.

These patients are often bright, pleasant, likable and eager to please. They may try to make their therapists feel that they are the only ones who truly understand them and show their gratitude by plying them with gifts, complimentary cards and praises. Yet these people are easily wounded by their therapists' remarks which may sound critical, or apparent lack of appreciation for the gifts. They become bitter and angry at their therapists easily. They demonstrate that anger through frequent crises that demand immediate attention. If they don't get it, they cut the therapists down with pejorative remarks, suicidal gestures, non-compliance with therapy, veiled threats of malpractice lawsuits and angry letters.

For example, one of my patients called and wanted to talk with me immediately. I was with a patient. My secretary determined that it wasn't an emergency and told her that I could call her back in five minutes. The patient simply hung up without responding. My secretary relayed the message and I called back immediately, but she had the phone off the hook. I called the police, asking them to check for a possible suicide attempt. They found her sulking. In response to their questions, she muttered that her psychiatrist doesn't really care about her; all she wants is her gifts and money.

Since that incident, I've made it a point not to accept gifts from patients, with the exception of inexpensive things like homemade cookies or candies, or cards or flowers when I am ill or hospitalized. At a time like that, when patients might begin to feel afraid and deserted, it's helpful for them to be able to make some kind of contact.

However, generally I repeat the need for boundaries at the beginning of each session with these kinds of patients. Also I remind them of their resilience and success in overcoming their abuse or revictimization, and encourage them to continue their successful recovery.

THERAPIST COUNTERTRANSFERENCE

Patients can have transference issues in which they project onto the therapist feelings they carry for someone in their past, thereby thwarting their own recovery. Although the projection is unintentional, rising as it does out of the subconscious, it can create a real barrier.

The same thing can happen to therapists and just as unconsciously. For example, a patient might have a gesture or facial expression that reminds me of a relative who was mean to me when I was a child. As a consequence, unconsciously I might feel resistance to the patient. If at any level I feel abused by a patient who is trying to overcome his or her abuse issues, I become the wrong therapist for this patient because I lose my objectivity. By the same measure, the patient can put an enormous strain on an already stressed therapist.

CONCLUSIONS

Although doing therapy with people recovering from sexual abuse can be enormously rewarding, it can be exhausting mentally, emotionally and physically. Any therapist who deals with patients who were sexually abused as children needs to be vigilant for possible pitfalls, both for patients and therapists. One of the more subtle pitfalls therapists need to be aware of is the possibility, indeed the probability, of transference and countertransference. It needs to be explored in the therapist's own mind, identified and discussed with patients, and never allowed to hinder the psychotherapeutic process.

It's tempting to feel omnipotent, to be proud of one's ability to gratify all of the patients' desires. Patients' gratitude and admiration encourages the inclination. But giving in to the tendency can impede the therapeutic process because it will backfire and self-satisfaction will rise up and bite at some inopportune moment. Either transference and countertransference issues will intrude, or a patient with borderline traits will impose unrealistic expectations.

Rather than avoiding any of these issues, it's best for both the patient and the therapist to understand the dynamics, expectations and frustrations possible. Setting and understanding healthy boundaries, learning to vent frustration and anger appropriately, identifying and dispelling unrealistic expectations and acting-out behavior, all help advance the therapeutic process and avoid therapist burnout. And the therapist's ace-in-the-hole anytime, is to allow him- or herself to feel free to seek a consult with one or more other therapists about a difficult case or difficult feelings.

CHAPTER SEVENTEEN

THERE IS HOPE

The evil that a sick human mind can devise to do to another is appalling and has the power to disturb deeply the victims and an ever widening circle of family and friends, including their therapists. There are those who debate the origin of such malevolence. It is a devil or the devil, they say. No, others say, there is nothing supernatural about it; it is behavior that is pitifully and completely a product of the human mind. Frankly, to me the point is moot. Instead of wasting time and energy arguing its origin, we can and must turn our attentions to *getting rid of a problem that we have the power to eliminate*. Abuse, like any kind of pollution, can be stopped at its source, which in this case is in the minds of survivors who otherwise will carry it forward into the next generation.

MESSAGES ABOUT RECOVERY

After the intense early healing takes place in frequent appointments and the upheaval of recovered memories, healing continues at a slower pace. During that time patients have appointments on a periodic basis or when they feel it necessary. Often they are moved to write to me to share their thoughts, their newly realized strengths, and their gratitude for new lives. Sometimes even their families are moved to write. I want to share a few such communications with you. I've created new names for them but I have edited the letters only minimally.

KATRA

When Katra became my patient four years earlier, she was having auditory hallucinations and paranoia. She had been in therapy and on medications for about six years without improvement. Her mother wrote to me first in response to my request for information about my patient's childhood. It was a long and candid letter, detailing the convolutions and denials involved in intergenerational child molestation and how it had reverberated through her family.

Katra, she said, had been a sensitive but happy child, but that she changed as the sexual abuse and friction between her parents took its toll. Her father's abusive behavior included inappropriate touching, tickling and pawing, peeping and questioning. After Katra was grown, he extended his behavior to his granddaughter, and changed his treatment of Katra to lies and emotional manipulation—treatment that previously he had reserved for Katra's mother.

The mother told that she was the daughter of a rigid, controlling workaholic and that now she understands how that made her vulnerable to "being exploited" by an abusive man. She told that Katra was attending the umbrella Twelve Step group that serves dysfunctional families, Adult Children of Alcoholics (ACOA). It was helping her understand and overcome the dynamics of sick relationships. Katra, her mother says, still carries "a lot of anger at my years of marriage with her father," but that she is confident "in time she will be at peace with herself."

A short time later I received an enthusiastic note from Katra:

> "Dear Doctor Callaghan,
> "You were so kind to take me on as a new client when your schedule was so full to begin with, and Linda you have literally SAVED MY LIFE AND I LOVE YOU SO MUCH I COULD CRY!!! I really mean this. I cannot believe how much better I am.

I am getting an A in English, writing some terrific papers, working on my second "love me" scrapbook and second journal, and still walking up to two hours a day. Work is great. I either receive nice compliments or presents (!) and the medication has surely turned me into a full-force human being again—with faults, charm, wit, emotion, love and happiness. You and your wonderful, loving therapy mean the world to me, because I feel sooooo happy, finally free of my sick dad, his sick abuse, and his sick paranoia. I am constantly writing to keep myself in the proper perspective and positive mental attitude. Most of the time it's easy.

With it being the time of the year for Easter and new beginnings, I just badly needed to write to THANK YOU for sincerely helping me and like I said literally saving my life. Linda, do you know that I NEVER THINK OF SUICIDE ANYMORE, NEVER . . . Before I came to you I thought about it every week at least once or twice! I haven't experienced a depression since last August, and I seldom cry about my father any more.

I feel like a whole new person with a whole new attitude and a lot of living to do. I cannot describe to you what this means to me, what I'm trying to say. Even if I spent the rest of my life alone, and never remarry, at least I have my peace of mind. What more could one ask for? My God, I was dying so bad emotionally. I'm so grateful to you, Linda; my best friends in life are God, my Mom and you.

Well I wish you a happy Easter and love and tenderness, and health. Because of you I dare to dream now and can feel relaxed at home, at work, whenever, no longer having to hide behind closed curtains with a brilliant brain yet inner sickness, no longer have to shower in the dark, hiding my lovely nakedness.

Linda, I truly love what your help has done for me. I LOVE LIFE. Do you know what it means to me to be saying it, writing, feeling it, experiencing it? It's like a dream come true. My prayers were answered with your guidance and conversations. I thank you from my entire heart for taking me into your arms and care."

At the time of this writing Katra has become self-sufficient and assertive. She recognized how her demeanor made her vulnerable to revictimization and has modified it. Now that she treats herself with more self-respect, her colleagues at work are more respectful, which, in turn, affirms her further. She wants no contact with her father, who is remarried, and communicated with me occasionally with short, positive and optimistic letters.

SARAFINA

Another patient, Sarafina, expressed many of the same feelings in a journal, which she showed to me. When she had begun therapy, her weight was over 250 pounds. At the time of the journal entry she had lost over 50 pounds and was still losing at a reasonable rate. She recorded two firsts: she was beginning to enjoy sex with her husband and she was able to drive to the city. Now she had energy, whereas previously she had been a "zombie." She had regained her love of horses and was looking forward to her mare foaling. She was feeling better than she ever remembered feeling in her life. Even though her therapy with me was finished, she wanted to keep in touch, she said.

DYANNE

As I reworked and expanded the contents of this book for the second edition, I received a touching, immensely powerful and healing letter from the survivor who wrote "Carnal Knowledge," offered in the Introduction on page 18. I'm replicating her entire letter below because to delete any of it would delete valuable insights into her recovery process.

I have been meaning to write to you for some time. I hope you are feeling well and enjoying life. [A concept she couldn't conceive during her abused years.]

You said to keep you posted of new memories and developments. I recovered the memory of the little stuffed cat I had as a little girl. I had known for some time that my favorite toy had come to a bad end, but didn't remember what. I must have told Sandy about it and then forgot about it—stuffed it into my inner child. [Sandy was her best friend, was also my patient, and has a history of severe sexual abuse as a child and a young adult.] It seems that my mother destroyed it in front of my eyes. She pulled out its blue eyes. Pulled out its long hair. Ripped out its insides. I told Sandy at the time that I felt like she was ripping my heart out. I loved that kitty so.

Last Christmas I bought a stuffed kitty for my kids, but then I gave it to myself. Somehow I understood that my little Annie [the name she has given her inner child] needed it to heal. At that time I hadn't recovered the memory of Mother murdering, destroying my favorite toy, but I must have been close to it.

I wonder how often I go into my inner child and never know it? I wouldn't know now if Sandy hadn't told me.

I've been quite contented considering the obstacles I'm up against. I have nothing to do with Ted's parents [Ted is her husband] I have seen his Mom a couple of times and am polite to her, but I don't have much affection for the protector of one of my living abusers. Sometimes I wonder what she thinks—no one in the family talks to me because I told Ted that Fred threatened Angel. [Fred is her father-in-law and one of her abusers. Angel is her daughter.] They give me a wide berth, and it pleases the hell out of me not to have to play their games.

I've talked about the abuse with my mother quite a few times and it has helped. But little Annie still feels afraid of her at times. I can say truly and without sadness that I love me. I used to cry when I said that—I had such shame.

On Thursday night I go to an ACOA meeting at a local church for an hour of lecture and a Twelve Step program afterwards. I went to a shame workshop a couple of weeks ago and began to learn about healthy boundaries, what they are and how they work to protect myself and others.

I know I'm healing when I can say I'm enjoying my journey. I have many to thank, I know, but especially you for not being afraid to hear my pain and my truth. I know that we were in an especially difficult situation with my husband's family being abusers, too. That's still rough for me—not feeling safe to confront Fred. (That rotten fucker. Still a little rage there. Not funny.) When we are either in control of [our] business, or I am self-supporting with my writing, then maybe I will feel free to confront him.

I finally got the guts to pick up *Inrage* [the first edition] and plan to read it soon. I was very afraid of my own pain; I could hardly stand to see my journal words in the Introduction.

I've enclosed additional work on my poem, "Carnal Knowledge." You already have a similar Part One that I wrote when I was feeling particularly great. Maybe that great feeling would have held on better if Ted hadn't been fighting so hard not to believe the abuse by his father. Now I know it's not so important what he believes. I can't control anyone's beliefs. What is important is what I believe, and what I do about it. Things are getting less black and white—all or nothing—and more shades of gray.

I put Part Two into "Carnal Knowledge" recently, and I feel it shows a lot of healing. What do you think? I'm proud of the poem and feel it could help others who are just beginning to learn about their abuse and their rage.

I just got going on my new computer and laser printer. I love it to pieces! We really couldn't afford it, but I knew that there was no way I'd ever get my career going without one. I did sell a horse to help out with the money and, thus, cut down on my stress.

My plans are going well to become a successful writer of juvenile novels. I really feel that's where I should and will be in the near future. For right now, I'm enjoying life, and that's most important. I don't have anything ready yet to submit to [to a publisher] because I've been working on my recovery. Also, it hasn't been easy having the "bastard" living next door for the summer. [She refers to her father-in-law again, with whom her husband works and co-owns the business, and who is also a neighbor.] I won't let him ruin my present or my future, though. He belongs to the past. He will meet his Creator alone and naked. Amen. I don't mean that I'm done with him, but I can't be obsessed with something I can do nothing about.

I love you, Linda.

With most sincerity,
Dyanne

P.S.
I just got up and had to tell you that I had a powerful dream about my father last night. He finally had enough guts to come to me in a dream. He didn't have enough guts to come sober, but at least he showed up. I confronted him verbally and really showed no mercy. I towered over him and wagged my finger in his face. He seemed shocked at first and then he wanted to make excuses to get me feeling sorry for him. I **told him there were no excuses and he never denied a word I said.**

Later on, you were holding me and told me that he had been a ghost. It felt good that you were there for me. I woke feeling very powerful.

P.P.S. (from my diary)

Yesterday was rough. Just got my computer yesterday and was trying to do too much, as usual. Got a stabbing pain in my chest, then a severe headache with nausea. I took aspirin right away, fixed lunch for Ted, and lay down for a little while. I felt better in a couple of hours, but it came right back before supper. I had been working on my "Carnal Knowledge" poem when the (stress or fright) attack happened, probably to prevent a memory block from loosening.

Linda, here is another dream that I felt was significant enough to record in my journal. Did I interpret the symbolism appropriately?

Last night I had a very upsetting and enlightening dream about Angel. In the dream she was about four and had grown a penis. I was upset. I knew I had to have it removed and wished that I'd had it done when it started to develop when she was two. I didn't know if she was really a girl or a boy now, but I knew that she had been born a girl.

After I woke, I was relieved that it was only a dream, but I know that dreams have subconscious symbolism, so I began to dig. I feel it symbolized my fear of her being born a girl and my inability to protect her, or teach her how to protect herself from violation by men. At that moment I felt sad that it isn't safe for my little girl, whom I love so much, to be a girl.

[Her symbolism and interpretation are correct as far as she goes; the girl in her dream represents both her daughter and herself. In addition, she has memories of her father-in-law sexually abusing her daughter when she was helpless to protect her. She felt that her father-in-law favors her son over Angel and, had Angel been a boy, she wouldn't have been sexually abused.

At the time of this letter her husband was angry at Dyanne and me because he didn't believe that his father

would abuse his wife and daughter. He believed, instead,
that I was supporting his wife's delusional thinking. However, as a child he, too, had been physically and emotionally
abused by his father and their prevailing relationship was an
uneasy peace.]

Angel seems to be doing well. She seldom wants the
light on at night anymore, and sometimes doesn't cover her
head. I'm trying not to attempt to control her emotions, but
it's hard. It would be easy to urge her to be happy too soon
after her loss [of innocence from sexual abuse] and not letting her do her grieving. That's probably because I wasn't
allowed to grieve my losses when I was a child. Reading
children's books and writing them should help me do better
with my inner child and with my children.

Clark [her son] is more difficult for me. He has so much
anger, in part, I think, from my over-protecting Angel. Also,
my body language may have been hostile. Who knows,
really? But I want to do what I can to help him be happy.
Last week I took him to an allergist, and he was allergic to
everything they tested him for. More stress and work, but
I'm dealing with it instead of imaginary worlds. [She refers
to financial stress that began when she quit working at the
family business. Currently her job is that of mother, homemaker and takes full responsibility for the family horses.]

CARNAL KNOWLEDGE

In memory of my father, E. H. B.

Born November 1917 Died Halloween 1983

PART II HEALING

The tiger no longer lurks in darkness,
    though he tries.
He is not proud,
    though he has many brothers
    huddled with him in separate hells.

I can see him with all his faces
Bright as neon on some nights
    arrogant, cruel
    sometimes smiling and passive.
I know what he has done.

I no longer pursue him with gun and knife,
But I wear the pistol and it carries real bullets,
And my knife hangs at my hip, sharper than any fang.
Never again will I lie down
In blind trust that he might
    love me.

Tenderly, piece by piece,
I have brought my heart back from the grave.
He just mutilated it.
It has been my hands that have nourished it . . .
    healthy enough to love."

THERE IS HOPE

My dictionary defines "hope" as "To wish for something with expectation of its fulfillment" and "to look forward to with confidence or expectation." Based on my psychiatric experience, even
with the horrific abuse I have described, I have hope.

    As I have listened to my patients relate the horrors of their
pasts, I have seen that the burden of their abuse had strengthened

them to access their emotional, mental, spiritual resilience. Then their therapy helped them understand that they could choose to transcend their pain and begin to heal. Those patients who released their anger appropriately—directing this anger is a critical function of the therapist that cannot be overstated—laying it squarely on the heads of their abusers and disregarding the risk of their abusers' further rejection, moved most quickly into healing. Likewise, releasing inappropriate guilt and shame allows them to move from the past into the present.

Invariably, I am moved deeply by my patient's courage, resilience and inner resources that helped them to survive. They have lost their innocence and watched their illusions die. They have gained wisdom, a new freedom to express themselves and to choose options they didn't know before that they had. But it's such a brutal tradeoff. It's so unfair. But, God bless them, they can and do heal. They have sensed, uncovered, processed and dealt with *inrage*.

RECOVERY

In the garden of life
there grows a tree
tall
strong
well rooted
Able to withstand storms
that now only sway it.

From that tree
seedlings of hope grow
protected
and life continues.

From the growth of the seedling
comes peace.
—Rose, an alter

APPENDIX I

The following piece, written by a DID patient, shows how she arrived at the names of her alters who arose from abuse. Samsara is a word used in the Upanishads referring to the cycle in the law of karma of transmigration: birth, death and rebirth.

SAMSARA

Born, emerged out of another's collapse
didn't know who she was
or what she was supposed to do
knew she was a channel
for the collapsed one
but knew there was more
began to realize
she had access to knowledge
knowledge of the system
about the past and the present
and she had anger, rage
worked very hard in her attempts
not to smash and crush verbally or physically
she had no name
no identity of her own
until she saw her name written
on an advertisement for a fragrance
"SAMSARA . . . .a touch of Serenity"
She knew Serenity
or at least knew of her
and

of her daily struggle for survival
her intense pain
and
her choice of a name that offered hope
She didn't know how she knew all this
didn't know how she came to have any of the knowledge
that floated in and out of her consciousness
questioned her own existence
took the word SAMSARA
and spent an entire day
looking up its meaning
knowing without understanding
that it would soon envelop her
even though the carefully copied definitions
didn't yet clarify her role

One day she witnessed the violence
and destruction of the souls
of the little girls
and the perfection demanded of them
and the reason for the existence
of the system of perfection
and of the system
of pain and the system of creativity

She wrote about what she saw
wrote with rage
and sought to destroy the perfection - the hypocrisy
of the ones outside the systems
She spattered their spotless world with blood
they turned and walked away
unwilling to face the destruction
her rage intense - unsatisfied
she turned again
to the definition of her name

saw that it felt right
it fit and enveloped her very being

She was SAMSARA!
it no longer mattered how she knew or what she knew
or where she came from
or why
or how long she would exist
She was SAMSARA

SAMSARA!
repeated cycles of
birth
misery
death

SAMSARA!
caused by Karma

Karma
doctrine that one's state in this life
is a result of
physical
mental
actions in past

SAMSARA!
She was - she existed
because of the actions
against the innocents
not only the abuse
but the demands for perfection

Karma
present can determine one's destiny

in the future

SAMSARA translates:
when the past has been grieved
with the grief including rage
there will be "liberation from rebirth"

"rebirth":
creation of new personalities

when we have grieved and raged
there will be no need for rebirth
we will transcend Karma
and will have Nirvana

Nirvana:
the liberation of bondage
to the repeated cycles of death and rebirth
("death" : collapsing)

Nirvana is attainable thru moral discipline
and the practice of Yoga

"moral discipline":
not destroying—controlling but still expressing
the rage, grief, pain

SAMSARA
repeated cycles of
birth, misery, death

SAMSARA knows she is part of this cycle
her "birth" stemmed from misery

SAMSARA knows she will transcend this cycle

she has the ability to see
and to rage at what she sees
she is forming relationships
slowly, carefully
she will not end in death (collapse)
she knows that her time may be limited
there may be a day when her intensity
will not be needed as it is needed now
but she won't end in death
the cycle will no longer go on and on
she has not all the answers
doesn't know how she knows what she knows
but it no longer matters
for today . . . ..
she is

SAMSARA!

©1989. Used with permission of the authors—the survivor and her alters.

APPENDIX II

A SATANIC CALENDAR

Delia gave me a Satanic calendar. As I looked it over I noticed that the dates of the major events corresponded with the dates on which my DID patients who had *not* achieved co-consciousness had particularly bad days.

January 7 St. Winebald Day. Blood ritual. Animal or human sacrifice by dismemberment. If human, victim must be a male, 15 to 31 years old.

January 17 Satanic Revels celebrated. Sexual ritual: oral, anal, vaginal. Victim, female, age 7-17.

February 2 Satanic Revels celebrated. Same as January 17.

February 25 St. Walpurgis Day. Blood ritual. Host of blood and dismemberment. Animal.

March 1 St. Eichatadt. Blood ritual. Drinking of human blood for strength and homage to the demons. Victim male or female.

March 20 Feast Day. Orgies. Spring Equinox. *See note below.*

April 19 - 26 Preparation for the sacrifice.

April 26 - 31 Grand climax. Da Muer. Necrophilia (intercourse with a corpse) female, 1-25 years old.

June 21 Feast Day. Orgies. Summer Solstice.

July 1 Demon Revels celebrated. Blood ritual, sexual, sensual association with demons. Female, any age.

August 3 Satanic revels. Sexual ritual. Oral, anal, vaginal. Female, 7-17.

September 7 Marriage to the beast Satan. Sexual Da Muer. Sacrifice, dismemberment. Female child under 21.

September 20 Midnight host. Blood ritual. Sacrifice, dismemberment. Female child under 21.

September 22 Feast Day. Orgies. Autumn Equinox

October 29 - 31 All Hallow's Eve. Blood and sexual rituals. Sexual climax, sensual association with the demons. Any human, male or female.
November 4 Satanic Revels. Sexual rituals. Oral, anal, vaginal. Female 7-17.

December 22 Feast Day. Orgies. Winter solstice.

December 24 Demon Revels. Da Muer. High Grand Climax. Male or female.

> *Note:* Celebrations of the solstices is a practice not confined to forms of Satanism, but is simply a marking of the sun's movement and is traceable to earliest cultures.
>
> Reference to "male or female" indicates choice of sacrifice victims.

APPENDIX III

FOR LILLITH

Written by The Recorder for Theodora

I'm not a make-believe thing in your mind,
I'm the splinter in your eye,
I'm the shiver in your heart.
And you thought that you could leave it all behind . . .
Well . . .

I'm back because your hand is on my throat
And I can see the outline of your fingers on that knife.
As you let me fall away
I turn to glass,
I splinter into lights and hide inside your mind . . .
Stained glass . . . .

You spilled my blood
And thought that you could have my life.
But . . .
When you wrapped your fingers around my heart . . .
Well . . .

Then . . . I truly died.

The poem refers to Theodora's claim that Lillith killed her five times. She's afraid of Lillith and hates her, too. She vowed to kill her, but two other alters weakened her resolve. She remembered having her throat slit, her "heart removed." They stole it, she cried.

APPENDIX IV

"An Overview of Cognitive Processes and Memory"

by Daniel J. Siegel, M.D.

By understanding important cognitive science concepts that relate to memory, one can begin to view memory processes as a part of general cognitive functions. This exciting academic area has a wealth of potential future applications to the clinical evaluation and treatment of children, adolescents and adults.

For those unfamiliar with thinking formally about memory, a few facts about memory and cognition will be helpful:

- Memory is not a unitary thing. At least two different forms of memory exist, which appear to rely on different brain structures.
- Memory is not photography. Remembering an experience is influenced by both the external aspects of an event and the internal biases during the experience. The details remembered may be accurate, though not complete, and then may be biased by postevent questioning.
- Memory and consciousness are not the same. Some information in memory is not easily accessed consciously, although it can be demonstrated to be influencing behavior. In fact, most "cognition" is nonconscious.
- Memory and narrative are not the same. What a child, adolescent or adult states is a language-based output that may re-

flect only a part of what is available to recall. Attachment experiences early in life may influence the way people remember and how they tell their autobiographical story.

- Memory processes, thought residing in the brain, are profoundly influenced by interpersonal experience.
- Cognition and interpersonal experiences during and subsequent to childhood trauma may have a unique impact on the ways in which memories for these events are processed and later accessed.
- Cognitive processes include such concepts as sensory imaging, attention, memory, thought, generalizations, differentiation, mental models and schema.

For the last three decades cognitive psychologists have used an information-processing model to conceptualize memory. Although linear in its architecture—despite a parallel structure of the brain—this basic model has proved useful both for designing productive research paradigms and for establishing a common vocabulary for talking about memory processes. A brief overview follows.

Input refers to the information or data coming into the system from the outer world. *Sensory imaging* is the ultrabrief (less than half a second) representation of sensory input. Attention directs the flow of information processing from the sensation stage onward. Information is processed and placed in short-term or working memory (not necessarily synonyms) for less than a minute. *Chunking* refers to the clustering of information bits to help further processing.

Working memory is said to be able to handle five to nine chunks of information. Information can be transferred from working memory to long-term memory with various rehearsal processes. The structure of long-term memory may be influenced by schematizations with various associative categorizations. Emotions may play a role in the associative links, forming the structure of long-term memory storage.

Encoding is the term for the sensory intake, perceptual processing and working-memory transfer to the storage stage in long-term memory. Once in storage, items may have various degrees of storage strength and retrieval strength. *Retrieval inhibition* is a crucial, normal function that prevents the voluminous (and perhaps unlimited) quantity of information in long-term storage from flooding into consciousness and working memory. Consciousness, focal attention and retrieval are thought to be serial processes that are both rate- and capacity-limited.

In this model, items retrieved from long-term memory are placed in working memory where they can be further processed and placed again, in altered form, in storage. Thus, retrieval can be divided into direct and indirect forms. Direct measures include spontaneous recall, cued recall and recognition tasks. Indirect measures include the speed of learning of a new task, word-stem completion and free-association tasks. These latter tasks do not require the subject to consciously recall having previously seen a test stimulus.

Differences in forms of retrieval may result from various factors including aspects of encoding, storage, retrieval and the conditions at time of questioning. Tulving's "encoding specificity principle" suggests that the conditions at the time of encoding influence which context at the time of retrieval will facilitate accurate recall.

The study of memory has resulted in the conceptualization of different systems or processes leading to two very different forms of memory. These forms have been described as implicit, procedural, or early memory versus explicit, declarative or late memory. Although the domains of these various classifications may not exactly overlap, for simplicity I will use the terms implicit versus explicit memory.

Implicit memory is the way in which the brain encodes an experience and then influences late behavior without requiring conscious awareness, recognition, recall or inner experience of a *retrieved memory*. Thus, the skill of riding a bicycle can be demonstrated even if a youngster has no recall of when he or she learned to ride. This is implicit memory without explicit recall. Implicit memory may also include somatic sensations derived from past experiences but devoid of a sense of their origins in the past. Implicit memory may be fundamental to repeated patterns of maltreatment and to transference phenomena.

Explicit memory is directly accessible to conscious awareness and can usually be stated with words. This may include memory for facts (semantic memory in Tulving's original model) and for personally experienced events ("episodic" memory). Episodic or autobiographical memory has the unique features of self and time, which distinguish it qualitatively from memory for facts that may have no source attribution or sense of when the fact was learned.

The medial temporal-lobe memory system, including the hippocampus and related brain structures, is thought to be essential for processing explicit memories. Controversy has developed over whether there is a separate autobiographical memory system although, functionally, factual and autobiographical memories are experienced differently. Lesions in the hippocampal formation can produce dissociations with impaired explicit and intact implicit memory. Other events with a similar dissociation may include childhood amnesia, hypnotic amnesia, surgical analgesia, benzodiazepine effects and divided attention phenomena. Elsewhere, I have hypothesized that posttraumatic stress disorder may involve the blockage of hippocampal processing, producing the classic findings of amnesia (explicit impairment) in the setting of specific avoidance behaviors, startle response and hyperarousal (intact, implicit memory). The possible role of divided attention in the impairment of explicit processing during trauma needs to be established by empirical research.

Hippocampal processing depends on a neurophysiologic event called "long-term potentiation." This event requires simultaneous activation of pre- and postsynaptic neurons and the diffusion of released nitric oxide (NO), and it is easily impaired by certain chemical inhibitors. Following this initial hippocampal processing, a "cortical consolidation" process occurs over time between the hippocampus and the cortex, making memories "permanent" and their retrieval independent of the hippocampus. This latter process may explain the phenomenon of retrograde amnesia seen in brain injury. Theoretically, cortical consolidation also may be intimately related to the language-based processing of autobiographical memory.

LEARNING AND MENTAL MODELS

Studies of perceptual abilities in infants reveal that the newborn is able to have complex cognitive operations from the beginning of extrauterine life. Two important abilities are those of "amodal perception" and "generalizations." In the former, the infant is able to perceive in one modality (e.g., the tactile sensation of a stuffed animal) and then recognize in another (e.g., seeing the stuffed animal). What is unclear is whether this amodal process includes a neural representation devoid of sensory systems (a nonmodal neural representation or whether a "transmodal" process interconnects sensory modalities. Despite this controversy in cognitive conceptualizations, it is uniformly accepted that humans are capable from birth of "mentally representing" the outside world.

A second cognitive capacity in early infancy is the process of generalization. Infants can note both similarities and differences across stimuli. Numerous research strategies have demonstrated that in infancy and onward, the human mind is able to establish a "summation" or "schematization" of prior stimuli and experiences. This unconscious cognitive process can be thought of as the creation of a "mental model" for a category of objects, persons or interactions. For example, infants can recognize a picture of a face that is a composite of several distinct faces previously seen.

Mental models are thus derived from the generalizations of past experiences. They, in turn, may influence present perceptions and help to determine future behavior. The evolutionary benefit of having a brain that can schematicize is evident in the survival value of being able to learn quickly about dangerous objects or events.

Thus, by extracting the salient features of, say, a dangerous lion, the brain can then generalize that "animals with big teeth are dangerous." When another large toothed animal approaches, the model is activated, the perception is classified as "dangerous" and the behavior initiated is to flee. The animal that survives reproduces, and the neural capacity is passed on.

Cognitive development therefore includes the early ability to learn from the environment by creating mental models. In a child or adult, the existence of these processes can only be measured indirectly. A mental model is always nonconscious; however, it may influence perceptions, thinking, emotional reactions and behavioral responses. Stern discusses the infant's development of a "representation of an interaction which is generalized," or RIG, as the summation of numerous interpersonal experiences with caregivers. These RIGs are thought to act as the building blocks of what Bowlby terms the "internal working model" of attachment, on which much of attachment theory and research have been based.

Mental models can be represented through various control processes and environmental triggers. Models for a given attachment figure may be conflictual or inconsistent, leading one to have cognitive difficulties in adaptation, including certain forms of insecure attachment and possibly predispositions to dissociation. Models may also profoundly influence behavior patterns by providing a cognitive link between the stimulus and action.

Mental models or schemata are also thought to form a basis for the organization of memory storage. The way in which a stimulus or experience is categorized will influence its "associative links" as well as the cognitive strategies necessary for retrieval. Learning is thus inextricably linked to perception schematization and memory.

STATE OF MIND

The concept of a "state of mind" has influenced the work of a number of researchers interested in memory and in trauma. The activation of a given mental model may be determined by environmental stimuli, internal control processes, specific memories and emotional states. A state of mind can include perceptual biases, dominant emotional tone, behavioral response patterns and increased accessibility of particular memories (either explicit or implicit).

Studies of mood and memory demonstrate that the state of mind at the time of encoding may determine the accessibility to later retrieval. For example, if one is presently sad, it may be easier to recall events experienced when one was sad in the past. How young children's relatively labile shifts in states of mind influence their memory processing is unclear. Studies of dissociative-disordered patients suggest that shifts in state of mind may be accompanied by various degrees of "memory" barriers.

For patients with multiple personality disorder (DSM-IV, dissociative identity disorder), alter identities can be conceptualized as distinct states of mind. Asymmetric access to memory across "amnestic barriers" raises intriguing questions about cognitive processes and dissociation.

NARRATIVE

Narrative, the telling of a sequence of events, is studied by academicians whose interests range from literature to developmental psychology. Bruner has described two basic modes of thought: narrative and paradigmatic (or logico-deductive). The narrative mode begins earlier in child development and is an important way in which children perceive and make sense of the world. Narrative takes into account the teller and listener, and can thus be considered a form of discourse. Genres of narrative include a schema, personal account or fictional. Perspectives include first, second and third person, and past, present or future. Narratives may include various levels of complexity from interactional descriptions to statements about intentions and inner emotional states.

For children, narratives can be co-constructed with their parents, allowing them to tell the story together. A similar process, "memory talk" between parent and child, focuses on the parents in the views and inner experience of the child. Studies suggest that child's ability to use language to spontaneously recall an event is greatly enhanced by and may be dependent upon the shared discussion of an event with others. Thus, narrative both establishes a sense of meaning for a child and is a shared process between parent and child that can shape the importance of the memory's content. A basic cognitive question is how narrative influences the encoding, storage and/or available retrieval strategies that allow for conscious access to memory.

An important independent set of studies has fascinating implications about the development of childhood memory. Attachment theory has a long history of its own stemming from ethnologic, psychoanalytic and developmental approaches to early parent-child interactions and subsequent behavioral patterns. Bowlby's idea of a secure base as an "internal working model" developing from consistent parent-child interactions led to Ainsworth's development of a research paradigm, the brief separation of a 1-year-old from its mother led to the attachment classification schema that has driven hundreds of Ph.D. dissertations and led to numerous longitudinal research projects. Main advanced the attachment-research paradigm by developing a semi-structured parental autobiographical narrative, the Adult Attachment Interview (AAI), whose classifications correlate with those of the ISS.

Attachment theory has numerous intriguing and controversial implications for understanding child development. Two general findings are especially salient. For the group of adults (dismissing) corresponding to the avoidantly attached children, there is a fascinating set of converging findings. In the initial ISS study, these infants' first year of life was marked by a mother-child relationship with emotional distance and rejecting behaviors. When these children were 2 years old, Beebe found that the face-to-face interactions of these dyads were characterized by a lack of the normal match between word use and affective facial expression. A study of 4-year-olds found that in problem-solving tasks, the parents of avoidant children did not join in at the level of the child's "zone of proximal development," essentially allowing the child to do the task on his or her own rather than through the requested joint effort. At 10 years of age, Main's sample of avoidantly attached children have a unique paucity in the content of their spontaneous autobiographical narratives. Interestingly, one of the characteristics of these children's parents is that they have a repeated insistence on not being able to recall their childhood experiences.

To outline: Avoidant children have limited autobiographical accounts. Dismissing adults insist they do not recall their childhood family experiences. Why is this? Are these genetically related individuals merely expressing the phenotype of impaired long-term memory for attachment experiences? Or, is there something about this attachment classification of emotional distance and rejection that leads to diminished encoding or impaired retrieval accessibility? Examining the importance of "memory talk" and co-construction of narrative may be important for future studies; perhaps these avoidant children are not engaged by their parents in either of these two processes, thus diminishing the accessibility of memories for experiences. This hypothesis needs research validation.

A second group relevant to child development and memory are those adults with the attachment classification of unresolved (trauma or grief). They display a disorientation and disorganization in response to specific cues in their narratives as assessed by the linguistic analysis of the AAI. Ainsworth found that the reported experience of trauma or loss was not statistically associated with the disorganizedly attached infants but that the finding of lack of resolution was. This disorganized behavior at the time of reunion in the ISS is unique in its chaotic, ineffective and bizarre nature. It has been suggested that frightening or frightened behavior by unresolved parents may cause this disorganized attachment status. The relationship among early conflictual attachment experiences, incoherent (conflictual) mental models and potential predispositions to dissociative phenomena needs further exploration.

It is important to note that this research paradigm supports the idea that "unresolved" trauma or grief may impair healthy parent-child interaction. From the memory perspective, this finding raises two questions: What is an "unresolved" memory, and what changes in the process of resolution?

REFLECTIVE PROCESSING

Reflective processing is an important concept in one useful model of memory called the "multiple-entry modular memory" (MEM) system. Johnson and Hirst describe the MEM model, which views memory as both a processor and subsystem organizer that encodes experiences with both perceptual and reflective components. Context and emotions are associated with both perceptual and reflective processing. Retrieval involves the reactivation of both components. In their model, a person develops a sense of self by reflecting upon the reflective processes.

The MEM model has been useful in examining a process called source monitoring in which the origin of a memory is assessed. One form of source monitoring, reality monitoring, is how "people discriminate, when remembering, between information that had a perceptual source and information that was self generated from thought, imagination, fantasy or dreams," according to Johnson. This process is hypothesized to use perceptual information, contextual information and supporting memories to determine the origin of a memory. This model may be useful for developing a scientifically based application of reality monitoring to assess "recalled" traumatic experiences in both children and adults, which would have important forensic uses. Further studies of the development of source and reality monitoring in children may advance our understanding of how a child's personal memory system is influenced by direct experiences; interpersonal talk about those experiences; and imaginal, dream and fantasy processes.

Research on childhood memory has revealed numerous findings potentially relevant to working with children and adolescents in the clinical and forensic arenas. Two broad academic areas in childhood memory research are basic developmental studies and applied memory investigations.

Developmental studies examine normal changes in the encoding and retrieval processes. In general, these studies suggest that children can remember accurately, although their spontaneous recall may be incomplete and inconsistent. Immature retrieval strategies may be present in young children and impair their ability to access information stored in memory. Interpersonal communication, such as in co-construction of narratives and memory talk, plays an important role in the creation of a personal memory system. Normal development changes in memory include the phenomenon of childhood amnesia.

Applied childhood memory research attempts to answer questions important to trauma and forensics. Fundamental queries include how pre-event information, intraexperience stress and bodily contact and/or postevent questioning influence children's recall. Ceci and Vruck's review provides a comprehensive historical analysis of the suggestibility of the child witness. In general, these studies suggest that even young children can accurately recall events and can retain information for long periods of time. However, these studies also demonstrate that pre- and postevent information may bias which details are reported and may even establish conviction that a nonevent occurred, which clearly has forensic implications regarding the interviewing of child victims or witnesses.

The issue of how childhood experiences are processed in memory and recalled in adulthood is of long-standing clinical importance. A fair proportion (5- 10% estimated in the U.S.) of adults may have a dismissing-attachment classification. The autobiographical narratives of this group of adults as assessed by the adult attachment interview tend to include an insistence that they do not recall details from their childhood family life. Whether they are not consciously aware of events stored in memory, have impaired encoding of these experiences or are merely not reporting these events is unclear. Another developmental finding, described by Rubin, is the "reminiscence" phenomenon in which adults age 35 and older tend, in response to neutral word-list cues, to recall more events from their childhood than in earlier adult years. Dismissing attachment and the reminiscence phenomenon are examples of impaired and amplified explicit autobiographical recall in nonclinical adult subjects. Clinical implications of these findings are that one should not necessarily interpret lack of recall as a pathognomonic indicator of "repressed" trauma. Also, an increased tendency to recall childhood in mid-life may be a normal developmental event and not a sign that something traumatic in childhood is "hidden" and is not intruding on consciousness.

The recent upsurge in societal interest in adults reporting delayed retrieval of childhood-trauma memories has led to a number of recent papers on the subject. Carefully designed retrospective studies on the experiences of amnesia ("Dissociation" and "repression" in clinical terms, "impaired explicit recall" in cognitive-science terms) in individuals with documented traumatic experiences in childhood are crucial. Even better would be the challenging establishment of prospective studies that follow traumatized children as they develop.

Attempts to integrate and understand the development of memory should encourage curiosity and inspire future collaborations between basic scientists studying development and memory and clinicians involved in the evaluation and treatment of children, adolescents and adults.

Dr. Siegel is acting director of training in child and adolescent psychiatry and medical director of the infant and preschool clinic at the University of California, Los Angeles, where he coordinates an interdisciplinary cognitive sciences study group. © 1994 *Psychiatric times*. Reprinted with permission. All rights reserved.

APPENDIX V

A THERAPIST'S EXPERIENCE

Historically, child sexual abuse is not a new phenomenon, as I discussed in chapter one, but the massive numbers of people seeking treatment is a relatively recent development. In the 1980s the numbers of survivors seeking therapy grew rapidly. For whatever reason, they refused to hide any longer. Soon the movement found its way into the celebrity population, the media got hold of it and the subject exploded into national attention. Very quickly heated denial rose in the form of the False Memory Syndrome movement alleging that over zealous therapists were implanting the memories and falsely linking child sexual abuse to other illnesses, such as eating disorders and dissociative disorders, PTSD (sometimes called Vietnam Veteran's Syndrome), depression, anxiety and personality disorders, and especially Borderline Personality Disorder.

In my experience these psychiatric problems were the presenting problems that brought patients into therapy and only after therapy was established did memories of their childhood abuse surface. For therapists whose training was eclectic and more biological than psychotherapeutic, like mine, the emergence of patients with long-repressed memories of childhood incest or abuse became problematic in my already overloaded practice. Nonetheless, as a psychiatrist and a member of the community, I felt responsible for helping these people whose needs were so great that they were overwhelming the therapists in our little town of Traverse City, Michigan. In addition to my regular patients, I was seeing quite a few patients adjunctively with other therapists for medications and to help with memory retrieval through hypnosis and sodium amytal. Every therapist in town had a crowded schedule and we kept getting more referrals daily. Despite my resolve to limit my practice, I found myself relenting when fellow therapists asked me to do co-therapy on difficult cases. I would pay dearly for my irresolution.

Dissociative clinics around the country began to advertise their expertise in dealing with this type of childhood trauma. Small area hospitals were geared only to short-term hospitalizations, so I referred some of my clients to these clinics, such as The Menninger Clinic in Kansas, the Columbine Hospital in Colorado, the Dissociative Clinic at Rush-Presbyterian St. Luke's in Chicago, Illinois. Some insurance companies balked at the cost of long-term hospitalization but were persuaded to reconsider when patients continued to exhibit self-destructive behavior.

In 1991, together with local therapists and a women's resource center from an adjoining town, I put together an ambitious Sexual Abuse Congress and invited experts in all fields of therapy, including religion and law enforcement. Response was terrific and I put out enormous amounts of work in addition to my full counseling schedule. Although the event was canceled abruptly at the last minute due to the outbreak of the Gulf War, response demonstrated the growing need to address the subject.

Nothing prepared the therapists, even my more experienced colleagues, for the veritable pandemic of child sexual abuse cases in our area, and especially the cases of DID and those claiming satanic ritual abuse. We were cautious, skeptical. Was there cross-fertilization of ideas between patients? Was it because we were surrounded by isolated, rural areas? Why now? Was our geographical area catching the fires raging around the rest of the country? Were these patients telling the truth or were we being used? According to Dr. Richard Kluft, director of the dissociative disorders program at the Institute of Pennsylvania Hospital, Philadelphia, "The truth is that most abuse still goes unrecognized, and most allegations are true in general if not in detail."[88]

The therapeutic community in our area aligned itself according to two polarities. The first group of therapists said their was no validity in the abuse charges and that the other group was poorly trained, suggesting false memories to their patients, encouraging clients to sue their abusers for damages, and using hypnosis and sodium amytal indiscriminately. The second group of therapists felt that repression of traumatic memories is not uncommon and careful questioning, hypnosis and even sodium amytal therapy can bring to the surface repressed memories of many years duration, and confronting the alleged abuser publicly or privately may be important to the healing process. Obviously, I was aligned with the second group.

Soon my caseload was filled almost exclusively with people with abuse histories and who were constantly in crisis. The stress of my heavy caseload and the kind of patients I was treating began to take a very heavy physical toll on me. I developed persistent, severe headaches, high blood pressure, and insomnia. My hours were long and stressful and patient payments were very poor. Instead of referring some of them to the local community mental health clinic, as advised, I continued with all of them because I knew there was a strong probability that they would feel abandoned and rejected for their inability to pay. Most of them had never before felt empowered to change their lives and now they were improving.

I received referrals from all over the country of patients, mainly women, who were recovering memories of satanic ritual abuse. They were dissociated, frightened, paranoid, and alienated from their families. They didn't look or sound psychotic, but the stories they told were of abuse so bizarre that it defied imagination. How could I say arbitrarily that the memories were untrue? How could the stories be confirmed when the alleged perpetrators were dead or the patients wouldn't allow me to talk with them? Of course, that refusal caused concern. Patient's spouses offered only confirmation of dissociative symptoms, and sometimes the spouses themselves were abusive and uncooperative. The lack of boundaries in

these patients' pasts was constantly reenacted in their relationships, even with unwary therapists. Also, I have learned in working with abuse survivors that they are extremely resilient and that
they can wield a lot of power and control over their therapists if
the therapists aren't constantly aware.

By the end of the day, and often at the end of individual sessions, I was a limp rag. My body was fighting against the pressure.
To give myself a little more time and relief from the lack of income, I moved my office into the walkout basement of our home.
Instead of easing the pressure, my hours grew longer because patients showed up at all hours. Prior to that time I'd been diagnosed with problems that were addressed with a cervical laminec-
tomy and fusion. Then in 1992 another surgery was called for,
and immediately after I was released I fell and broke my hip, but
was sent home and told to take it easy, so I went home and resumed my practice.

Then one morning in April I woke and tried to get out of bed
and found I couldn't. I was paralyzed from the neck down with a
condition called Brown-Sequard Syndrome, and told I would never
walk again. More surgery was necessary, which was botched and
required still another. My colleagues tried to cover for me by taking my patients into their practices, and they were appalled to
discover the patient load I had been carrying. I was furious, helpless and hopeless, and what made me angrier still was that I sensed
that I had done this to myself.

Although I did recover, and I am walking and soon will be
practicing again, during the time that I was disabled an action was
initiated against me by a DID patient who felt abandoned and
was out to retaliate, and an assistant to the State's Attorney General believed her and took up her cause. While her charges were
groundless, she added energy to the machinery of my destruction.
Meanwhile, I had no choice but to turn all my energies to my
recovery.

It appalled me to think that the very people I worked myself
almost to my own destruction would turn on me. The fact that

they would and did affirmed to me that psychiatrists are not sav-
iors but healers, and that the healing needs to take place within
carefully set and maintained boundaries. Patients who have been
abused carry a load of anger that can and does spill over onto
innocent people. Commonly, people who are ill go to a physician
with the conviction that the doctor will "fix it," will take away the
pain and the fear that goes with it. I believe that people with
psychiatric illnesses aren't much different and when the doctor
can't "fix it" with a few magical words or potions, the fear rises
again and behind the fear is the anger of helplessness. *That* is the
anger that struck out wearing the cloak of law, and while I understand and can forgive it, it would be better if boundaries had been
maintained and the painful lesson never had to be learned.

BIBLIOGRAPHY

Ammerman, R. T. and Hersen, M., eds. *Children at Risk: An Evaluation of Factors Contributing to Child Abuse and Neglect*. Plenum, 1990.

Anderson, Bill. *When Child Abuse Comes to Church*. Bethany House, 1992.

Badger, Lee W., et al. *Child Abuse in the Deep South: Geographical Modifiers of Abuse Characteristics*. Institute for Social Science Research Monograph Ser.: No. 2. Univ. of Alabama Press, 1988.

Bass, Ellen and Davis, Laura. *The Courage to Heal: A Guide for Women Survivors of Child Sexual Abuse*. HarperCollins, 1988.

Bass, Ellen and Thornton, Louise, eds. *I Never Told Anyone: Writing by Women Survivors of Child Sexual Abuse*. HarperCollins, 1983.

Baxter, Arlene. *Techniques for Dealing with Child Abuse*. C. C. Thomas, 1986.

Bentovim, Arnon, et al. *Child Sexual Abuse Within the Family: Assessment and Treatment*. Butterworth-Heinemann, 1988.

Berrick, Jill D. and Gilbert, Neil. *With the Best of Intentions: The Child Sexual Abuse Prevention Movement*. Guilford Press, 1991.

Besharov, Douglas J. *Recognizing Child Abuse: A Guide for the Concerned*. Free Press, 1990.

Breiner, S. J. *Slaughter of the Innocents: Child Abuse through the Ages*. Plenum, 1990.

Burgess, Ann W. et al. *Sexual Assault of Children and Adolescents*. Free Press, 1978.

Christiansen, James. *Educational and Psychological Problems of Abused Children*. R and E Pubs., 1980.

Ciba Foundation Staff. *Child Sexual Abuse Within the Family*. Routledge, Chapman and Hall, 1984.

Clark, Robin E. and Clark, Judith F. *Encyclopedia of Child Abuse.* Facts on File, 1989.

Cleveland, Dianne. *Incest: The Story of Three Women.* Free Press, 1986.

Conte, Jon R. and Shore, David A., eds. *Social Work and Child Sexual Abuse.* (Journal of Social Work and Human Sexuality Ser.: Vol.1 and 2). Haworth Pr., 1982.

Courtois, Christine A. *Healing The Incest Wound: Adult Survivors in Therapy.* W. W. Norton, 1988.

DeCamp, John W. *The Franklin Cover-Up: Child Abuse, Satanism and Murder in Nebraska.* AWT Inc., 1992.

Engel, Beverly. *The Right to Innocence: Healing the Trauma of Childhood Sexual Abuse.* Ivy Books, 1990.

Faller, Kathleen. C. *Child Sexual Abuse: An Interdisciplinary Manual for Diagnosis, Case Management and Treatment.* Col. U. Pr. 1989.

—*Understanding Child Sexual Maltreatment.* Sage, 1990.

Finkelhor, David. *Child Sexual Abuse: New Theory and Research.* Free Press, 1984.

—*Sexually Victimized Children.* Free Press, 1981.

—*A Sourcebook on Child Sexual Abuse.* Sage, 1986.

Garbarino, James and Gilliam, Gwen. *Understanding Abusive Families.* Free Press, 1984.

Gaylor, Annie L. *Betrayal of Trust: Clergy Abuse of Children.* Freedom Religious Foundation, undated.

Giaretto, Henry. *Integrated Treatment of Child Sexual Abuse.* Science and Behavior, 1992.

Girard, Linda W. *My Body Is Private.* A. Whitman, 1984.

Glaser, Danya and Frosh, Stephen. *Child Sexual Abuse.* Brooks-Cole, 1988.

Goldstein, S. *Sexual Exploitation of Children.* CRC Press, 1986.

Gomes-Schwartz, Beverly, et al., eds. *Child Sexual Abuse: The Initial Effects.* Sage, 1990.

Greven, Philip. *Spare the Child: The Religious Roots of Punishment and Psychological Impact of Physical Abuse.* Random, 1991.

Grubman-Black, Stephen D. *Broken Boys, Mending Men: Recovery from Childhood Sexual Abuse.* Ivy, 1992.

Hayden, Dawn C., ed. *Out of Harms Way: Readings on Child Sexual Abuse, Its Prevention and Treatment.* Oryx Pr., 1986.

Hancock, Maxine and Mains, Karen. *Child Sexual Abuse: A Hope for Healing.* Shaw Pubs., 1987.

Haugaard, Jeffrey J. and Reppucci, N. Dickon. *The Sexual Abuse of Children: A Comprehensive Guide to Current Knowledge and Intervention Strategies.* Jossey-Bass, 1988.

James, Beverly and Nasjleti, Maria. *Treating Sexually Abused Children and Their Families.* Consulting Psychol., 1983.

Jarvis-Kirkendall, Carol and Kirkendall, Jeffery. *Without Consent: How to Overcome Childhood Sexual Abuse.* Swan Pr., 1989.

Johnson, Clara L. *Child Abuse in the Southeast: An Analysis of Eleven Hundred Seventy-Two Reported Cases.* Regional Inst. Social Welfare, 1974.

Kempe, C. Henry and Kempe, Ruth. *The Common Secret: Sexual Abuse of Children and Adolescents.* W. H. Freeman, 1984.

Mayer, Adele. *Sexual Abuse: Causes, Consequences and Treatment of Incestuous and Pedophilic Acts.* Learning Pubns., 1985.

Mead, James, et al. *Investigating Child Abuse.* 2nd ed. R.C. Law & Co., undated.

Miller, Alice. *Breaking Down the Wall of Silence: The Liberating Experience of Facing the Painful Truth.* NAL-Dutton, 1991.

Mrazek, Patricia B. and Kempe, C. H. *Sexually Abused Children and Their Families.* Pergamon, 1982.

Project Impact Staff. *Child Sexual Abuse: Impact and Aftershocks.* Project Impact, 1989.

Rossetti, Stephen J. *Slayer of the Soul: Child Sexual Abuse and the Catholic Church.* Twenty-Third, 1990.

Rush, F. *The Best Kept Secret: Sexual Abuse of Children.* McGraw-Hill, 1981.

Sgroi, Suzanne H. *Handbook of Clinical Interventions in Child Sexual Abuse.* Free Press, 1981.

Tobin, Pnina, et al. *Keeping Kids Safe: A Child Sexual Abuse Prevention Manual.* Learning Pubns., 1990.

LL

Ward, Fred and Ward, Betty. *About Sexual Abuse: A Program for Teens and Young Adults.* Unitarian Univ., 1990.

CHILD MOLESTATION

Adams, Caren and Kay, Jennifer. *Helping Your Child Recover from Sexual Abuse.* U. of Wash. Press, 1992.

Bagley, Christopher and King, Kathleen. *Child Sexual Abuse: The Search for Healing.* Routledge, 1989.

Barnard, George W., et al. *The Child Molester: An Integrated Approach to Evaluation and Treatment.* Brunner Mazel, 1989.

Bass, Ellen and Davis, Laura. *Beginning to Heal: The First Book for Survivors of Child Sexual Abuse.* Harper Collins, 1993.

Baxter, Arlene. *Techniques for Dealing with Child Sexual Abuse.* C. C. Thomas, 1986.

Barry, Jason. *Lead Us Not Into Temptation: Catholic Priests and the Sexual Abuse of Children.* Doubleday, 1992.

Breer, William. *The Adolescent Molester.* C. C. Thomas, 1987.

Calof, David L. with Leloo, Mary. *Multiple Personality and Dissociation: Understanding Incest, Abuse and MPD.* 1993, Parkside.

Campagna, Daniel S. and Poffenberger, Donald L. *The Sexual Trafficking in Children: An Investigation of the Child Sex Trade.* Greenwood, 1987.

Child Sexual Abuse: A Special Issue of Social Casework. Families Intl., 1987.

Crnich, Joseph E. and Crnich, Kimberly A. *Shifting the Burden of Truth: Suing Child Sexual Abusers—A Legal Guide for Survivors and Their Supporters.* Recollex, 1992.

Crowley, Patricia. *Not My Child: A Mother Confronts Her Child's Sexual Abuser.* Avon, 1991.

Daly, Lawrence W. *Innocence: The Ragged Edge.* Daly Consulting, 1988.

Driver, Emily and Droisen, Audrey, eds. *Child Sexual Abuse: A Feminist Reader.* NYU Press, 1989.

Emans, S. Jean and Hager, Astrid H., eds. *Evaluation of the Sexu-*

ally Abused Child: A Medical Textbook and Photographic Atlas. OUP, 1992.

Ennew, Judith. *The Sexual Exploitation of Children.* St. Martin, 1986.

Faller, Kathleen C. *Understanding Child Sexual Maltreatment.* Sage, 1990.

Finkelhor, David. *Child Sexual Abuse: New Theory and Research.* Free Pr., 1984.

—*A Sourcebook on Child Sexual Abuse.* Sage, 1988.

Finkelhor, David, et al. *Nursery Crimes: Sexual Abuse in Day Care.* Sage, 1988

Gardner, Richard A. *Sex Abuse Hysteria: Salem Witch Trials Revisited.* Creative Therapeutics, 1991.

—*True and False Accusations of Child Sex Abuse.* Free Press, 1992.

Goffman, Jerry M. *The Man Program: Self-Help Counseling for Child Molesters.* Batterers Anon., 1986.

Goldman, Renitta and Garguilo, Richard, eds. *Children at Risk: An Interdisciplinary Approach to Child Abuse and Neglect.* PRO-ED, 1990.

Gomez-Schwartz, Beverly, et al., eds. *Child Sexual Abuse: The Initial Effects.* Sage, 1990.

Goodman, Gail S. and Bottoms, Bette L., eds., *Child Victims, Child Witnesses: Understanding and Improving Testimony.* Guilford Pr., 1993.

Hancock, Maxine and Mains, Karen. *Child Sexual Abuse: A Hope for Healing.* Shaw Pubs., 1987.

Hart-Rossi, Janie. *Protect Your Child from Sexual Abuse: A Parent's Guide.* Parenting Pr., 1984.

Hillman, Donald and Solek-Tefft, Janice. *Spiders and Flies: Help for Parents and Teachers of Sexually Abused Children.* Free Pr., 1990.

Hindman, Jan. *Impact: Sexual Exploitation Interventions for the Medical Profession.* AlexAndria OR, 1985.

—*Step By Step: Sixteen Steps Toward Legally Sound Sexual Abuse Investigations.* AlexAndria OR, 1987.

Hollin, Clive R. and Howell, Kevin, eds. *Clinical Approaches to Sex Offenders and Their Victims*. Wiley, 1991.

Hunter, Howard. *Man-Child: An Insight into Child Sexual Abuse by a Convicted Molester, with a Comprehensive Resource Guide*. McFarland & Co., 1991.

Huskey, Alice. *Stolen Childhood: What You Need to Know About Sexual Abuse*. InterVarsity, 1990.

Hyde, Margaret O. *Sexual Abuse: Let's Talk About It*. John Knox, 1987.

Kehoe, Patricia. *Something Happened and I'm Scared to Tell: A Book for Young Children Victims of Abuse*. Parenting Pr., 1987.

Kempe, C. Henry and Kempe, Ruth. *The Common Secret: Sexual Abuse of Children and Adolescents*. W. H. Freeman, 1984.

Kitchens, James A. *Beyond the Shame: Understanding and Treating the Child Molester*. Ads-Co., 1991.

La Fontaine, Jean. *Child Sexual Abuse*. Blackwell, 1990.

Loontjens, Lois. *Talking to Children—Talking to Parents about Sexual Assault*. ETR Assoc., 1984.

Lydeen, Lottie F. *Sexual Abuse of Children: Index of Modern Information*. ABBE Pubs Assn., 1990.

McCoy, Diana L. *The Secret: A Child's Story of Sex Abuse. Ages 7-10*. Magic Lantern, 1986.

Maney, Ann and Wells, Susan, eds. *Professional Responsibilities in Protecting Children: A Public Health Approach to Child Sexual Abuse*. Greenwood, 1988.

Masson, Jeffrey M. *The Assault on Truth: Freud's Suppression of the Seduction Theory*. HarperCollins, 1992.

Mead, Thimothy. *The Mind of the Pedophile: Child Sexual Abuse and the F.C.R.* Vantage, 1992.

Miller, Deborah. *Coping With Incest*. Rosen Group, 1992.

Montegna, Donna. *Prisoner of Innocence*. Launch Pr., 1989.

Myers, John E. *Evidence in Child Abuse and Neglect Cases*. 2 vols. Wiley, 1992.

O'Donohue, W. T. and Geer, J. H., eds. *The Sexual Abuse of Children*. 2 vols. L Eribaum Assoc., 1991.

Patton, Michael Q. *Family Sexual Abuse: Frontline Research and Evaluation*. Sage, 1991.

Plummer, Carol A. *Preventing Sexual Abuse: Activities and Strategies for Those Working with Children and Adolescents*. Learning Pubns., 1984.

Reid, Kathryn G. and Fortune, Marie M. *Preventing Child Sexual Abuse: A Curriculum for Children Ages 9-12*. Pilgrim OH, 1989.

Renvoize, Jean. *Innocence Destroyed: A Study of Child Sexual Abuse*. Routledge, 1993.

Rush, Florence. *The Best-Kept Secret: Sexual Abuse of Children*. TAB, 1991.

Russell, Diane E. *Sexual Exploitation*. Sage, 1984.

Salter, Anna C. *Treating Child Sex Offenders and Victims: A Practical Guide*. Sage, 1988.

Sanderson, Christiane. *Counselling Adult Survivors of Child Sexual Abuse*. Taylor and Francis, 1990.

Sanford, Doris. *I Can't Talk About it: A Child's Book about Sexual Abuse*. Multnomah, 1986.

Satullo, Jane, et al. *It Happens to Boys Too. . . .* Berkshires, 1989.

Schetky, Diane H. and Green, Arthur H. *Child Sexual Abuse: A Handbook for Health Care and Legal Professionals*. Brunner-Mazel, 1988.

Tower, Cynthia C. *Secret Scars: A Guide for Survivors of Child Sexual Abuse*. Viking Penguin, 1989.

Tzeng, Oliver C., et al. *Theories of Child Abuse and Neglect: Differential Perspectives, Summaries and Evaluations*. Greenwood, 1991.

Ward, Elizabeth. *Father-Daughter Rape*. Grove, 1985.

Ward, Fred and Ward, Betty. *About Sexual Abuse: A Program for Teens and Young Adults*. Unitarian Univ., 1990.

Webster, Linda, ed. *Sexual Assault and Child Sexual Abuse: A National Directory of Victim Services and Prevention Programs*. Oryx, 1989.

Young, Mary de. *Child Molestation: An Annotated Bibliography*. McFarland & Co., 1987.

INCEST

Abramson, Paul R. *Sarah: A Sexual Biography*. (Sexual Behavior Series) State U NY Pr., 1984.

Arens, W. *The Original Sin: Incest and Its Meaning*. Special issue of International Journal of Family Therapy. Human Sc. Pr., 1984.

Barnes, Patty D. *The Woman Inside: From Incest Victim to Survivor*. Mother Courage, Nov. 1989.

Birts, Amber B. *Mama, Why Didn't You Help Me?* Hughes Pub., 1991.

Butler, Sandra. *Conspiracy of Silence: The Trauma of Incest*. Volcano, 1985.

Cleveland, Dianne. *Incest: The Story of Three Women*. Free Pr., 1986.

Courtois, Christine A. *Healing the Incest Wound: Adult Survivors in Theory*. Norton, 1988.

Dabney, Melodye L. *Incest Annotated Bibliography*. Dabney, 1984.

Forward, Susan and Buck, Craig. *Betrayal of Innocence: Incest and Its Devastation*. Viking Penguin, 1988.

Fox, Robin. *The Red Lamp of Incest: An Enquiry into the Origins of Mind and Society*. U of Notre Dame Pr., 1983.

Ganzarian, Ramon C. and Buchele, Bonnie J. *Fugitives of Incest: A Perspective from Psychoanalysis and Groups*. Intl. Univs. Pr., 1988.

George, King. *Sex in the Family*. Yassam, 1989.

Gordon, Linda. *Heros Of Their Own Lives: The Politics and History of Family Violence*. Viking Penguin, 1989.

Herman, Judith. *Father-Daughter Incest*. HUP, 1981.

Hobson, Nancy. *Cry Uncle*. MAC, 1990.

Houle, Georgia B. *You Will Plant Your Vineyards Once More*. Consortium, 1986.

Imbens, Annie F. *Christianity and Incest*. Fortress, 1992.

Justice, Blair and Justice, Rita. *The Broken Taboo: Sex in the Family*. Human Services Press, 1979.

Kane, Evangeline. *Recovering From Incest: Imagination and the Healing Process*. Sigo Pr., 1989.

Kleiman, Dana. *A Deadly Silence: The Ordeal of Cheryl Pierson—A*

Case of Incest and Murder. Dutton, 1989.

Lydeen, Lottie F. *Incest—Acts, Myths and Facts: Index of Modern Authors and Subjects with Guide for Rapid Research*. ABBE Pubs Assn., 1991.

McNaron, Toni R. and Morgan, Yarrow, eds. *Voices In The Night: Women Speaking About Incest*. Cleis Pr., 1982.

Maltz, Wendy. *Sexual Healing Journey: A Guide for Survivors of Sexual Abuse*. Harper Collins, 1991.

Maltz, Wendy and Holman, Beverly. *Incest and Sexuality: A Guide to Understanding and Healing*. Free Press, 1986.

Mayer, Adele. *Incest: A Treatment Manual for Therapy with Victims, Spouses and Offenders*. Learning Pubn., 1983.

Meiselman, Karin C. *Incest: A Psychological Study of Causes and Effects with Treatment Recommendations*. Jossey-Bass, 1978,

—*Incest: A Psychological Study of the Causes and Effects with Treatment Recommendations*. Jossey-Bass, 1992.

—*Resolving the Trauma of Incest: Reintegration Therapy with Survivors*. Jossey-Bass, 1990.

Mey, Vander, Brenda J. and Neff, Ronald L. *Incest As Child Abuse: Research and Applications*. Greenwood, 1986.

Nancy E. *Once I Was A Child and There Was Much Pain: A Glimpse Into the Soul of an Incest Survivor*. Frog in Well, 1989.

Poston, Carol and Lison, Karen C. *Reclaiming Our Lives: Adult Survivors of Incest*. Little, Brown, 1989.

Quina, Kathryn and Carlson, Nancy. *Rape, Incest and Sexual Harassment: A Guide for Helping Survivors*. Greenwood, 1989.

Randall, Margaret. *This Is About Incest*. Firebrand Bks., 1987.

Renshaw, Domeena C. *Incest: Understanding and Treatment*. Little, Brown, 1992.

Renvoize, Jean. *Incest: A Family Pattern*. Routledge, 1985.

Russell, Diana E. *The Secret Trauma: Incest in the Lives of Girls and Women*. Basic, 1987.

Santiago, Luciano P. *The Children of Oedipus, Brother and Sister Incest in Psychiatry Literature, History and Mythology*. Libra, 1973.

Sisk, Sheila L. and Hoffman, Charlotte F. *Inside Scars: Incest Recov-*

ery As Told by a Survivor and Her Therapist. Pandora, 1987.

Stein, Robert. *Incest and Human Love: The Betrayal of the Soul in Psychotherapy.* Spring, 1973.

Thorman, George. *Incestuous Families.* C. C. Thomas, 1983.

Trapper, Terry S. and Barrett, Mary J. *Systemic Treatment of Incest: A Therapeutic Handbook.* Brunner-Mazel, 1989.

Twitchell, James B. *Forbidden Partners: The Incest Taboo in Modern Culture.* Col. U. Pr., 1989.

Ward, Elizabeth, *Father-Daughter Rape.* Grove, 1989.

Wilson, Earl D. *A Silence to Be Broken: Hope for Those Caught in the Web of Incest.* Multnomah, 1986.

Wisechild, Louise M. *Obsidian Mirror: An Adult Healing from Incest.* Seal, 1988.

INCEST VICTIMS

Amber. *Daddy, Please Say You're Sorry.* CompCare, 1992.

Ashley, Sand. *The Missing Voice: Writings by Mothers of Incest Victims.* Kendall-Hunt 1992.

Blaha, Dionne C. *The Singing Bird Will Come: Living with Love, Strength and Joy, a Book for Incest Survivors.* Wiley, 1990.

—*Secret Survivors: Uncovering Incest and Its Aftereffects in Women.* Ballantine, 1991.

Brohl, Kathryn. *Pockets of Craziness: Identifying Yourself as an Adult Survivor of Incest.* Free Pr., 1991.

Dinsmore, Christine. *From Surviving to Thriving: Incest, Feminism and Recovery.* State U NY Pr., 1991.

Edwards, Katherine. *A House Divided: The Secret Betrayal of Incest.* Zondervan, 1990.

Feldmeth, Joanne R. and Finley, Midge H. *We Weep for Ourselves and Our Children: A Christian Guide for Survivors of Childhood Sexual Abuse.* HarperSanFrancisco, 1990.

Hooper, Carol Ann. *Mothers Surviving Child Sexual Abuse.* Routledge, 1993.

Johnson, Janis T. *Mothers of Incest Survivors: Another Side of the Story.*

Ind. U. Pr., 1992.

Kramer, Selma and Akhlar, Salman, eds. *The Trauma of Transgression: Psychotherapy of Incest Victims.* Aronson, 1991.

Lew, Mike. *Victims No Longer: Men Recovering from Incest and Other Childhood Sexual Abuse.* HarperCollins, 1990.

Miller, Alice. *Thou Shalt Not Be Aware: Society's Betrayal of the Child.* NAL-Dutton, 1986.

Miller, Deborah. *Coping with Incest.* Rosen Group, 1992.

Mones, Paul. *When A Child Kills.* PB, 1991.

Neie, Winifred C. *The Princess and Sorcerer: Recovering from Incest Through the Use of Fairy Tales and the Imagination.* Sigo Pr., 1991.

Paddison, Patricia L., ed. *Treatment of Adult Survivors of Incest.* Am Psychiatric, 1993.

Peterson, Betsy. *Dancing With Daddy: A Childhood Lost and a Life Regained.* Bantam, 1991.

Poston, Carol and Lison, Karen. *Reclaiming Our Lives: Hope for Adult Survivors of Incest.* Bantam, 1990.

Roth, Nicki. *Integrating the Shattered Self: Psychotherapy with Adult Incest Survivors.* Aronson, 1993.

Spohn, Terry, ed. *Growing Through the Pain: The Incest Survivor's Companion.* Parkside, 1989.

Westerlund, Elaine. *Woman's Sexuality After Childhood Incest.* Norton, 1992.

Wiehe, Vernon R. *Sibling Abuse: Hidden Physical and Sexual Abuse.* Free Pr., 1990.

Wiehe, Vernon R. and Herring, Teresa. *Perilous Rivalry.* Free Pr., 1991.

INCEST VICTIMS—BIOGRAPHY

Fraser, Sylvia. *My Father's House: A Memoir of Incest and of Healing.* HarperCollins, 1989.

Galey, Iria. *I Couldn't Cry When Daddy Dies.* Mother Courage, 1988.

Hobson, Nancy. *Cry Uncle.* MAC, 1990.

LL

Lee, Kate. *Tender Heart: An Incest Survivor's Story in Poetry.* Children Light Pub., 1991.

VARIOUS

Brune, Frank. *Twisted Love.* Detroit Free Press, 1991.

Caul, D. "Group and Videotape Techniques for Multiple Personality Disorder." *Psychiatric Annals,* Vol. 14, 1980, pp. 43-50.

Eisler, Riane. *The Chalice And The Blade: Our History, Our Future.* HarperSanFrancisco, 1987.

Ferenczi, S. "The Confusion of Tongues Between Adults and the Child." *International Journal of Psychoanalysis,* 30:225-230, 1949. (Published previously in Int. FUR PSA 19:5-15, 1933 as "The Passions of Adults and Their Influence on the Sexual and Character Development of Children").

Gabbard, Glen O. "Psychodynamics of Sexual Boundary Violations." *Psychiatric Annals,* Vol. 21, No. 11, Nov. 1991. pp. 651-660.

Komrad, Mark S., M.D. "Should We Believe Patients' Claims of Satanic Cult Abuse?" *The Psychiatric Times; Medicine and Behavior.* April 1992, Vol. IX, No. 4, p. 54-55.

Loew, Clemens A., Grayson, Henry, Loew, Gloria Heiman. *Three Psychotherapies.* Brunner/Mazel, 1975.

Mechatie, Elizabeth. "Child Abusers Are Sometimes Children Themselves." *Clinical Psychiatry News.* October, 1992. P. 8, Vol 20, No. 10.

Sherman, Carl. "Bean-Bayog Surrenders Medical License on Eve of Board Hearing." *Clinical Psychiatry News,* Vol. 20, No. 11, Nov. 92, pp. 3-9.

"APA's Handling of Ethics Case Criticized." *Clinical Psychiatry News.* Vol. 20, No. 11., Nov. 1992. pp. 1-18.

Singer, Erwin. *Key Concepts in Psychotherapy.* 2nd edition. Basic Books, 1970.

Spiegel. D. "Multiple Personality As A Post-Traumatic Stress Disorder." *Psychiatric Clinics of North America*, 1984, pp. 101-110.

Peck, M. Scott, M.D. *People Of The Lie*. Simon & Schuster, 1983.

Von Leeuwen, Kato, M.D. "Countertransference With Patients Sexually Abused As Children." *The Psychiatric Times; Medicine and Behavior*. May, 1992. Vol. IX, No. 5. p. 28-29.

Weis, Virginia G., J.D. "Child Abuse Reports Aid Patient Healing." *The Psychiatric Times*. Vol. IX, No.4, April 1992.

ENDNOTES

1 See endnote #16 for a brief discussion of the term "mental illness" applied specifically to MPD.

2 "Child rape is fueling AIDS' spread in Africa." *Star Tribune*, August 23, 1998

3 "'Utah's dirty little secret': The bonds of polygamy," by Julie Cart, *Star Tribune*, August 24, 1998.

4 Ibid.

5 Quoted from a letter dated January 9, 1989, from Beverly J. Cuthbert, Director of the Department of Social Services, Grand Traverse County, Michigan.

6 Renshaw, M.D., Domeena. *Incest: Understanding and Treatment*. New York: Little Brown, 1982.

7 Pedophilia is an adult preference for children as objects of sexual activity, although not all child sexual abuse is committed by pedophiles.

8 See page 253.

9 Singer, Erwin. *Key Concepts In Psychotherapy*, Second Edition. New York: Basic Books, 1970.

10 *Man, Myth and Magic: Illustrated Encyclopedia of Mythology, Religion and the Unknown* (NY, Marshall Cavendish, 1995).

11 *The Satanic Bible*. Whippany, NJ, Wehman Brothers, 1972, paperback edition Avon Books, 1989.

12 The woman Delia knew as her mother was not her biological mother.

13 Paul Tillich, *The Courage To Be* New Haven, Yale University Press, 1952.

14 As noted earlier, the woman Delia knew as her mother was not her birth mother.

15 The words in quotes in this paragraph are unconscious responses.

16 Multiple Personality Disorder commonly is called "mental illness." In *his Multiple Personality and Dissociation: Understanding Incest, Abuse and MPD*, David L. Calof, a psychotherapist who specializes in DID, says that rather than mental illness, DID is a creative response to unendurable trauma that would overwhelm a less resilient personality. I concur. Sharon's MPD is reactive, caused by her abuse in the cult, by her parents and other extended family members. True mental illness, I believe, derives from a biological condition that is genetically transmitted and is usually due to a chemical imbalance in the brain.

17 Derek Freeman, *Margaret Mead and Samoa: The Making and Unmaking of an Anthropological Myth* Cambridge, Harvard University Press, 1983.

18 I averaged two to three sodium amytal interviews each week.

19 Actually, this isn't unusual behavior for adolescent girls who, first, initially don't know the power of their own sexuality and may protest loudly when first told to be more modest, and second, who aren't above testing that power once they're aware of it. These nubile children feel, and rightly so, that father should be a safe person to test in this way. The difference in this case is that Ray's daughter's seductive behavior continued beyond what might be considered a testing period. This entire incident shows how sexual abuse becomes intergenerational.

20 These figures were garnered from *The Journal of Clinical Psyuchiatry*, Volume 55, March 1994, and *Menninger Perspective*, Number 4, 1994.

21 Both poems are used with Betty's permission.

22 Daniel B. Kessler and Philip Hyden, *The Clinical Symposia*, CIBA-GEIGY, Vol. 43, No. 1, 1991.

23 What I'm pointing to here, without attempting to pass judgment on any of the parties involved, is the *response* of the women who watched Professor Hill being questioned by committee members. The nationwide roar of outrage from women is a clear demonstration of a generation of women growing too

strong and aware to remain victims of the centuries-old power structure. The fact that the Senate committee was so clumsy about it simply made it easier to identify. The roar of outrage signifies the slim chance that it will happen again.

24 Report to the President and Congress by the United States Merit System Protection Board. 1988. Indexed under Sex Crimes.

25 Ibid.

26 Gross, Jane. *New York Times.* July 14, 1991, Section 1, page 10.

27 Maltz, Wendy. *Sexual Healing Journey: A Guide for Survivors of Sexual Abuse.* New York: HarperCollins, 1991.

28 Ibid.

29 *Psychiatric News*, September 20, 1991, pp. 16-27.

30 Ibid.

31 I am grateful to Riane Eisler who developed this concept historically and conceptually in her 1987 benchmark book *The Chalice And The Blade* (San Francisco, Harper & Row). Partnership, she showed, is a model humanity lived for millennia until the domination, or war model, of male-dominant societies crushed it. We can return to the partnership prototype, she demonstrates.

32 McClellan, Barbara. "Kids Molesting Kids." *Detroit Free News*, September 19, 1989, pp. 1-6C.

33 Ibid.

34 Ibid.

35 Ibid.

36 Finkelhor, David. *Child Sexual Abuse: New Theory & Research.* Free Press, 1984.

37 Johnson, op. cit.

38 Ibid.

39 Ibid.

40 Ibid.

41 Bruni, Frank. "Twisted Love." *Detroit Free Press*, August 31, 1991.

42 Ibid.

43 Morey, Ann-Janine. "Blaming Women for the Sexually Abusive Male Pastor." *The Christian Century*, October 5, 1988, p. 42-45.

44 Newspaper accounts were first of clergy child sexual abuse and then later of clergy malfeasance involving adult females. I followed it in *The Detroit Free Press* in the latter half of 1992, but newspapers all over the country were reporting on the case of former Minnesota priest, James Porter who was finally charged with over 30 counts of child molestation. That case, like the Hill-Thomas harassment case, was the match that lit the kindling in more cases as people spoke out saying that it had happened to them too. Suddenly, to their surprise, their words were given credence.

45 Ibid.

46 Ibid.

47 Morey, op. cit.

48 Morey, op. cit.

49 Legal action against former priest James Porter is still pending at the time of this writing.

50 Description of counselors who have sexually exploited their patients, as identified by Schoener and Gonsiorek. Quoted from a conference handout from Parkside Pastoral Counseling Center, Chicago, Illinois.

51 Courtois, Christine. A. *Healing the Incest Wound: Adult Survivors In Therapy* (New York: Norton, 1988), p. 8-9

52 This material was adapted from Courtois' book (see note above) for a conference on Sexual Misconduct and Clergy by Parkside Pastoral Counseling Center in 1991.

53 Ibid

54 Rediger, G. Lloyd. *Ministry and Sexuality: Cases, Counseling and Care.* Minneapolis: Fortress Press, 1990.

55 Ibid.

56 Ibid.

57 Ibid.

58 Ibid.

59 Gabbard, Glen O., "Love Cure Fantasy Found in Female Therapists." *The Psychodynamic Letter*, June 1991. *Psychodynamic Letter* is a house publication of the Menninger Memorial Hospital.

60 From a private conversation with a woman who is recovering from such abuse and wants to remain anonymous.

61 Marmor, Judd. "No Psychotherapist Can Be All Things To All Patients." Clinical Psychiatry News, Vol. 19, No. 4, April 1991, pp. 3, 22A-22B.

62 "Betrayal," 1978, directed by Paul Wendros, starring Lesley Ann Warren and Rip Torn.

63 Stephanson, Joan. "AMA Rules On Recovered Memories." *Clinical Psychiatry News*, Vol. 22, No. 27, July, 1994.

64 Kandel, Minouche and Eric Kandel, "Flights of Memory." *Discover Magazine*, May 1994, p. 34.

65 For a distinctly biased but thorough discussion, see Hollida Wakefield and Ralph Underwager. *Return Of The Furies: An Investigation into Recovered Memory Therapy.*" Chicago, Open Court, 1994), pp. 342-344. Since religion is one of the remaining strongholds of patriarchy, it's noteworthy that Underwager was for many years a Lutheran pastor. Wakefield is a psychologist, a field clearly she rates superior.

66 Fallon, Sadik, Saoud and Garfinkel. *Journal of Clinical Psychiatry*, 55:10, October 1994, pp. 424-428.

67 "Academic Highlights," Op. cit., pp. 461-462.

68 Rabkin, Wagner and Rabkin. Op. cit., pp. 433-438.

69 Rauch, Savage, Alpert, et al., *Archives of General Psychiatry*, Vol. 52, January 1995, pp 20-28.

70 Greist, Jefferson, Kobak, et al., Op. cit., pp. 53-60.

71 Roberts, Paul. "My Life As A Hexagon." *Psychology Today*, November-December 1993.

72 Ibid.

73 Craig, Judith L. "Remembering Abuse: What Are The Facts?" *Menninger Perspective*, Volume 25, No. 4, 1994, p. 25.

74 Ibid.

75 Double-blind studies have been done on the incidence of these illnesses that have yielded statistics as varied as the discipline that contracted to have them done: sociology, psychology, social work, addictionology, law enforcement, theology, neuropsychology, psychiatry, obstetrics, gynecology, and so on. In my opinion, due to the natural bias occurring in a study contracted or conducted by a certain field of expertise, and the integrity of the administrators of the study, these studies are not useful in the controversy under discussion.

76 For example, reported in the December 18, 1994 Star Tribune, scientists at the Salk Institute in San Diego and the University of Iowa College of Medicine have discovered that a part of the brain called the amygdala plays a central role in discerning social signals. The organ is an almond-sized structure located near the base of the brain's three-pound, gelatinous sponge of tissue. If the amygdala is damaged, a person loses a vital social skill, the ability to recognize and interpret the play of emotions in facial expressions. Further, laboratory studies have pinpointed that the amygdala is the site where adrenaline and other hormones affect memory.

77 Kandel, Minouche and Eric. "Flights of Memory," *Discover*, May 1994, pp. 32-38.

78 From the annual meeting of the American Psychiatric Association, quoted in *Science News*, June 4, 1994, p. 365.

79 Ibid.

80 Ibid.

81 See Chapter 16, Therapy and Therapists, for more discussion about this.

82 To provide an excellent comprehensive and professional discussion and overview of memory, in Appendix, I have reproduced an article by Daniel J. Siegel, M.D., that was featured in the professional journal *Psychiatric Times*. It serves a twofold purpose. One, to understand basic concepts of memory. Two, to identify how this area of research can apply to clinical evaluations and treatment.

83 These associations include The International Association For Social Psychiatry, The American Psychiatric Association, The American Academy of Psychoanalysis, and The Society for Biological Psychiatry.

84 Noel, Barbara, with Kathryn Watterson. *You Must Be Dreaming*. New York: Poseidon Press, 1992.

85 Sherman, Carl. "Bean-Bayog Surrenders Medical License on Eve of Board Hearing." *Clinical Psychiatry News*, Vol. 20, No. 11, Nov. 1992, pp. 3-9.

86 Ibid.

87 Ibid.

88 Reported in *Clinical Psychiatry News*, Vol. 21, #3, March 1993.

Printed in the United States
3959